THE
{CHEAP
Bastard's}
G U I D E ™
to
Boston

HELP US KEEP THIS GUIDE UP TO DATE

Every effort has been made by the author and editors to make this guide as accurate and useful as possible. However, many things can change after a guide is published—establishments close, phone numbers change, hiking trails are rerouted, facilities come under new management, etc.

We would love to hear from you concerning your experiences with this guide and how you feel it could be improved and kept up to date. While we may not be able to respond to all comments and suggestions, we'll take them to heart and we'll also make certain to share them with the author. Please send your comments and suggestions to the following address:

The Globe Pequot Press
Reader Response/Editorial Department
P.O. Box 480
Guilford, CT 06437

Or you may e-mail us at:

editorial@GlobePequot.com

Thanks for your input, and happy travels!

CHEAP BASTARD'S™ SERIES

THE
{CHEAP}
Bastard's
GUIDE™
to
Boston

Secrets of Living the Good Life for **FREE**

Kris Frieswick

INSIDERS' GUIDE®

GUILFORD, CONNECTICUT
AN IMPRINT OF THE GLOBE PEQUOT PRESS

The prices, rates, and hours listed in this guidebook were confirmed at press time. We recommend, however, that you call establishments to obtain current information before traveling.

To buy books in quantity for corporate use
or incentives, call **(800) 962–0973**
or e-mail **premiums@GlobePequot.com.**

INSIDERS' GUIDE®

ISSN: 1934-2586
ISBN-13: 978-0-7627-4280-6
ISBN-10: 0-7627-4280-1

Manufactured in the United States of America
First Edition/First Printing

{ CONTENTS }

SECTION 3:
Exploring Boston

{ ACKNOWLEDGMENTS }

"The finest inheritance you can give to a child is to allow it to make its own way, completely on its own feet."

—Isadora Duncan

We are all the product of our parenting, and that is the main reason that this book exists. For four decades, I studied with the Master, the King, the high Oracle of Cheap, my father, Sidney Frieswick. I hope that this book serves as fitting testimony to him. I didn't fully appreciate his unique approach to life as a child (and sometimes I still don't), but it made me what I am today. He's one of the two best men I've ever known.

I'd also like to acknowledge and thank my late mother, Priscilla Frieswick, for showing me that it is possible to have grace, class, style, and a sense of humor, even while living La Vida Cheap. Mom, I miss you every day.

This book literally would not have happened if it had not been for the tireless efforts of my excellent assistant, Christine Walsh, who agreed to help me despite the fact that she had no idea how much work lay ahead, and how quickly it would all need to be done. She is intelligent, thorough, tireless, and a pleasure to work with. Any publication in America would be lucky to have her—I know I was. Thank you, Christine, from the bottom of my heart.

I'd like to thank Clif Garboden, managing editor at the *Phoenix* and longtime inspiration, for suggesting my name to the editors at Globe Pequot to write this book. Thanks also go to Mike Urban for his support and guidance and for talking me down from the ledge whenever I felt overwhelmed.

Heartfelt thanks go out to my friends, especially Jim and Nan Wolfe, Karen DeTemple, Ken Dietz, the C U Next Tuesday Club, and the Lifers for offering moral support when the lifting got heavy, for bringing beer when the temperature in my office started to climb, and for making me laugh when my brain turned to mush. But most of all, I want to thank my husband, Andrew Robinson, the other one of the two best men I've ever known. I still wake up every morning amazed I married such a catch, a man who makes all the good things in my life possible and who doesn't have a Cheap bone in his body.

{ INTRODUCTION: }
The Land of the Free

"Give us a good cheap twenty-four-hour day,
No part of which we'd have to waste."

—*Robert Frost*

Ever since the Puritans set foot on our rocky soil in 1620, Bostonians have spent a great deal of time and energy trying to live on the smallest amount of money possible. For centuries that meant eschewing the finer things in life and making do with only the basic necessities—and having the basic necessities patched, resewn, resoled, or shellacked when they eventually fell apart. The Puritans may be gone, but the Puritan ethic is still alive and well in the City on the Hill. Today, that ethic has created a new kind of Puritan—the Cheap Bastard Bostonian.

Such was the situation in the Frieswick home. We were not poor. Yet my father, the king of the Cheap Bastards, refused to turn on the heat in our house before Thanksgiving, and he shut it off promptly after Easter (even when Easter fell in mid-March). In the intervening winter months, he kept the heat turned down so low that, as a child, it was not uncommon for me to wake up and find a thin sheet of ice on the water in the toilet. If anything in a can was on sale at the grocery store, he bought so much of it that our pantry resembled that of a well-stocked fall-out shelter. On more than one occasion, he came to near blows with the cashiers at Shaw's and Stop 'n' Shop if the advertised sale price on tuna fish differed by even one penny from the price on the can. (He gained a bit of a reputation locally, and some cashiers closed their aisle when they saw him coming.) To this day, he'll drive to a different state to save sales tax on a $50 pair of pants.

For my father, and those of his ilk, getting a deal is a moral imperative. The point of being cheap isn't only saving money. Cheap Bostonians simply believe that there's no reason to buy an expensive version of something when the extremely cheap version does the job just as well, even if they must launch a Crusade to find it. The deal is all the sweeter if it is free. "Free" is the Cheap Bastard Holy Grail.

I, like any teenager worth her salt, was mortified by my father's Cheap Bastard ways. But age and experience, living solely on the fruits of my own labor for the past couple of decades, and the fact that half my genetic material comes from a

Cheap Bastard have at last taken their effect. So it was inevitable that I would be charged with creating the definitive Cheap Bastard's Guide to our fair city, Boston, the Hub of the Solar System (as Oliver Wendell Holmes once described it), a cultural, educational, and medical mecca and, more important, the home of Filene's Basement and its automatic markdowns.

Unfortunately for anyone who didn't grow up here, the first rule of Cheap Boston is not to talk about Cheap Boston. Bostonians find it unseemly to talk about money: either how much we spend, or how much we earn. We would much rather talk about an embarrassing medical condition. This makes it a lot harder for newcomers, visitors, and even longtime residents to find bargains. That is why this book was crying out to be written—to help everyone find the way toward Cheap Living. In a city that has seen prices skyrocket on everything from real estate to movie tickets in the past decade, it's getting harder and harder to find good stuff cheap or free. The good news is that it's out there for the taking.

Lots of Bostonians are cheap, but that doesn't mean we'll take any old thing just because it's free. We have standards, and I dare say they're fairly high. As such, this book is by no means a comprehensive overview of every single free or very cheap thing in the city—that would take volumes. What I've tried to do is to weed through as much of the free Boston universe as I could and to highlight things worth your time and effort. In fact, I like to think that what you hold in your hand is a guide to some of the best places, things, and experiences that the city of Boston has to offer. That they're free or cheap is a nice side benefit.

First, some definitions. Most of the listings in this book are free. By *free,* I mean that absolutely no money will change hands. But as anyone will tell you, there are two kinds of free: totally free, and free with strings attached. Strings, in this book, often involve some investment of something other than money to procure the object of your desire. Often that investment is your time—for instance, volunteer ushering to get theater tickets or arriving extra early to avoid a cover charge. And since time is money, I've made sure to call out any deals that come with a catch. (I've done that by boldly highlighting "The Catch" in any listing that has one.)

The second type of listing in this book is for things that are obscenely, ridiculously cheap, things that are such a profound bargain that I thought you'd really want to know about them—like $25 massages or cut-rate mortgages. Cheap Bastards appreciate that sometimes, to get a true value, you must part with a little green.

I've tried to include listings that would appeal to everyone who finds themselves in Boston proper: vacationers who must offset the cost of their expensive hotel room by economizing on everything else, residents who want or need to economize, or just people, like my father, who can't think of a good reason to spend more money than is absolutely necessary. Some listings will be more appropriate for full-time Bostonians—for instance, anything that requires a long lead time (like volunteer ushering)—but many other things are perfect for anyone who just needs a quick fix of free.

All the listings in this book are located in Boston proper unless otherwise indicated. The information contained here was accurate as of press time, but things are always changing. Make sure to call ahead to confirm dates, times, and whether the deal is still on offer before you venture out.

As you're experiencing all the free and cheap goodness that Boston has to offer, remember that half the fun of being a Cheap Bastard in Boston is uncovering bargain treasures that no one else knows about. If you do find some good cheap stuff that didn't make it into this book, please let me know about it or, at the very least, tell some friends. We've been entirely too closed-mouthed about our cheap little gems in this town, and it's my hope that this book will put an end to the first rule of being a Cheap Bastard in Boston.

I hope you enjoy this book and that it helps you discover a whole new side of a city that is getting a big reputation as one of the most expensive places in the United States to live. That's true only if you don't know where to look.

Live free or die (trying),
Kris Frieswick

{ SECTION 1: ENTERTAINMENT } IN BOSTON

{ MUSIC: }
BARGAIN BEATS

"Extraordinary how potent
cheap music is."

—*Noel Coward*

Boston has long been an incubator for raw musical talent, thanks to the presence of the Berklee College of Music, the New England Conservatory, Longy School of Music, and the Boston Conservatory and strong music programs at our universities. Our bars and lounges have hosted the fledgling incarnations of the best rock 'n' roll the world has ever seen. There is also a dizzying variety of completely free outdoor concerts in the summer, featuring everything from alternative and jazz to classical and oldies.

What follows is by no means a comprehensive list, as lounges and bars are adding and subtracting live music from their mix all the time, sometimes depending on the season. Below we've listed the places that are known for the high quality (and regularity) of the free tunes they showcase. Unless otherwise noted, venues listed here have no cover and no minimum. It's good to be a music-loving Cheap Bostonian.

ROCK/POP/FOLK/ALTERNATIVE

Abbey Lounge

3 Beacon Street
Somerville
(617) 441–9631
www.abbeylounge.com

THE CATCH

} Get to the pub side before 9:00 P.M. to hear the main stage show for free. No minimum, but expect to buy at least one drink to keep the barkeep happy.

This grungy locals' haven has a pub in one half, a tiny stage in the other half. Music plays at both six nights a week (on Sunday they rest, although sometimes they have a show on the main stage, so check the Web site for details). The pub features free music starting at around 7:00 P.M. that plays until the main stage show starts, usually around 9:00 P.M. The club charges a cover to enter the main stage area, but once the main stage show starts, you can hear the show just fine from the pub side without paying a cover.

All Asia Cafe

334 Massachusetts Avenue
Cambridge
(617) 497–1544
www.allasiabar.com

THE CATCH } Occasionally, shows have a drink minimum and/or cover. Check Web site for schedule.

This longtime locals' favorite offers a number of no-cover musical acts nearly every night (music sometimes gives way to an open-mic or comedy night, so check the Web site before heading out). Acts range from modern rock to jazz to alternative. And when the munchies hit, there's Asian cuisine just a waitress away. In rare cases, this bar has a drink minimum and a cover.

Asgard

350 Massachusetts Avenue
Cambridge
(617) 577–9100
www.classicirish.com

THE CATCH } Cover charge on holidays like New Year's Eve and St. Patrick's Day.

This newly renovated space is open and airy but gets down with a wide selection of musical acts, including jazz, funk, pop, and rock. There's no cover, except on some holidays. The live music is on Friday and Saturday nights, and shows begin around 9:00 P.M. They also sometimes have live music on Wednesday and Thursday. Updated music schedules are on their Web site.

The Black Rose

160 State Street
(617) 742–2286
www.irishconnection.com

THE CATCH } On Friday and Saturday nights, there's a $5.00 cover.

This staple of Boston's Irish community features no-cover traditional Irish music Sunday through Thursday. The bands start at 9:30 P.M. seven nights a week. On Saturday and Sunday there's no-cover music from 4:00 to 7:00 P.M.

The Cantab Lounge

738 Massachusetts Avenue
Cambridge
(617) 354–2685
www.cantab-lounge.com

THE CATCH } There's a $3.00 cover on Thursday and a variable cover on Friday and Saturday nights.

The Cantab has been around forever and is a beloved, though noisy, local watering hole. Monday night features folk and acoustic music at 8:00 P.M. Tuesday is bluegrass night, starting at 8:00 P.M.

Sunday and Wednesday feature the blues, starting at 9:00 P.M. On Thursday night there's a soul review band that goes on at 9:00 P.M. On Friday and Saturday nights, Little Joe Cook and the Thrillers hold court at 9:30 P.M., as they have done for the past thirty years.

Dick's Last Resort
Quincy Market at Faneuil Hall Marketplace
(617) 267–8080
www.dickslastresort.com

If you don't mind noise, flying napkins, waiters sporting too much "flair," a warehouselike ambience, and the hordes of ridiculously attired bachelorette parties that swamp this place on the weekends, you can actually hear some pretty good music seven nights a week. Shows begin between 8:00 and 8:30 P.M. and are typically acoustic guitar cover bands. Classic rock cover bands take the stage during the weekend, when shows start between 9:00 and 9:30 P.M.

The Green Dragon Tavern
11 Marshall Street (near Faneuil Hall Marketplace)
(617) 367–0055
www.somersirishpubs.com

THE CATCH
> There's a $5.00 cover on Friday and Saturday nights, but if you're in the bar before 10:00 P.M., you can see the show free.

This is one of the oldest continuously operating pubs in Boston, dating back to Revolutionary War days, and now it's a popular hangout for the young and restless professional crowd that flocks to this part of town for the nightlife. Free rock cover bands take the small corner stage on Tuesday, Wednesday, and Thursday at 9:00 P.M. and on Friday and Saturday at 10:00 P.M. Sunday features live band karaoke at 10:00 P.M.—this is your long-awaited chance to front your own rock band, if only for one song. Leave that hairbrush at home, 'cause they let you use a real mic and everything.

Hennessy's
25 Union Street
(617) 742–2121
www.somersirishpubs.com

THE CATCH
> There's a $5.00 cover on Friday and Saturday.

Seven days a week, bands perform light rock, hits from the '70s, '80s, and '90s, and Top 40 covers at this hopping pickup joint in the Quincy Market area. Shows start at 10:00 P.M. on Friday and Saturday and at 9:00 P.M. on other nights.

Kinsale

2 Center Plaza (across from City Hall Plaza)
(617) 742–5577
www.classicirish.com/kinsale_music.html

Live shows without a cover occur on Tuesdays, some Fridays, and most Saturdays. On Tuesday the shows begin at 7:30 P.M. and feature Irish music. On Friday and Saturday the shows begin at 9:30 P.M. and are mainly cover bands.

Lucky's Lounge

355 Congress Street (at the corner of A Street)
(617) 357–5825
www.luckyslounge.com

This hip, happening underground bar (there's no sign, so look for the mysterious stairs on the corner of A Street and Congress Street going down into a basement) has a cool '60s vibe that attracts lots of artists and writer types from the surrounding Fort Point Channel arts community. Appreciative of the fact that they're mostly starving artists, Lucky's offers up free live music on every night except Monday and Tuesday, all without a drink minimum. On Wednesday it's jazz at 9:00 P.M. On Thursday Lucky's features 1960s, 1970s, and soul music at 9:30 P.M. Friday nights feature local bands at 10:00 P.M., and on Saturday there's a jazz trio at 10:00 P.M. But save yourself for the big daddy of them all—Sinatra Sunday, starting at 8:30 P.M.

Matt Murphy's

14 Harvard Street
Brookline
(617) 232–0188
www.mattmurphyspub.com

This teensy Irish bar boasts free live music Thursday through Tuesday nights, starting at 10:30 P.M. On offer are jazz, reggae, fusion, and everything else in between. Get there early or prepare to stand, possibly in someone else's back pocket. This place really packs 'em in.

Middle East

474 Massachusetts Avenue
Cambridge
(617) 492–9181
www.mideastclub.com

The Middle East is actually four spaces in one: Upstairs, Downstairs, the Corner, and ZuZu. Upstairs and Downstairs are performance spaces that feature top-notch national and local acts. Ticket prices vary from $10 to $15. ZuZu and the Corner serve eclectic Middle Eastern food and host a variety of free live music and other types of entertainment, like art openings and belly dancing with live musical accompaniment on Wednesday nights. Dates and times vary, and there is sometimes a small cover charge, so check the Web site before venturing out. Entertainment starts around 10:00 P.M. in both spaces.

Mr. Dooley's Boston Tavern

77 Broad Street
(617) 338–5656
www.somersirishpubs.com

Traditional Irish music fills this pub on Friday from 5:00 to 9:00 P.M. and on Friday and Saturday at 9:30 P.M. An Irish *seisuin,* a traditional Irish music gathering, happens on Sunday from 4:00 to 7:00 P.M.

Paddy O's

33 Union Street
(617) 263–7771
www.somersirishpubs.com

THE CATCH
There's a $5.00 cover on Friday and Saturday evenings after 9:00 P.M.

Light rock and Top 40 covers are on tap at this small locals' place on Wednesday and Thursday at 9:00 P.M. and on Friday and Saturday at 10:00 P.M., and an Irish *seisuin* happens on Sunday from 4:00 to 7:00 P.M. The completely incongruous Reggae Night starts at 9:00 P.M. on Sunday.

Toad

1912 Massachusetts Avenue
Cambridge
(617) 497–4950
www.toadcambridge.com

THE CATCH
There's a cover on Friday and Saturday evenings after 9:00 P.M.

This phenomenal little bar is so small that it is sometimes necessary to ask the bass player in the band to step aside if you want to get to the bathroom behind the stage. The quality of the musicians that this place draws just never ceases to amaze—lots of Berklee grads trying out new stuff call Toad their home away from home. Get there early and claim your spot at the door end of the bar. Rock, jazz, and blues are the staples here. Shows start seven nights a week after 7:00 P.M. Check the Web site for nightly details.

JAZZ AND BLUES

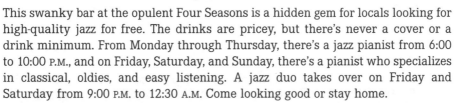

Bristol Lounge
The Four Seasons Hotel
200 Boylston Street
(617) 351–2052
www.fourseasons.com/boston/lounge_35.html

This swanky bar at the opulent Four Seasons is a hidden gem for locals looking for high-quality jazz for free. The drinks are pricey, but there's never a cover or a drink minimum. From Monday through Thursday, there's a jazz pianist from 6:00 to 10:00 P.M., and on Friday, Saturday, and Sunday, there's a pianist who specializes in classical, oldies, and easy listening. A jazz duo takes over on Friday and Saturday from 9:00 P.M. to 12:30 A.M. Come looking good or stay home.

Good Life Downtown
28 Kingston Street
(617) 451–2622

A recent renovation has left this bar/restaurant without much of its previous Rat Pack cool, but the music is still hot. Jazz takes over the downstairs lounge on Friday and Saturday from 9:00 P.M. to 1:30 A.M.

Les Zygomates
129 South Street
(617) 542–5108
www.leszygomates.com

This gorgeous French bistro was one of the first restaurants to colonize the previously dodgy "Leather District" of Boston, and its reputation is one of the reasons that most nights are still standing room only here. The stage features live jazz music, often with a vocalist, Wednesday through Saturday from 8:00 P.M. to midnight. Sit at the bar and relax. There's no drink minimum (but there is an excellent wine list if you feel so inclined). Tables are reserved for diners.

Top of the Hub
Prudential Tower
800 Boylston Street
(617) 536–1775
www.selectrestaurants.com/tophub/index.html

Top of the Hub offers live jazz, seven nights a week, and the best view in town—from the fifty-second floor of the Prudential Center, the second-tallest building in the city. Shows begin at 8:30 P.M. during the week, 9:00 P.M. on Friday and Saturday, and 8:00 P.M. on Sunday.

Wally's Cafe

427 Massachusetts Avenue (near Huntington Avenue)
(617) 424–1408
www.wallyscafe.com

Since 1947 Wally's Jazz Club, a dingy, dubious-looking hole-in-the-wall in a not-great section of Massachusetts Avenue, has been the undisputed king of the Boston jazz scene. Wally's has live music seven nights a week and never has a cover. It regularly hosts some of the best jazz, funk, Afro, and Latin musicians in the world. It is also a proving ground for each year's new crop of Berklee grads (the school is just a couple of blocks up Mass. Avenue). If there's a world-famous musician in town, chances are high that he or she will make the required pilgrimage to Wally's. Music starts at 9:00 P.M. each night, with a jazz jam on Saturday at 5:00 P.M. and on Sunday at 4:00 P.M.

CLASSICAL/CHAMBER/EARLY MUSIC

Boston Lyric Opera

45 Franklin Street, fourth floor
(617) 542–4912
www.blo.org

You can hear the BLO at many of the Waterfront Performing Arts Series nights in Columbus Park during the summer (see listing below). You can also hear them for free if you are willing to volunteer your time. The organization actively seeks volunteers in their administrative and ticket offices, at performances, and to staff their gala fund-raising events. Contact the BLO directly to let them know you're interested in helping out.

Boston Symphony Orchestra

Community Chamber Concert Series
(617) 638–9300
www.bso.org
education@bso.org

Sunday at 3:00 P.M. at various sites, roughly once a month, October through May.

Admission is free, but you must reserve tickets two weeks prior to the concert. Call or e-mail for dates, times, and tickets.

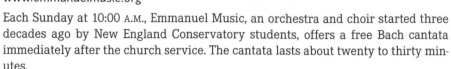

Emmanuel Music

at Emmanuel Church
15 Newbury Street
(617) 536–3356
www.emmanuelmusic.org

Each Sunday at 10:00 A.M., Emmanuel Music, an orchestra and choir started three decades ago by New England Conservatory students, offers a free Bach cantata immediately after the church service. The cantata lasts about twenty to thirty minutes.

King's Chapel

64 Beacon Street
(617) 227–2155
www.kings-chapel.org

THE CATCH } Suggested donation of $3.00.

Free recitals are offered on Tuesday at 12:15 P.M. They run about thirty to forty minutes and feature all types of music—jazz, folk, classical, world music.

MIT Chapel

84 Massachusetts Avenue
Cambridge
(617) 253–2826
www.mit.edu/mta/www/music/events.html

There are free noontime performances each Thursday in this hauntingly beautiful chapel designed by world-renowned architect Eero Saarinen. The music is mostly classical or baroque.

Newton Free Library

330 Homer Street
Newton
(617) 796–1360
www.ci.newton.ma.us

Every concert is free and open to the public. The classical concerts are typically on Sunday at 2:00 P.M., but check out their Web site for special events.

Old South Meeting House

310 Washington Street
(617) 482–6439
www.oldsouthmeetinghouse.org

Some musical events offered here are free. Best to check the Web site for full information. Musical styles vary from classical violin to acoustic guitar with Latin rhythms. Very global, very eclectic.

Rutman's Violin Shop

11 Westland Avenue
(617) 578–0066
www.rutmansviolins.com

THE CATCH } Rutman's gratefully accepts donations for attending performances. } This store, which specializes in string instruments, doubles as a performance space. In its tiny recital area, which holds up to fifty people, you can see the classical stars of tomorrow today. Performers are often students from Berklee or the New England Conservatory. The easiest way to find out what's coming up is to call the store.

PUBLIC CONCERTS AND FESTIVALS

Walking through Boston in the summertime sometimes sounds like walking through a concert hall; there is music absolutely everywhere—downtown, along the river, tucked into plazas great and small, sometimes even in a train station at the peak of rush hour. Most public concert series begin in mid-June, when the weather finally turns consistently warm, but Boston's outdoor music lovers know that no matter what it's doing when you leave your house, always pack some rain gear. Public concerts are enormously popular in Boston—especially the ones that take place on the Esplanade—so go early, bring a folding chair, and enjoy all those gloriously free tunes!

Boston Blues Festival

www.bluestrust.com

Last weekend of September, noon to 6:00 P.M.

This festival is a free, two-day concert, and the grand finale of Boston Blues Week, which features concerts by blues royalty at venues in the city and surrounding communities.

Cambridge River Festival

Memorial Drive
Cambridge
(617) 349–4380
www.cambridgeartscouncil.org/community_river.html

Second or third Saturday in June, noon to 6:00 P.M.

A revered annual event in Boston, the River Festival occurs along a milelong stretch of Memorial Drive between JFK Street and Western Avenue that is closed down especially for the party (be prepared for traffic snarls). It features music from around the globe, arts, crafts, and food, all by the side of the Charles River. The festival is organized by the Cambridge Arts Council.

Fourth of July Celebration

The Hatch Memorial Band Shell
Charles River Esplanade (access by Fiedler Footbridge off Mugar Way at Beacon and Arlington Streets)
www.july4th.org

Concert is at 8:30 P.M. on July 3 and July 4.

This is the big daddy of outdoor concerts, the one that attracts over a million people who line both sides of the river just to be near the concert by the Boston Pops Orchestra, the dramatic cannon finale of the "1812 Overture," and, of course, the world-class fireworks display. The concert is broadcast around the world and has come to be known as "America's Fourth of July Celebration." This event caps off a weeklong series of happenings that occur throughout the city. If you don't like crowds, it's a good week to go out of town.

Die-hards who want to be as close as possible to the performance by the Pops and their special guests arrive at the Hatch Shell well before 9:00 A.M. to snag one of the 8,000 wristbands given out that allow in-and-out access to the Oval, the grassy seating area immediately in front of the Hatch Shell. Once the wristbands are gone, and they usually are by mid-morning, everyone else must find seating outside of the Oval. But not to fret—the view of the fireworks from the Oval isn't that great. The best of all worlds is to find a seat farther down the Esplanade where you have a clear view of the area directly over the river as well as the show. Small blankets and low beach chairs are allowed in the Oval, as are coolers, but alcohol is strictly prohibited throughout the Esplanade, and security guards check.

For those who are in it just for the music, the Pops does the same concert at the Hatch Shell on July 3, starting at 8:30 P.M. (but without the "1812 Overture," cannons, and fireworks).

Harborfest

(617) 227–1528
www.bostonharborfest.com

Event locations throughout Boston.

It's a precursor to the big Fourth of July celebration, and it takes over the city for seven days leading up to July 4. Harborfest happens all along the Boston Harbor waterfront, from the Charlestown Navy Yard to Castle Island. There are Revolutionary reenactments, tall ship tours, walking tours, and concerts. Many of the events charge a fee, but most of the concerts are free. Consult the Web site for all time and location information.

Waterfront Performing Arts Series

Christopher Columbus Park
Atlantic Avenue (in the North End, next to Marriott Hotel)
(617) 635–3911
www.cityofboston.gov/arts/default.asp

Tuesday evenings during summer, 6:00 to 8:00 P.M.

Local performing arts organizations, like the Boston Lyric Opera and the White Heat Orchestra, are showcased during this popular outdoor concert series.

WBOS EarthFest

The Hatch Memorial Band Shell
(617) 822–9600
www.earthfest.com

EarthFest is a free annual concert that started out to celebrate Earth Day, but since April 22 is usually cold and rainy here in Boston, the sponsoring radio station started holding this event in May. It starts about 10:00 A.M. and goes on until 6:00 P.M. The day is filled with popular live music acts, food-sampling opportunities, and education. There are over a hundred booths set up on the Charles River Esplanade with the purpose of educating people about the environment and nonprofit ecological organizations.

WBOS Copley Square Concert Series

Copley Square
www.boston.com

Thursday at 6:00 P.M., mid-July through August.

Some of the top alternative and pop artists in the country, including Howie Day, Aimee Mann, and Tracy Bonham, take the stage in the middle of Copley Square for this wonderful concert series that draws thousands (and really gnarls up traffic on the surrounding roads—so take the subway to the Copley stop on the Green Line, which lets you out directly across the street).

WCRB Classical Concert Series

(781) 893–7080
www.wcrb.com

Copley Square Plaza (at Dartmouth and St. James Streets, across from Boston Public Library)

Each Thursday at noon during June.

The Hatch Memorial Band Shell

Every Wednesday at 7:30 P.M., late June through early September.

Classical music in a classical setting.

MAKING BEAUTIFUL (FREE) MUSIC

The proliferation of competitive music schools in the Boston area means that it is a veritable embarrassment of riches for Cheap music lovers. The music schools and university music departments regularly host student recitals, and these aren't your garden-variety students—think Itzhak Perlman in his younger days. There are also frequent instructor recitals as well as workshops offered by visiting musicians. All of the schools listed below hold frequent free performances. Dates and times vary, so check out the Web sites for the latest offerings.

Boston Conservatory
8 The Fenway
(617) 912–9222
www.bostonconservatory.edu
The Conservatory offers lots of free performances from students, faculty, and visitors. Senior projects are also free and open to the public.

Boston University
Tsai Performance Center
685 Commonwealth Avenue
(617) 353–8724
www.bu.edu/tsai
The Tsai hosts frequent student and school organization musical performances, most of them free.

Longy School of Music
One Follen Street
Cambridge
(617) 876–0956
www.longy.edu
Concerts typically take place at the Edward M. Pickman Concert Hall, 27 Garden Street, Cambridge, but sometimes they take place in the different Longy recital rooms, also located on Garden Street.

New England Conservatory
Jordan Hall
30 Gainsborough Street
(617) 585–1260
www.concerts.newenglandconservatory.edu
The Conservatory's Jordan Hall is a lovely combination of opulence and intimacy, and it is arguably one of the most beautiful places to hear classical music played by those who have made it their life.

WFNX Concert Series

City Hall Plaza
Cambridge Street
(781) 595–6200
www.fnxradio.com

Various dates, usually 6:00 to 9:00 P.M.

Love alt rock and heavy metal? These concerts are just packed with your musical compadres, and things can get mighty lively when the speakers get turned up to 11. Each show features several bands. WFNX's largest free show is the Disorientation Tour—a welcome-back concert for students in September. The event kicks off in the early afternoon and is filled with music and booths—an alternative festival. Check the Web site for updates on artists and times.

WODS Concert Series

The Hatch Memorial Band Shell
(617) 787–7000
www.oldies1033.com

Each year for the past two decades, Oldies 103.3 has held their free summer concerts at the Hatch Shell. There are typically five concerts per summer, and they feature the "oldies but goodies" of the '50s and '60s. Past shows have featured Gloria Gaynor, Frankie Valli, and KC and the Sunshine Band. Shows start at 7:00 P.M. Oldies 103.3 is at the Hatch Shell as early as 2:00 P.M. with their advertising clients, giving away free goodies, so you can make a day of it. Bring blankets and lawn chairs. Shows run between two and three hours. Check the station's Web site for info on dates and performers.

{ THEATER: }
THE PLAY'S
THE THING

"If you must have motivation, think
of your paycheck on Friday."
— *Noel Coward's advice to actors*

Boston's theater scene has exploded in the past few years. Once the province of a few well-known theaters that hosted traveling productions of Broadway favorites, Boston is now home to a slew of new, smaller theaters featuring homegrown productions—a trend powered by local elites hungry for more homegrown cultcha (that's "culture" to those not from Boston). The city is now packed with brand-new and refurbished historic theater spaces, some ornate and some basic.

Today, there is something out there for everyone who loves theater, especially if you are a Cheap Bastard. That's because much of the best is free. When it's not free, it's available on the cheap. If you are willing to usher during a performance, the universe of free Boston shows grows even larger. Ushering is a great way to sample all the diversity (and, sometimes, perversity) in Boston's vibrant, eclectic, and active theater scene.

IT'S SHOWTIME!

The best way to figure out what shows are heading our way is to consult one of the many Web sites devoted to Boston theater. Among the most comprehensive is from Stage Source (www.stagesource.org), which maintains a quarterly listing of every performance going on in the area. It lists the hottest coming shows and their performance dates so you can get your name on the volunteer list in advance. Other good resources for keeping yourself in the know are Theatre Mania (www.theatremania.com), Boston Theatre Scene (www.bostontheatrescene.com), The Boston Globe (www.boston.com), and The Phoenix (www.thephoenix.com).

VOLUNTEER USHERING

Can you walk and chew gum at the same time? If so, you're already halfway to a lucrative part-time career as a volunteer theater usher. Most of the theaters and performance troupes in Boston are actively seeking people to help out in a variety of ways, and, in exchange, they're willing to let you stick around and see the show for free.

Some of the most well-known spaces in town, like the Wang Theatre, the Wilbur Theatre, the Colonial Theatre, and the Opera House, use unionized ushers and do not use volunteers. Most of the rest of the city's stages welcome volunteer ushers with open arms. The job couldn't be much easier, given the perks. After helping the paying ticket holders (poor suckers) to their seats, ushers are often allowed to fill whatever seats are left empty once the doors are closed, the lights fall, and the curtain rises. If no extra seats are available, many theaters will make folding chairs available, or, in rare instances, ushers will have to stand during the performance. But that's a small price to pay to watch award-winning thespians do their thing.

The dress code varies from formal to casual. Ushers are usually required to show up about an hour before the show to learn the seating plan, get familiar with the layout of the theater itself, get basic information so that they can answer theatergoers' questions—and then its go-time. Some theaters also ask that volunteers participate in some light cleanup after the show, so don't make any early dinner plans.

There's a very active ushering subculture in the city of Boston, so if you're interested in joining in, make your interest known well in advance. Ushering slots usually fill up quickly, especially for the most popular shows (like musicals). Most theaters that use ushers have a hotline, or an e-mail address, and will let you reserve your preferred date and performance up to three weeks in advance. Some will even allow you to book entire parties of ushers for a particular night, so it's a terrific way for a gang of friends to go to a show for a grand total of nada. And that's right in our price range, isn't it?

If the show or company that you're interested in isn't listed here, try giving them a call anyway (most administrative offices open at or after 10:00 A.M.). Theaters are constantly changing their policies, so you never know when they might start using volunteer ushers. There might also be other volunteer opportunities (such as administrative or marketing help) available that will also net you free seats for shows. Above all, don't be the least bit shy about asking—it's not the Cheap Bastard way!

Actors Shakespeare Project
(617) 661–9622, ext. 704 (house manager)
www.actorsshakespeareproject.org
ushers@actorsshakespeareproject.org

Ushers per performance: 3–4

This Shakespearean troupe performs in a variety of spaces throughout the city (mostly in Cambridge), winning awards and accolades from far and wide, including kudos from such unlikely observers as *New York* magazine (which cited actor Alvin Epstein's performance as King Lear as "The Best Performance New York Missed" in its December 2005 Culture Awards). If you don't want to miss it, too, make sure to call or e-mail the house manager at least a month in advance. The house manager keeps a database of ushers that they've used in the past, and he contacts them several weeks before a new performance starts to see who is interested. That's a list on which you definitely want to be.

Alarm Clock Theatre Company
476 Franklin Street, #1 (administrative offices)
Cambridge
www.alarmclocktheatre.org
info@alarmclocktheatre.org

Ushers per performance: 2

The Alarm Clock Theatre, one of the resident theater companies at the Boston Center for the Arts complex (see listing below), uses a variety of the stages there. It arranges its own ushers for its performances, however, so contact the company's managing director to get a chance to see one of its critically acclaimed performances, which have included plays by Israel Horowitz and other world-renowned writers, as well as plays by its own award-winning resident playwright, Dan Stroeh.

American Repertory Theatre
Loeb Drama Center
64 Brattle Street
Cambridge
(617) 496–2000, ext. 8817 (volunteer usher hotline)
www.amrep.org

Ushers per performance: 2–4

The grande dame of local theater, the ART has been offering award-winning plays in Cambridge since 1979. Founding director Robert Brustein and creative director Robert Woodruff have earned the ART the reputation as "one of the best three theater companies in the country," according to a review in *Time* magazine. Classic theater and cutting-edge premieres are the name of the game here, and there is a long list of regular ushers who make it a point to get in early for upcoming shows— so don't dawdle if you want to see the ART for free. Ushers don't seat people at this venue; they just hand out programs, take tickets, greet guests, and answer questions. Call the volunteer usher hotline two weeks before a show opening to reserve your spot. Make sure to leave two dates that you can usher. The house manager checks the hotline on Monday mornings.

Another Country Productions

P.O. Box 560192 (administrative offices)
West Medford, MA 02156
(617) 939–4846
www.anothercountry.org
lyralenkaye.acp@gmail.com

Ushers per performance: 1–4

Another Country Productions, which is in residence at the Devanaughn Theatre (see listing below), is a fringe theater favorite in Boston. Creators of SLAMBoston, a monthly, high-octane, short-play competition, ACP features regular productions that deal with diversity, inclusion, and gender issues. Contact the company's artistic director, Lyralen Kaye, via e-mail to volunteer for an usher spot. ACP prefers to hear from volunteers up to a month before a scheduled show, but Kaye encourages people to call at any time, as usher vacancies sometimes crop up at the last minute.

As Yet To Be Theatre Company

P.O. Box 410154 (administrative offices)
East Cambridge, MA 02141
(781) 258–0275
www.aytb.org
volunteers@aytb.org

Ushers per performance: 1

This small theater company is aiming its work at a younger audience (defined as thirty and under) and seeks to challenge conventional boundaries of what theater can be. It presents classics and new works, mostly at the Devanaughn Theatre stage. One weekend a year, it performs a series of one-act plays by local playwrights. Ushers should make their interest known via e-mail.

Blue Man Group

Charles Playhouse
74 Warrenton Street
(617) 426–6912
www.blueman.com

Ushers per performance: 12

They're wacky, they're rhythmic, they're blue. This show, which defies anything like description, has been packing the Charles Playhouse and creating delighted, and slightly confused, audiences for nearly twenty years. Although the theater uses a lot of ushers, make sure to call well in advance, as some shows (weekends, holidays) book up fast. Ushers must wear all black, but take our word for it: Don't wear anything that you don't want to get drenched with paint and other drippy stuff. Open-toed shoes are also verboten. Arrive an hour before showtime to get a briefing on seating, usher for about half an hour, then enjoy the show—and keep your head down! Volunteers stay behind to help the house staff clean for about twenty minutes after the show.

Boston Center for the Arts

539 Tremont Street
(617) 933–8673 (volunteer hotline)
www.bcaonline.org

Ushers per performance: varies

This theater and visual arts complex, which was completely redesigned in 2005, is home to several different performance spaces, including the BCA Plaza Theatre, the Black Box Theatre, the Stanford Calderwood Pavilion (which houses the main stage Virginia Wimberly Theatre), and the Nancy and Edward Roberts Studio Theatre. It is has five small resident theater companies that collectively represent some of the most cutting-edge (and multi-award-winning) theatrical talent around. From Celtic-themed plays to slapstick to drag, the BCA has become the theatrical hub of the Hub. In addition to the resident companies, the BCA hosts a variety of visiting companies. Shows change out frequently, so call the hotline to get a list of the shows for which usher spots are available.

Boston Playwrights' Theatre

949 Commonwealth Avenue
(617) 353–5443
www.bu.edu/bpt

Ushers per performance: 2

This theater company and performance space showcases the original works of local playwrights, many of whom have gone on to greatness. The theater space is also the home of the Boston University Graduate Playwriting Program. The theater's resident acting company participates in the Boston Theatre Marathon, a series of ten-minute plays staged in May. Many visiting theater companies also use the space (most make their own usher arrangements), so check the production calendar on its Web site and call the main number to make your reservations, which are taken up to three weeks in advance.

Boston Theatre Works

325 Columbus Avenue, Suite 11 (administrative offices)
www.bostontheatreworks.com
volunteer@bostontheatreworks.com

Ushers per performance: 2

The Boston Theatre Works has become a vibrant, important, and acclaimed player on the local theater scene. With shows like *Pulp,* a musical that explores the world of 1950s lesbian pulp fiction, to *Take Me Out,* about a baseball player's coming out, the BTW pushes the theatrical envelope while also embracing classics such as *Othello* (which it staged in cooperation with the lauded Shakespeare & Company of Lenox, Massachusetts). But BTW doesn't just act—it makes you think, with after-show discussions and Q&A sessions with actors. Once a year, the BTW stages BTW Unbound, a festival of new plays featuring local writers. Ushers should contact the theater two to four weeks in advance by e-mailing the volunteer coordinator.

Cambridge Multicultural Arts Center

41 Second Street
Cambridge
(617) 577–1400
www.cmacusa.org

Ushers per performance: varies

Theater and dance troupes, jazz musicians, and comedians perform regularly at this renovated former courthouse. The building also houses an art gallery with a rotating schedule of exhibits. The performance space manager books ushers for about half the shows that take place here. Check the Web site for the current performance schedule.

Company One

19 Littell Road (administrative offices)
Brookline
(617) 277–7032
www.companyone.org

Ushers per performance: 2

Company One bills itself as a "diverse fringe theatre for young diverse urban audiences." Launched in 1998 as a creative project between five friends, the company now regularly performs in the Boston Center for the Arts performance spaces—the big time here in Boston. They polished their fringe cred when they started the Boston Fringe Festival, which brings together smaller theater companies to perform short, one-act plays that push the limits of human experience, in works both familiar and original. Ushers should contact the house manager directly at the company's main number.

Devanaughn Theatre and Theatre Company

The Piano Factory
791 Tremont Street
(617) 247–9777
www.devtheatre.com

Ushers per performance: 2

The Devanaughn is home to its own fringe theater group (called the Devanaughn Theatre Company), which has tackled everything from Chekhov to Pinter and focuses its productions on works that dig down deep into the human psyche and look hard at whatever one finds there. Call the main number and leave your contact information for the executive director two weeks in advance to reserve an usher spot. Other theater companies also use the Devanaughn stage, and they generally arrange for their own ushers.

The Footlight Club

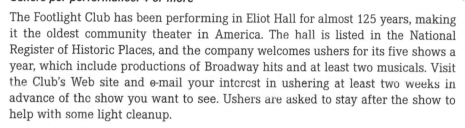

Eliot Hall
7A Eliot Street
Jamaica Plain
(617) 524–6506
www.footlight.org

Ushers per performance: 4 or more

The Footlight Club has been performing in Eliot Hall for almost 125 years, making it the oldest community theater in America. The hall is listed in the National Register of Historic Places, and the company welcomes ushers for its five shows a year, which include productions of Broadway hits and at least two musicals. Visit the Club's Web site and e-mail your interest in ushering at least two weeks in advance of the show you want to see. Ushers are asked to stay after the show to help with some light cleanup.

The Gold Dust Orphans

The Theater Machine (aka the Ramrod Center for the Performing Arts)
1256 Boylston Street
(617) 265–6222
www.thetheatermachine.com

Ushers per performance: 2

This all-male comedy drag troupe, fronted by writer/performer Ryan Landry, creates some of the funniest and most irreverent interpretations of the Great Canon of American Theater that you're likely to find anywhere, such as their critically acclaimed production of *Death of a Saleslady*. Landry and his posse perform in a small theater downstairs from a gay bar, the Ramrod, ensuring one of the most entertaining and provocative nights of theater in the city. Call Landry at least two weeks before the show for which you want to usher. Landry cautions that ushering opportunities go fast, so call sooner rather than later.

The Huntington Theatre Company/Boston University Theatre

264 Huntington Avenue
(617) 273–1666 (house manager)
www.huntingtontheatre.org

Ushers per performance: 8–10

The Huntington Theatre Company has received three Tony Award nominations for productions staged here and then transferred to Broadway, as well as six Elliot Norton Awards for Outstanding Production. As one of the premier theater companies in the country, the Huntington has produced over fifty American and world premieres, as well as reinventing productions of works by Shakespeare, Molière, Cole Porter, and Steven Sondheim. Needless to say, it's one of the most coveted volunteer usher opportunities in the city. Call early. Call often. Phone the house manager's line for volunteer details

Jewish Theatre of New England

333 Nahanton Street
Newton
(617) 558–6580 (main office)
www.lsjcc.org

Ushers per performance: 6–8

This local theater space hosts four to six shows by visiting performers each year, including musicals, drama, cabaret, comedy, and dance. Most feature a Jewish theme or Jewish performers. Past events have included monologist Rain Pryor, comedian Judy Gold, and the Klezmer Conservatory Band. Volunteers are asked to call the main office number to make usher reservations.

The Longwood Players

Cambridge Family YMCA Theatre
820 Massachusetts Avenue (Central Square)
Cambridge
(617) 566–3513 (Longwood Players house manager)
www.longwoodplayers.org
info@longwoodplayers.org

Ushers per performance: 2–4

The Longwood Players bring the biggest musical hits to Cambridge, including *La Cage aux Folles, West Side Story,* and *Singing in the Rain.* Call or e-mail no more than one month before a performance to reserve your ushering spot.

The Lyric Stage

140 Clarendon Street, second floor
(617) 585–5675 (box office)
www.lyricstage.com

Ushers per performance: 4

The Lyric Stage performance company puts on seven shows a season, including musicals and at least one play written by a Bostonian. The Lyric has routinely garnered the top awards from the Boston Theatre Critics Association and the Independent Reviewers of New England for its productions of such eclectic plays as *The Underpants,* by comedian Steve Martin, and *Sunday in the Park with George.* Ushers will greet, seat, and help patrons negotiate their way across the stage during intermission—a logistical necessity at this intimate performance space. Call the main box office number between noon and 5:00 P.M., and they'll put you on the list.

The Metro Stage Company

Cambridge Family YMCA Theatre
820 Massachusetts Avenue (Central Square)
(617) 524–5013 (Metro Stage administrative offices)
www.metrostagecompany.com

Ushers per performance: 2–4

This brand-spanking-new theater company is looking for volunteers for all of its performances, which have included *Godspell* and *Nunsense*. It is also willing to accommodate groups of friends or family members who want to usher together, as space allows. Call the Metro Stage administrative offices to reserve an ushering spot.

The New Repertory Theatre

The Arsenal Center for the Arts
321 Arsenal Street
Watertown
(617) 923–7060 (administrative offices)
www.newrep.org
usher@newrep.org

Ushers per performance: 9

The New Rep, now in its second decade, has received numerous awards for its productions of locally written plays as well as the classics. It is the resident theater company at the newly built Arsenal Center for the Arts in Watertown, just west of Boston. Its first season there included productions of *Romeo and Juliet*, *True West*, and *Ragtime*. The company needs lots of ushers, and you can reserve your spot as soon as the lineup for the new season is announced, usually in early March. (The season starts each September.) The best way to reserve is via e-mail. Couples or groups that want to usher together are very welcome. Public transportation is available to the Arsenal Square area from downtown Boston.

The Nora Theatre Company

Box 382034 (administrative offices)
Cambridge, MA 02238
(617) 491–2026
www.thenora.org
info@thenora.org

Ushers per performance: varies

By the time you read this, the critically acclaimed Nora Theatre Company will be snugly tucked into their new theater in Central Square in Cambridge. The company intends to use ushers for some, but not all, of its performances, so call or e-mail several weeks before a show opens to determine what their ushering needs will be. Try to usher on a Wednesday when the company hosts its free post-performance wine tastings. Post-play discussions take place after Thursday shows. You're not required to stay for either, but it's a nice way to end your theatrical evening.

PAY WHAT YOU WANT NIGHT

The Theatre Offensive, Up You Mighty Race Performing Arts Company, and the Zeitgeist Theatre Company have regular "Pay What You Want" nights as part of every show run. On these special nights, theatergoers may literally pay whatever they want to see the show. Nights vary by performance, so check out the companies' Web sites for information on the specific nights when you can be as cheap a bastard as you wanna be.

Queer Soup
(617) 824–4297
www.queersoup.net
info@queersoup.net

Ushers per performance: 1–2

This fringe theater company performs locally written plays, mostly comedy, about gay, lesbian, bisexual, and transgender issues. It has made a name for itself as a creative, edgy, extremely funny company that performs at the Black Box Theatre at the Boston Center for the Arts, the Boston Playwrights' Theatre, and other spaces throughout the city. To reserve an ushering spot, contact the company via e-mail.

The Regent Theatre
7 Medford Street
Arlington
(781) 643–4488
www.regenttheatre.com

Ushers per performance: 4

This ninety-year-old theater space was built as an E. M. Loew's vaudeville house, so it has showbiz in its very bones. The newly formed CORE Stage Company, which specializes in musicals like The Who's *Tommy,* took up residence here last year. The Regent also hosts musical and traveling company performances. In 2004 the Regent made local headlines with the performance of *Sin: A Cardinal Deposed,* a play about the sexual abuse lawsuits against the Archdiocese of Boston, performed by the Bailiwick Repertory of Chicago. In a real rarity for these parts, the Regent has free parking across the street. Ushers should call between noon and 5:00 P.M. during the week to reserve a spot. Join the e-mail list for a monthly newsletter of upcoming events and bargain ticket opportunities.

Roxbury Center for the Arts at Hibernian Hall

182-186 Dudley Street
Roxbury
(617) 541–3900, ext. 2324 (performance space manager)
www.rcahh.org

Ushers per performance: varies

The newly refurbished Hibernian Hall is now home to the Roxbury Center for the Arts, which hosts several small local theater companies that specialize in African-American–themed performances. The space manager at the RCA coordinates some, but not all, of the usher opportunities at the Hibernian, so call ahead to find out which shows they're booking ushers for. If they're not booking ushers for a particular show you want to see, the RCA's manager is happy to direct you to the correct volunteer contact person at the theater company staging the performance.

Stuart Street Playhouse

200 Stuart Street
(617) 426–4499, ext. 13
www.stuartstreetplayhouse.com
HouseManager@stuartstreetplayhouse.com

Ushers per performance: varies

Housed in the Radisson Hotel on Stuart Street, the Stuart Street Playhouse and company have distinguished themselves in the past ten years by performing and hosting an eclectic selection of off-Broadway hits (such as *Stomp* and *Forever Plaid*), provocative social commentary (like the long-running *I Love You, You're Perfect, Now Change* and *Menopause, the Musical*), and standards (*Jacques Brel Is Alive and Well and Living in Paris*). To volunteer, call the house manager or e-mail your ushering desires.

Sugan Theatre Company

75 Garfield Street (administrative offices)
Cambridge
(617) 497–5134
www.sugan.org
peter@sugan.org

Ushers per performance: 1

Introducing Boston audiences to Celtic- and Irish-themed theater, as well as Irish and Celtic writers, directors, and actors, is the mission of the Sugan Theatre Company. Considered one of the best local theater companies in the city, the Sugan has earned rave reviews for its productions of *Tom Crean—Antarctic Explorer, Talking to Terrorists,* and *Women on the Verge of HRT*. Ushers are encouraged to sign up one to two weeks before the show is scheduled to begin. To reserve a spot, e-mail the company's managing director, Peter O'Reilly.

The Theatre Offensive

(617) 621–6090
www.thetheateroffensive.org
joinus@thetheateroffensive.org

Ushers per performance: 2–4

They're here, they're queer, and they're on the offensive. The Theater Offensive, a resident company at the Boston Center for the Arts, has been celebrating gay, lesbian, bisexual, and transgender culture and politics for over fifteen years, gathering an impressive lineup of local theater awards along the way. It also produces the *OUT ON THE EDGE* Festival of Queer Theatre, *Plays at Work*, new works by queer and local artists, *True Colors Out* Youth Theater, and *A Street Theater Named Desire*. Ushers should contact the company's office phone number or e-mail them.

Turtle Lane Players

283 Melrose Street
Newton
(617) 244–0169

Ushers per performance: up to 3

The Turtle Lane Players do one thing and do it well: musicals. This small local theater troupe has previously performed everything from Gilbert and Sullivan's works to *The Full Monty*. To reserve an ushering spot, call the box office between 11:00 A.M. and 5:30 P.M. on weekdays. Ushers will be asked to help clean up after the show.

Up You Mighty Race Performing Arts Company

8 Pleasanton Street (administrative offices)
Dorchester
(617) 427–9417
www.upyoumightyrace.org

Ushers per performance: 2–4

This company, which derives its name from a quote from civil rights leader Marcus Garvey, focuses on black classic theater. Now in its sixth year, the company was founded by Akiba Abaka, a local woman who was discouraged with the lack of outlets for black-themed theater in the Boston area. The company has staged performances of August Wilson's work, as well as *Joe Turner's Come and Gone, Raisin,* and other classic plays written by renowned black playwrights. The company also does pro bono and reduced-price performances. Contact Abaka directly at the main office number at least three weeks in advance to reserve an usher spot.

Wheelock Family Theatre
180 The Riverway
(617) 879–2000 (main number)
(617) 879–2147 (volunteer usher coordinator)
www.wheelock.edu/wft/wft.asp

Ushers per performance: 4–8

The WFT has won just about every award that a family-themed theater company can win, with its lively productions of *Tuck Everlasting, Alice in Wonderland,* and *Pippi Longstocking.* The company also produces at least one musical and one adult drama during the season. Ushers' dress code is casual. Call the volunteer usher coordinator directly to make a reservation.

Zeitgeist Stage Company
116 West Newton Street (administrative offices)
(617) 759–8836
www.zeitgeiststage.com
ZeitgeistStage@aol.com

Ushers per performance: 1–2

The Zeitgeist Stage Company has been electrifying Boston audiences since 2002 with plays that explore controversial subjects like racism, mental health, and war. The company won the 2005 Elliot Norton Award for Outstanding Local Fringe Theatre Production from the Boston Theatre Critics Association for its production of *Blue/Orange.* The company is in residence at the Boston Center for the Arts, where it performs mainly in the complex's Black Box Theatre. Ushers should e-mail the artistic director to reserve a spot two to three weeks in advance of the desired production. The earlier the better—ushering opportunities at Zeitgeist are one of the hottest tickets in town.

CHEAP TICKETS

Free is the bomb, but cheap is good, too. If ushering isn't your bag, there are plenty of ways to see theater in Boston—including the most popular productions at a reduced price.

Bostix Ticket Booths
Copley Square (corner of Boylston and Dartmouth Streets)

Hours: Monday through Saturday, 10:00 A.M. to 6:00 P.M.; Sunday, 11:00 A.M. to 4:00 P.M.; closed Patriots Day, Thanksgiving, and Christmas.

Faneuil Hall Marketplace (Congress Street)

Hours: Tuesday through Saturday, 10:00 A.M. to 6:00 P.M.; Sunday, 11:00 A.M. to 4:00 P.M.; closed Monday, Thanksgiving, and Christmas.

www.artsboston.org

THE CATCH

} Tickets available at the booths are cash only.

Bostix, operated by ArtsBoston, is the best way to score half-price, same-day tickets to some of the city's most coveted shows. You must show up in person on the day of the show to take advantage of the half-price deal. Lines can be long, so bring a cup of coffee, something to read, and a fistful of dollars. If you hate lines, check out the Bostix Web site at www.artboston.org, where you can buy reduced-price (although not half-price) tickets for future shows. Sign up on the Bostix Web site for the e-mail newsletter to receive a sneak peek at the next day's bargain theater opportunities before anyone else.

Stage Source

88 Tremont Street, Suite 714
(617) 720–6066
www.stagesource.org

THE CATCH

} Membership in Circle of Friends is $50.

Although it was created to service the theater community—performers, artists, and theaters—Stage Source has become the theater lover's best friend. By joining its Circle of Friends, you receive a special membership card that will get you two-for-one ticket deals for over fifty different theater companies in the metro-Boston area. It's even tax deductible. Stage Source also maintains a list of all the theater performances in Boston, and members get a heads-up on free or reduced-price performances throughout the year.

Wheelock Family Theatre

180 The Riverway
(617) 879–2000 (main number)
www.wheelock.edu/wft/wft.asp

Because it is a family-oriented theater company and understands that taking your entire brood out for a night of wholesome theatrical entertainment can put a strain on the wallet, the Wheelock Family Theatre has a policy of never turning away anyone because of inability to pay. They won't ask for proof, but this offer should be used by those who really need it. The theater also has half-price deals for members of many local organizations and employers, so call ahead to see if you qualify for the deal.

IN A RUSH

Many theaters in the Boston area offer reduced-price tickets an hour before the show, called rush tickets. Come bearing cold, hard cash (that's all most theaters will take for rush tickets) and score some really cheap seats. The tickets are on an availability basis, so if you're in a large party, you might not all get seated together. Call the theater ahead of time to find out its policies.

ALWAYS FREE

Commonwealth Shakespeare Company
Boston Common
270 Tremont Street (administrative offices)
(617) 532–1252
www.freeshakespeare.org
info@freeshakespeare.org

It has become an annual ritual as beloved as the Fourth of July—free Shakespeare on the Boston Common. For three glorious weeks each July into August, the Commonwealth Shakespeare Company performs one of the Bard's classics for all to enjoy. The performances draw thousands to the grass of the Common (on the Charles Street side), and the entire park becomes a theater for three hours.

If you plan to attend, go early. Shows start promptly at 8:00 P.M. on Tuesday through Saturday and at 7:00 P.M. on Sunday (on Monday they rest). By late afternoon, devoted fans are already staking their claim by the front of the stage. Bring a low chair or a blanket (chair rentals are available), a picnic supper, and nonalcoholic beverages (booze is forbidden) and bask in the glory of great free theater.

If free isn't good enough for you, you Cheap Bastard, then volunteer to help the CSC put on their mammoth productions, and you'll get special VIP seating at a performance for yourself and a guest. For more information about volunteering, e-mail.

Theatre Is Alive
www.tcg.org

Been dying to see a show at a particular theater, but just never got around to it? Well, sometimes, procrastination pays. In this case, Theatre Is Alive will give you a chance to finally see a show at that theater—for free. This special one-night national event, which happens in October every year, lets you see a performance free in any participating theater as long as you have never been to a show at that theater before. It is up to the individual theaters to figure out how to keep track of that (we suspect that all will be welcome on this special night). Started in 2005 by the Theatre Communications Group, a nonprofit theater-arts organization, the free-theater-athon idea was expanded to Boston in 2006. Information on participating venues and dates is available on the group's Web site.

{ DANCE: }
FREE-FORM

"Your love for yourself is only shown
when you are dancing freely."

—*Anonymous*

Whether it's to keep warm during our cold winter months, or to pay homage to the blessed arrival of spring and summer, Bostonians are always dancing. There's an enormous culture of dance in the city, with dozens of tiny dance companies holding free performances at venues great and small, and free dance festivals scheduled throughout the year. Clubs and impromptu participatory dance events are easy to find, and their motto is always the same—the more the merrier. For those who picture themselves as the next Nureyev, dance education at many of the studios and schools in the area is also free for the asking for those willing to put in some hours in trade. So strap on your dancing shoes and enjoy all that this great dance city has to offer.

WATCHING IT

Big Moves
(617) 869–2970
www.bigmoves.org
info@bigmoves.org

THE CATCH } Volunteers, especially those willing to put up show flyers, can see shows for free.

This organization welcomes people of all sizes for classes in most forms of dance and movement. Big Moves also fields a dance troupe of fifteen dancers who perform hip-hop, modern, jazz, and ballet at spaces around town. Big Moves does not currently have a home studio, but a schedule of classes and shows, with locations, is available on its Web site or by e-mailing the address listed above. Send e-mail to the same address to volunteer.

BoSoma Dance Company
50 North Beacon Street (administrative offices)
Brighton
(978) 500–3057
www.bosoma.org
company@bosoma.org

Ushers and volunteers can see the shows for free. } BoSoma has made a name for itself with its modern, highly athletic form of dance that blends classical ballet, Indian, West African, and jazz to push the limits of the human body. Its shows are always a popular ticket in town, and the company uses volunteer ushers when it performs at such prestigious venues as the Tsai Performance Center at Boston University. Volunteers are also needed to help with marketing and publicity and to get the word out to the community about this innovative troupe. Contact the company through its Web site to find out more about ushering or volunteer opportunities.

The Boston Conservatory

31 Hemenway Street (main stage theater)
(617) 536–6340
www.bostonconservatory.edu

Founded in 1867, this preeminent fine arts school hosts several free full-length student performances each year—two in the spring and several more in the fall. Check the Web site for dates and times.

Cambridge Dance Month

Venues throughout Cambridge
(617) 547–9363, ext. 15
www.dancemonth.com

Every May.

Although many events are already free, volunteers can attend every event for nothing. Call in early February to sign up. } The mayor of Cambridge and the Dance Complex, a local teaching and performance studio that promotes dance throughout the area, host this monthlong celebration of movement. The events kick off at a special ceremony on the first Saturday of May, when the mayor declares it Dance Month. Dance events include free classes, performances, and studio open houses. The most compelling part of Dance Month is "Dance Distractions," which event organizers call "outbreaks of movement in an unusual or choreographically underused location, a spontaneous frolic evoking a joyous response." Such locations have included bank lobbies, city council meetings, and major intersections during red lights. Most Dance Month events are free or suggest a small donation. The rest cost between $1.00 and $30.00. The Dance Month calendar is posted at the beginning of April.

Charles River Dance Festival

The Dance Complex
536 Massachusetts Avenue
Cambridge
(978) 239–1135 (volunteer coordinator)
www.riversidedancecompany.20m.com

Two days every March.

THE CATCH

Volunteer before the event to see the shows for free. Call in early February.

This two-day event has featured many of the best small dance companies in town, like Dance Edge, BoSoma, Amara, Caroline Patterson, and Synergy Dance Company. Tickets are usually $15, but the event's organizers need lots of help before the show to get the festival off the ground. To volunteer, contact organizers directly in February at the number listed above.

Collage Dance Ensemble

16 Braeland Avenue (administrative offices)
Newton Centre
(617) 795–2468
www.collageusa.org
info@collageusa.org

THE CATCH

Ushers and volunteers can see the shows for free.

This acclaimed performance company, which blends folk and contemporary dance, performs at some of the largest theatrical spaces in town, so they're always looking for ushers. They're also eager for help in all aspects of production—everything from running lights and ironing costumes backstage to writing grants and marketing. Not only do ushers and volunteers get to see the shows for free, but volunteers are also allowed to take classes with the dance troupe, a unique treat reserved only for those who are a part of the dance company's organization.

Dance Across the City

Shubert Theatre
265 Tremont Street
(617) 532–1263
www.danceacrossthecity.org

January (date varies each year); registration at 8:00 A.M. on the day of the event.

This free, one-day event features classes and performances by some of the world-famous dance companies that call Boston home. In the past the event has featured workshops and performances by members of the Boston Ballet, the Mark Morris Dance Company, and the Snappy Dance Theatre. Registration for the event takes place in the reception area of the Wang Center for the Performing Arts (next to the Shubert), and attendance is on a first-come, first-served basis. This series is hosted by the Wang Center for the Performing Arts and the Bank of America Celebrity Series, and it is one of the most popular events in town for dance lovers of all ages. Get there early and expect a line well before registration begins. The schedule is posted at least a month in advance.

Monkeyhouse Dance Company

www.monkeyhouselovesme.com
MonkeyhouseLovesMe@gmail.com

Various times and venues throughout the city.

This innovative, humorous modern dance trio does free performances throughout the city as part of their Princess Pamplemousse Project. The princess is a character that Monkeyhouse founder Karen Krolak invented to help explain dance choreography to audiences. The troupe also presents regular free performances for those who want to skip the lesson and get straight to the narrative-driven, sometimes zany dance for which this company is known.

Prometheus Dance

536 Massachusetts Avenue, Studio 6 (The Dance Complex)
Cambridge
(617) 576–5336
www.prometheusdance.org
info@prometheusdance.org

THE CATCH
} Ushers see the shows for free.

This award-winning and highly acclaimed modern dance ensemble actually consists of two groups: the main troupe and the elders ensemble, composed of fifty-somethings and above who give the youngsters a run for their money. Both troupes do free shows around town from time to time. A listing is available on their Web site. Rehearsals are also open to the public. The main troupe rehearses on Tuesday and Thursday from noon to 2:00 P.M. The elder group's rehearsal times vary, so call ahead for information. The main troupe uses ushers for its paid performances, which have taken place at the Boston Conservatory Theatre and the Dance Complex. Call the house manager at the main number if you want to see the show for free as an usher.

Sayat Nova Dance Company of Boston

Newton
(617) 923–4455
www.sayatnova.com

THE CATCH
} Volunteers and ushers can see the show for free.

Armenian folk dance is a swirl of colors and emotions celebrating the ancestral home of many Bostonians. This twenty-year-old, award-winning company, which tours the world, does a number of local shows at such prestigious venues as the Emerson Majestic Theatre. Sayat Nova uses ushers frequently for its Boston-area performances. The job requires taking tickets, selling items at the company's concession stand in the front of the house, and seating guests. Volunteers should call about a month before a show to participate. Volunteers are also needed year-round to get the word out about this company's activities.

DOING IT

Boston Swing Dance

The St. James Armenian Church
465 Mt. Auburn Street (corner of School Street)
Watertown
(978) 440–7832 (volunteer line)
www.bostonswingdance.com
claire@bostonswingdance.com (volunteer e-mail)

Usually second Saturday of the month, September through June; lessons at 8:00 P.M.; social dance 9:00 P.M. to midnight.

THE CATCH

} Volunteer for one hour at the dance to get in for free.

This monthly event is very popular with the Boston swing dance community, thanks to a combination of great live swing bands and a fantastic wood floor. It's $13 to take part, but you can dance and take lessons for free if you volunteer to sell tickets and drinks for an hour during the night. Contact the volunteer coordinator, and she'll put you on a list of volunteers. There are a lot of regulars, but eventually your name will be called up and you'll be assigned a one-hour shift. Check the Web site for the full schedule.

Free Swing at Copley Square

Dartmouth Street at St. James Street
www.fiveguysnamedmike.org
www.itsallswing.com

Every other Sunday, June through September, 1:00 to 4:00 P.M.

This free swing dance happening is an impromptu event pulled together by the local swing dance community, spearheaded by five guys from Boston named Mike who love swing dancing. Updates on dates of the events, scheduled deejays, and rain dates are available on their Web site or on www.itsallswing.com, another swing dance Web site for local hoofers.

MIT Folk Dance Club

Massachusetts Institute of Technology
MIT Student Center
84 Massachusetts Avenue
Cambridge
(617) 253–3655
http://web.mit.edu/fdc/www/

Second and fourth Tuesday of the month, 8:00 to 10:30 P.M.; Wednesday and Sunday, 8:00 to 11:00 P.M.

$5.00 suggested donation for non-students. } The Folk Dance Club at the Massachusetts Institute of Technology, started over forty years ago by students, offers three different types of folk dances to keep you in touch with the motherland. Dances from around the world can be found on Sunday night, Israeli dances on Wednesday night, and America's homegrown Contra dances every other Tuesday night. The dances are usually held in the fourth floor of the MIT student center but are subject to change, so check the Web site before venturing out. Organizers say that the donation is "just a suggestion." It helps pay for the cookies and lemonade that are available at some of the dances. Beginners are welcomed, and introductory lessons are given at the start of each class.

MIT Lindy Hop Society

Massachusetts Institute of Technology
MIT Student Center
84 Massachusetts Avenue (various classrooms)
Cambridge
http://web.mit.edu/swing
http://mit-swing.blogspot.com

Wednesday night, 8:30 to 11:30 P.M.

The dance is free, but they sometimes ask all participants for donations. } Lindy hop, swing, and sometimes even salsa are the *raison d'être* of this student-run dance club. Introductory classes usually start at 7:30 P.M., and the social dance starts after that. The room location changes from week to week, and sometimes so does the lesson start time, so check the Web site for up-to-the-minute scheduling info.

Tango by Moonlight

Weeks Pedestrian Bridge (over the Charles at the intersection of Memorial Drive and DeWolfe Street)
(617) 699–6246 (tango line)
www.bostontango.com

Full-moon nights from May through September, 7:30 to 11:00 P.M.

Imagine the sight of more than a hundred people, locked in the classic tango embrace, swirling across a historic footbridge over the Charles River in the moonlight. Even if you don't tango, it's a sight worth seeing. This magical dance event, organized by the Tango Society of Boston, has become a blockbuster event that draws people from all over the metro area. A fifteen-minute tango lesson precedes the festivities.

GET YOUR GROOVE ON

With all the options, keeping track of what's happening in the dance community in Boston can be a daunting task, but several good Web sites will keep track of it all for you. Visit these sites for great information on free and low-cost dance events going on all over town.

The Boston Dance Alliance

www.Bostondancealliance.org
This is the premier dance advocacy organization in Boston promoting dance. Here you'll find a list of upcoming performances and links to most of the area's dance organizations, troupes, and performance spaces.

Have to Dance

www.havetodance.com
There's a very comprehensive monthly calendar of all Boston dance events on this site, as well as links to dance clubs and studios. One-stop shopping for all your dance needs!

West African Dance in Boston (WADaBo)

www.wadabo.com
This organization promotes West African dance and culture in the Boston area and maintains a list of free performances taking place around the city. It's also an online gathering place for teachers of African dance.

WORK-STUDY

Whether your dream is a life in a tutu or in a pair of tap shoes, work-study programs at local dance studios can help make it come true for very little money. Some of these programs are more formal than others, and some involve a fairly extensive training program before you're allowed to take part. But once you've got a regular gig, you will be allowed to exchange all your hard work for classes taught by some of the best dancers in the area. Next stop—Theatre District!

Be One Studios

62 Warren Street
Roxbury
(866) 442–2411
www.beoneboston.com
info@beoneboston.com

This new studio offers yoga, modern and urban dance, and martial arts classes for free to people who will help out on a regular basis. The studio asks for a regular weekly time commitment for those people wishing to take regular classes.

CasaNia Studio

46 Porter Road (off Massachusetts Avenue at Porter Square)
Cambridge
(617) 491–5144
www.casania.com

Nia, a combination of modern dance, martial arts, and healing arts, is the specialty at CasaNia. Work-study participants can exchange one hour of work for a one-hour class. The studio also offers over twenty-seven classes per week in forms such as modern, African, ballroom, salsa, and belly dance. Work-study duties include activities such as assisting teachers with attendance and cleaning up studios after class.

Dance Complex

536 Massachusetts Avenue
Cambridge
(617) 547–9363 (volunteer line: ext. 11)
www.dancecomplex.org

The Dance Complex has more than seventy classes a week in all forms of dance in its six studios. It has a formalized work-study program that awards students one class-hour credit or one hour of rehearsal space for each hour worked. There's a four-week training period for work-study participants, for a total of about eight hours, after which the studio asks for a minimum sixteen-week commitment of two to three and a half hours per week. They also ask that you commit to the same time each week and make arrangements to have your shift covered if you can't make it.

There are two main types of volunteer positions available: the front desk and facility maintenance. The front-desk position involves answering phones, taking reservation requests for classes and performances at the Dance Complex, and handling all cash transactions. The facility-maintenance job involves cleaning and maintenance of the building. There is usually a waiting list for both of these positions, but there is turnover, so the sooner you get on the list, the sooner you can start hoofing!

{ COMEDY:
CHEAP LAUGHS }

"Always laugh when you can . . .
it is cheap medicine."

—*Lord Byron*

Boston has spawned more than its share of world-famous comics: Jay Leno, Conan O'Brien, Denis Leary, Janeane Garafalo, Anthony Clark, Steve Sweeney, Dane Cook, Paula Poundstone, Steven Wright . . . and they all started at one of the many comedy clubs in Boston. Sadly for Cheap Bastards, free laughs in this town are hard to find. Most clubs charge at least $8.00 to $10.00 for a show (and most of the time, the comics see very little of it . . . ah, such is showbiz). Still, some of the best and most innovative humor in the city can be had for free, sometimes with a catch, sometimes without. Either way, you've got a very good chance of catching a rising star at one of these comedy shops.

CLUBS

All Asia Bar

332 Massachusetts Avenue
Cambridge
(617) 497–1544
First Tuesday of the month, 7:30 P.M.
www.allasiabar.com
www.stashcomedyjam.com

THE CATCH

There is a one-drink minimum, but it can be cola or spring water.

The All Asia is the site of the underground comedic stylings of Stash and his crew of merry henchmen, all of whom take over the bar at the All Asia once a month to do whatever takes their comedic fancy—which doesn't really leave much out, so leave the kids at home.

TALK FUNNY TO ME

Comedy MeetUps
http://comedy.meetup.com/cities/us/ma/boston/

THE CATCH

} You must be eighteen or older to register.

Sometimes, the best laughs come from just hanging around with funny people. If you'd like to connect with some funny people in Boston, then MeetUp is the best way to do it for free. MeetUp.com, a Web site that facilitates in-person gatherings for people with similar interests, has a very active Boston comedy meetup group. Register on their Web site, and then log into one of the many Boston comedy meetups (there's one for sketch comics, improv comics, and stand-up comics). The group moderator will schedule the meetups off-line, and if you're registered, you'll be in the know. You're not required to say funny things when you meet up with the comics, but they're all Cheap Bastards too, and if you don't hold your own, you could get stuck with the tab.

Emerald Isle Bar and Lounge

1501 Dorchester Avenue
Dorchester
(617) 288–0010
Open mic: Wednesday at 8:30 P.M.
Comedy show: Sunday at 8:30 P.M.

THE CATCH

} These nights fill up, so get there around 7:30 P.M.

This is one of the best comedy clubs in the city because it's run by Rich Gustavson, an accomplished comic in his own right and a great friend to the Boston comedy scene. There's no cover or drink minimum for either of these shows. Word is that the kitchen even shovels out a few free pizzas for the crowd on Wednesday nights.

The Green Dragon Tavern
11 Marshall Street (near Faneuil Hall Marketplace)
(617) 367–0055
www.somersirishpubs.com

Monday at 10:00 P.M.

Comedians duke it out in an open-mic format for cash prizes at this historic pub in the heart of the Quincy Market/Faneuil Hall area.

Sally O'Brien's Bar

335 Somerville Avenue (Union Square)
Somerville
(617) 666–3589
www.sallyobriensbar.com

Titters Comerdy Club, Monday at 7:30 P.M.

"Hungry comedians will joke for food" is how this night of free comedy is sold to the masses. A roster of local comics compete for a free dinner, and the audience votes on who wins. With a free meal at stake, suffice it to say that some of these guys will never be funnier.

Sweetwater Café

5 Boylston Place
(617) 351–2515

Wednesday at 9:30 P.M.

In the lower level of the Sweetwater is a little oasis of funny along the busy "Alley," a club and restaurant arcade in downtown Boston. There is no drink minimum. The show is made up of prescheduled comedians, but occasionally there are open-mic opportunities, so find the person in charge before the show starts if you're eager to try out your new "material" on an unsuspecting crowd.

THAT VOODOO THAT YOU DO

Mystery Lounge at the Comedy Studio

Upstairs at the Hong Kong Restaurant
1236 Massachusetts Avenue
Cambridge
(617) 661–6507
www.mysterylounge.com

Tuesday, 7:00 to 8:00 P.M.

The Comedy Studio, just outside Harvard Square, has been called the greatest comedy club in the world. While we can't prove this, we can prove that it is the only place in town to see a live magic cabaret show. The Mystery Lounge, started by local magicians in 1997, takes place in the Comedy Studio on Tuesday nights at 8:00 P.M. and costs $10. But you can get a sneak peek at the magic to come by heading to the second-floor lounge to see one hour of jaw-dropping "close-up" magic—card tricks, pulling things out of people's noses—for absolutely free. There is no drink minimum. And who knows, maybe one of the close-up magicians will pull $10 out of your ear so you can go upstairs and see the stage show, too.

COMEDY FESTIVAL

Boston International Comedy and Movie Festival
119 Braintree Street (administrative offices)
Allston
(617) 782–8100
www.bostoncomedyfestival.com
Eight days in mid-September.

Although most of the performances and movie screenings surrounding this acclaimed comedy festival, which was launched in 2000, cost money (and the tickets are getting harder to get every year), the festival plans at least one large, free event to bring comedy to the downtrodden masses. The location and the date vary, so check the Web site for details. The schedule is usually posted by early August.

WORK IT OUT

The smell of the greasepaint, the roar of the crowd, the humiliation of running out of funny things to say—such is the world of improv. Improvisational comedy is one of the most popular types of entertainment in the city. The shows pack up night after night, with some improv troupes doing two or more shows, six nights a week. And now you—yes, you—can be part of this exciting world! In exchange for a few hours of work a week, two local improv groups will make you part of their slightly dysfunctional family. They'll let you watch as much improv as you can stomach, and maybe even teach you the tricks of the trade.

ImprovBoston
1253 Cambridge Street
Cambridge
(617) 576–1253
www.improvboston.com
www.improvboston.com/training/scholarship.html (Matt Carey Scholarship)

One of the best improv troupes in the city, ImprovBoston is looking for people to work in the box office for a minimum of three shows per month and do some light office work. Not only will you get a small stipend (that's right, they're paying you), but you will also get an ImprovBoston membership card that will let you see as many shows as you want for free. The troupe performs two to three shows a night (except for Mondays). ImprovBoston also offers an annual scholarship in honor of former alum Matt Carey, who died in 2004. The scholarship covers the cost of ImprovBoston workshops and a master class for an undiscovered improv talent in training.

The Tribe

Tribe Theater
67 Stuart Street
(617) 510–4447
www.tribeboston.com
workstudy@tribeboston.com

THE CATCH

> You must be nineteen or older to attend shows at The Tribe Theater.

This improv and sketch comedy group has an innovative work-study program for people interested in learning improv. You'll need to enroll in the program and work at least eight hours per week (as an usher, member of the stage crew, box office staff, or intern in other departments). In return, you can see an unlimited number of shows for free and even take free improv training classes. The Tribe offers four different levels of training, and you need to log at least twelve hours of work per level. Shows are on Thursday and Friday, with other shows on occasional Saturdays and Sundays. Shows typically begin at 8:00 P.M.

{FILM:}
CELLULOID ZEROES

"We're so poor, we don't even have a
language! Just a stupid accent!"

—*Mel Brooks*, Robin Hood: Men in Tights

Remember the good old days, when a family of four could head to the local drive-in to see the latest Hollywood blockbuster for just five bucks a car? Neither do I. But don't despair. Despite the conventional wisdom that it costs an arm and a leg to see a film in Boston, there are plenty of ways to see lots of movies for free, or darned near it. Take your pick of the cherished classics, latest releases, and even those impenetrable foreign films (with distracting subtitles) throughout the city of Boston. Most places, especially the outdoor venues, encourage you to bring your own snacks, so you'll spend as much for a big night out as you would have if you'd just stayed home on the couch in front of the tube—again. Films are a lot more enjoyable when you see them on the really big screen, like their makers intended, and even more so when they're free!

ALWAYS FREE

Boston Public Library
700 Boylston Street (Copley Square)
(617) 536–5400
www.bpl.org/news/upcomingevents.htm

Film events and series are ongoing.

You could spend the next month in the Boston Public Library and still find new things to do every day. It hosts a variety of film series throughout the year featuring such diverse cinematic offerings as short films by acclaimed local documentary director David Sutherland and a series of full-length feature films on life in China. Founded in 1848, the Boston Public Library was the first large free library in the United States, which makes it a hallowed place near and dear to our cheap little hearts. In addition, the following branch libraries have regularly scheduled adult and children's films. Many other branches have randomly scheduled films, so check the main BPL Web site listed above for the latest schedules for each branch.

CHARLESTOWN
179 Main Street; (617) 242–1248; children's film on Tuesday at 10:30 A.M.

DORCHESTER
Lower Mills Branch, 27 Richmond Street; (617) 298–7841; children's film on Friday at 10:30 A.M. (schedule varies; consult Web site for details).

EAST BOSTON
276 Meridian Street; (617) 569–0271; children's film on Friday at 10:00 and 11:00 A.M.

JAMAICA PLAIN
Connolly Branch, 433 Centre Street; (617) 522–1960; children's film on Wednesday at 10:30 A.M.

MATTAPAN
10 Hazelton Street; (617) 298–9218; children's film on Thursday at 10:30 A.M.

NORTH END
25 Parmenter Street; (617) 227–8135; children's film on Monday at 11:00 A.M.; adult film time and dates vary.

ROSLINDALE
4238 Washington Street; (617) 323–2343; preschooler film on Monday at 10:30 A.M.

ROXBURY
Dudley Branch, 65 Warren Street; (617) 442–6186; preschooler film on Tuesday at 10:30 A.M.; adult film series on Thursday at 5:30 P.M.

Egleston Square Branch, 2044 Columbus Avenue; (617) 445–4340; preschooler film on Monday at 10:30 A.M.; adult film on Thursday at 1:00 P.M.

Parker Hill Branch, 1497 Tremont Street; (617) 427–3820; preschooler film on Tuesday at 10:30 A.M.

SOUTH BOSTON
646 East Broadway; (617) 268–0180; children's film every other Wednesday at 10:30 A.M. and noon; adult film on Thursday at 6:00 P.M.

SOUTH END
685 Tremont Street; (617) 536–8241; preschooler film on Monday at 10:30 A.M.; monthly Tuesday-night film for teens and tweens at 6:00 P.M. (see Web site for schedule).

WEST END
151 Cambridge Steet; (617) 523–3957; children's and adult films (schedule varies; consult Web site for details).

WEST ROXBURY
1961 Centre Street; (617) 325–3147; adult films (schedule varies; consult Web site for details).

Film Series at the Scandinavian Living Center

Nordic Hall
206 Waltham Street
Newton
(617) 527–6566
www.slcenter.org/default.asp

First Thursday of the month at 7:30 P.M., September through June.

THE CATCH } These are free, but donations are "gratefully accepted." Be warned: Nobody can lay on the evil eyeball like an old Finn.

And you thought Scandanavians were all about glögg and saunas. There's some mighty fine cinema coming out of those chilly little countries, and much of it can be seen for free at the Scandanavian Living Center, an assisted living community. If you attend one of these monthly free film screenings, you will notice that most of the people in the room will not need to read the graciously provided subtitles, which will lend the whole experience some elusive authenticity in a world gone ersatz.

Free Friday Flicks

Hatch Shell (at the Esplanade along the Charles River, by Arthur Fiedler Footbridge)
(617) 787–7200 (movie hotline)
www.wbz1030.com

Starts at sunset every Friday, mid-June through August.

THE CATCH } Because of copyright issues, WBZ can't release the name of the film until the Monday before the show.

This free, kid-friendly film series, hosted by local radio station WBZ 1030 AM, has become a Boston institution. Movies begin at sunset. Bring a picnic, a blanket, and the kids. Remember that, like all public parks in the city, alcoholic beverages are not allowed.

Free Movie Night at ZUZU!

474 Massachusetts Avenue
Cambridge (Central Square)
(617) 864–3278, ext. 237
www.mideastclub.com/zuzu/index.html

Randomly selected Monday nights at 10:30 P.M. (check Web site for schedule).

This restaurant/bar in the middle of the world-famous Middle East entertainment complex in Central Square is one of the hippest places in town, period. But throw in a free movie night about every two weeks, and the cool quotient goes through the roof. As befits a place this mod, the "movie" is shown on a small TV at the bar, and the sound is turned off (there's usually a live band or deejay doing their thing). But if watching a spaghetti western or Woody Allen comedy with a punk rock soundtrack doesn't sound like a good way to spend a Monday night, I don't know what does. Movie lip-reading is easiest from seats at the bar.

Lucy Parsons Center Radical Film Night
Lucy Parsons Center
549 Columbus Avenue (South End)
(617) 267–6272
www.lucyparsons.org

Every Wednesday night at 7:00 P.M.

If the Man is getting you down, you'll find lots of like-minded company at the Lucy Parsons Center. Although Parsons, a strident activist, early anarchist, eventual Communist, and prolific writer, died in 1942, her spirit lives on at this small, collectively run bookstore devoted to direct citizen action. Every Wednesday, the center screens a film that deals with progressive, activist, or radical issues. Come angry or stay home.

Movies by Moonlight
Boston Harbor Hotel
70 Rowes Wharf
(617) 439–7000
www.bhh.com/PR_movies.cfm

Starts at sunset every Friday, mid-June through August.

What a freebie! Just as the glow from another spectacular sunset fades over Boston Harbor, the opening credits begin to roll on the huge portable movie screen assembled in front of the Boston Harbor Hotel's Intrigue outdoor cafe. You can enjoy the movie for free if you sit along the docks on either side of the cafe seating area, which is reserved for people who plan on eating or drinking something off the cafe's menu. Come early and bring a chair—this annual film series is one of the most popular public events in the city. Most movies are classic comedies and dramas geared for an adult audience (like *The Big Sleep, The Sting,* and *To Kill a Mockingbird*). Check the hotel's Web site for a listing of films.

FREE MOVIE MADNESS

The powers that be in Hollywood have identified Boston as a prime location to get intelligent feedback before movies go into general release. The mar-

keters' cluelessness about what makes good cinema is our gain. There are a number of ways to score free tickets to these screenings. In most cases, even though you will be holding a free ticket, seating is first-come, first-served on screening nights. Make sure to arrive at least one hour prior to movie time to ensure that you and your date can find a seat.

Another tip for movie lovers: If there's a movie coming out that you know you want to see, go to the promotional Web site for that movie (usually the name of the film with a dot-com added at the end, but a simple Web search will usually find the link to the studio's official movie Web site). Many of these studios' sites offer free advance-screening tickets.

Entertainment Weekly Free Screenings

www.ew.com/freescreening

Brought to you by Entertainment Weekly, *this site periodically has free tickets to local advance screenings. You'll have to check back frequently, because the site goes dark when a screening is over or all the tickets have been given away.*

Free Movie Screenings

www.freemoviescreenings.net

This Web site compiles and lists the Web site links to movie studios' free screening offers. Most of the ticket links allow you to print out the tickets directly. Some tickets require you to enter personal info to qualify to be entered into a free ticket drawing.

Wild About Movies

www.wildaboutmovies.com/screenings/index.php

This great movie lovers' site has reviews, a critics' forum, and access to free screening tickets. Unlike other sites, it even has a listing of upcoming films for which it will be offering free screening tickets, so you can plan way ahead. You'll have to search out listings for free screenings in the Boston area, but there are plenty of them in there. The site also has links to win free DVDs.

VOLUNTEERING

The Harvard Film Archive
Carpenter Center
24 Quincy Street
Cambridge
(617) 495–4700
www.harvardfilmarchive.org
rmeyers@fas.harvard.edu (volunteer coordinator: Rebecca Meyers)

The Harvard Film Archive, part of Harvard University's Library of Fine Arts, is a rare and precious gem for film lovers. Its archives are among the most exhaustive and well preserved in the country, and it is recognized nationwide as a leader in the study of film. The HFA hosts frequent screenings, forums, and director lectures by groundbreaking talents such as Atom Egoyan, British director Terence Davies, actor-directors John Malkovich and Tommy Lee Jones, and the "Father of African Cinema," Ousmane Sembene. Its bulletin, available online, gives in-depth overviews of screenings and a listing of other upcoming events.

The HFA hosts frequent free events, and when they're not free, screenings are $8.00, and special events are $20.00. If that's too rich for your blood, the HFA does use volunteer ushers. By ushering at screenings one night a week, volunteers get free admission to all HFA screenings. Contact the volunteer coordinator directly to sign up. If you love film, this is the volunteer gig of a lifetime.

Museum of Fine Arts

465 Huntington Avenue
(617) 369–3040 (volunteer line)
www.mfa.org/about/index.asp?key=1342 (volunteer application)

The Museum of Fine Arts hosts some of the most exciting film series and director lectures in the city every year, including series featuring international women's films, French films, and gay and lesbian films, but they're not cheap. The best way to get in on the action for free is by volunteering to become a movie usher. All volunteer candidates are required to fill out an application (the link is provided above). The museum will send you a list of volunteer opportunities—if their current needs include theater ushers, you're golden. The museum operates with a staff of more than 1,200 volunteers and is looking for a fixed time commitment from those who want to join the ranks.

{READINGS AND LECTURES: FREE VERSE}

"No entertainment is so cheap as reading, nor any pleasure so lasting."

—*Mary Wortley, Lady Montagu*

Boston is a city that lives by the belief that the pen and mouth are mightier than the sword. We like to think we came up with the idea, actually. Our Old South Meeting House was one of the first places where the natural right to free speech was tested—the result was the Boston Tea Party and the Revolutionary War. So it's no surprise that you can find readings and lectures at venues large and small throughout the metro area, featuring people exercising their precious right to say whatever the heck they want as long as it doesn't incite a riot. As becomes free speech, most of these events are free, although some come with a small price tag. On any given night you can hear some of the most accomplished writers, thinkers, and movers and shakers in the country. Boston has long been known as the Athens of America, and it ain't 'cause we wear togas.

BOOKSTORE READINGS

Most bookstores in the Boston area host readings from time to time, but we've weeded through the many to present you with this list of gems, known for both the frequency and quality of their events.

Barnes and Noble, Boston University
660 Beacon Street
(617) 267–8484
www.bu.bkstore.com

This bookstore dominates Kenmore Square, near Fenway Park, and serves the tens of thousands of Boston University students who descend on the area each September. But there are plenty of treats here for nonstudents, too. The store hosts readings and author discussions in its special reading room, usually at 7:00 P.M., on various dates throughout the year. The volume drops off a bit after May, when the hordes return to wherever it is they're from, but the quality of the events suffers not a whit. Some events are hosted off-site at the Boston University School of Management at 595 Commonwealth Avenue, and for those events, tickets are sometimes required. They can be obtained (they're often free) at the School of Management building after 5:00 P.M. the day of the event.

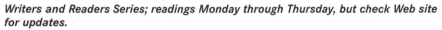

Brookline Booksmith

279 Harvard Street
Brookline
(617) 566–6660
www.brooklinebooksmith.com

Writers and Readers Series; readings Monday through Thursday, but check Web site for updates.

Brookline Booksmith, which has been around for over forty years, was one of the first bookstores in the area to make author readings look like celebrity events. The names they draw in are so large that the bookstore often moves the festivities to nearby Coolidge Corner Theatre, where admission is a paltry $2.00 for author events, and that's just to cover the cost of renting the theater. Past author readings have included Margaret Atwood, Elmore Leonard, Zadie Smith, David Sedaris, Irvine Welsh, P. D. James, Michael Chabon, Margaret Cho, and George Carlin.

Harvard Book Store

1256 Massachusetts Avenue
Cambridge
(800) 542–READ
www.harvard.com/events

Harvard Book Store was founded in 1932 by Boston native Mark Kramer with $300 he borrowed from his parents. Since then, it has become one of the most well-known and prolific sources of author readings, discussions, and literary events in the city. It hosts events at its store, as well as at locations throughout Cambridge. Some off-location events, such as those at the Brattle Theatre in Harvard Square, cost $3.00. There is something happening at the Harvard Book Store nearly every day of the week, so check the events calendar frequently to see what's new.

The Harvard Coop

1400 Massachusetts Avenue
(617) 499–2000
www.thecoop.com

The Harvard Coop Author Series; check Web site for details.

Students started the Coop (or Cooperative) back in 1882. In the beginning the Coop was simply a place to buy books, school supplies, and coal or wood for those cold Cambridge winters. The Coop is now one of the biggest bookstores in the state and hosts author readings and discussions nearly every day. Reading times and locations at the Coop vary, so make sure to check the Web site for details.

Newtonville Books

296 Walnut Street, Newton; (617) 244–6619
www.newtonvillebooks.com
Books & Brews series.

107 R Union Street, Newton Centre; (617) 964–6684
Newtonville Books in The Attic series.

The owner of Newtonville Books, Tim Huggins, has taken book readings up a notch with his wonderful Books & Brews series. He hosts author readings, discussions, and book signings in a special room at his bookstore, predominantly featuring local writers, with a nationally touring writer thrown in from time to time. Afterward, all attendees are invited to stroll to a local bar for free appetizers and a free drink. It's like the Trifecta of Cheap! He also cohosts author readings at a local restaurant/nightclub, The Attic at the Union Street Bar and Grille, where guests can enjoy a full meal and bar service (not free) during the readings. Reservations for these events are recommended, but standing room along the bar is available if you aren't interested in sitting down for a meal.

Porter Square Books

Porter Square Shopping Center
25 White Street
Cambridge
(617) 491–2220
www.portersquarebooks.com

Readings Thursday and Friday at 7:00 P.M., but events happen throughout the week, so check Web site for updates.

This independent bookstore and coffee shop prides itself on featuring the works of local writers, and there is an entire section devoted to the works of Boston's own talent. This store is located right at the Porter Square T stop on the Red Line and offers plenty of free parking.

SALONS AND SLAMS

Cantab Lounge

738 Massachusetts Avenue
Cambridge
(617) 354–2685
www.slamnews.com/cantab/schedule.html

Poetry Slam at the Cantab Lounge every Wednesday at 8:00 P.M.

THE CATCH · Cost to watch or participate is $3.00, and you must be eighteen or older with valid photo ID.

The Cantab (short for Cantabrigian, which is what you are if you live in Cambridge) hosts a weekly poetry slam, a fast-paced, winner-take-all competition in which members of the audience judge the competing poets on their performed poetry. Poetry Slam International rules are always in effect: Poems are the poet's original work of three minutes or less, no props, no costumes, no musical accompaniment.

Center for New Words

7 Temple Street
Cambridge
(617) 876–5310
www.centerfornewwords.org

This feminist organization is a hotbed of grrrrl power and gives authors and thinkers a forum to showcase their work. Free readings take place throughout the week and include programs like Conversations with Authors, Feminism & Dessert (a salon with sweets!), and New Voices Open Mic Night (which suggests a $5.00 donation).

Four Stories

The Enormous Room
567 Massachusetts Avenue (Central Square)
Cambridge
www.fourstories.org

THE CATCH · The series goes on summer hiatus from mid-April to September. You must be twenty-one or older to get in.

Started by local writer Tracy Slater in 2005, the Four Stories reading series rapidly became one of the hottest gatherings in the city. Built around the idea of a salon, Four Stories features a happening deejay, a cool club space, hip locals, and readings by four accomplished authors on the first Monday of every month. Each reading has a theme (such as Down and Out in Chestnut Hill, Light and Dark). Get there early—they fill to capacity nearly every night they run.

Grub Street, Inc.

160 Boylston Street
(617) 695–0075
www.grubstreet.org

This literary organization is the center of writers' life in the city of Boston. Its membership and faculty reads like a who's who of Boston literary elite. Throughout the year it offers courses, free workshops, seminars, and free readings at venues throughout the city, as well as at its headquarters on Boylston Street. Check out their Web site for a complete listing of upcoming events.

Out of the Blue Art Gallery

106 Prospect Street
Cambridge
(617) 354–5287
www.outoftheblueartgallery.com

THE CATCH

} The gallery suggests a $3.00 to $5.00 donation for Open Bark.

This art gallery/social gathering place for the alternative crowd is also an active participant in Boston's rich literary landscape. It hosts a variety of evening reading, art, and music events; all either request a donation or charge a flat fee. Open Bark, an open-mic night every Saturday at 8:00 P.M., allows just about any form of expression.

MUSEUMS AND LIBRARIES

Boston Public Library

700 Boylston Street (Copley Plaza)
(617) 536–5400
www.bpl.org/news/upcomingevents

What better place to go for a free reading than the first free large public library in the country? There are readings, discussions, and lectures nearly every day at the library's main Copley Square location; most are held in the roomy Rabb Lecture Hall. All of the library's neighborhood branches host author events as well. For a complete listing of events at all branches, see the Web site listed above (see Appendix B for a list of addresses and phone numbers for all branches).

The French Library and Cultural Center

53 Marlborough Street
(617) 912–0400
www.frenchlib.org

THE CATCH } You must RSVP for free public events. Many other events are free only to members. Membership costs $60 a year.

Love the French? Bostonians do. The French came to New England to help out in that little clash with the British back in the 1700s, and we never forgot the favor. There are statues of our French heroes all over town. The French Library, which occupies two historic mansions in the Back Bay, is a cultural and educational institution that seeks to perpetuate the love affair, through parties, readings, and other events, many of which are free to all. Others require a membership. Readings occur on no set schedule, so consult the French Library's Web site for more information.

John F. Kennedy Presidential Library and Museum

Columbia Point
Dorchester
(866) JFK–1960
www.jfklibrary.org

THE CATCH } You must register in advance for all forums. Seating in the main hall is first-come, first-served. Doors open an hour before the forums begin.

It is a sobering yet uplifting site—the John F. Kennedy Presidential Library and Museum standing white and gleaming along the shore where the Atlantic Ocean meets the Neponset River. The museum is not only a fitting tribute to our late president, who was born in Brookline, but also the home of the Kennedy Library Forums, a series of political, historical, and cultural "conversations" that feature some of the most powerful and influential voices in our country. Forum events are free and happen on selected Mondays from 5:30 to 7:00 P.M., but you are required to register in advance.

Museum of Afro-American History

14 Beacon Street, Suite 719 (administrative offices)
46 Joy Street (museum galleries)
(617) 725–0022
www.afroammuseum.org/events.htm

THE CATCH } Admission is $3.00. The series takes a break from June through August.

Between 1800 and 1900, the north side of Beacon Hill was home to most of the black population in the city of Boston. From there, they worked to help free their brothers and sisters in the rest of the country in the years before Emancipation. That proud history is captured at the Museum of Afro-American History. Frequent lectures, readings, and educational gallery tours are available to all comers.

LECTURES

Blacksmith House
Cambridge Center for Adult Education
56 Brattle Street
Cambridge
(617) 547–6789
www.ccae.org

Some of the best poets and authors from, or coming through, town make a stop to read at the Blacksmith House Poetry Series on Mondays at 8:00 P.M. The readings take place at the historic site of Cambridge's village smithy (also the inspiration for Longfellow's 1839 poem "The Village Blacksmith"). Tickets may be purchased forty-five minutes prior to the reading.

Cambridge Forum
3 Church Street
Cambridge
(617) 495–2727
www.cambridgeforum.org

Cambridge Forum is one of public radio's longest-running public affairs programs. It is recorded live every week in Harvard Square for broadcast by WGBH radio. Dates, locations, and times vary, so check the Web site for more information. Topics run the gamut from Saudi oil reserves to gay marriage. Tapings are free and open to the public.

Ford Hall Forum

716 Columbus Avenue, Suite 565 (administrative offices)
(617) 373–5800
www.fordhallforum.org

The Ford Hall Forum, founded in 1908, is the nation's oldest free lecture series. It schedules lectures and debates in venues throughout the city, including at the Old South Meeting House and Faneuil Hall, the site of early gatherings of the men who would lead the American Revolution. Previous speakers have included Noam Chomsky, Alan Dershowitz, Robert Frost, Henry Kissinger, Martin Luther King Jr., Rosa Parks, Ayn Rand, Robert Reich, Eleanor Roosevelt, Pete Seeger, and Malcolm X. All lectures are free and open to the public. Check the Web site for a calendar of upcoming events.

The Old South Meeting House

310 Washington Street
(617) 482–6439
www.oldsouthmeetinghouse.org

THE CATCH — Although many events are free to all, some require you to pay museum admission of $5.00. } Angry about a tax on tea, 5,000 colonials gathered on December 16, 1773, at the Old South Meeting House to devise a way to make sure their displeasure was duly noted by King George. Someone suggested tossing all that tea into the ocean, people seemed to like the idea, and the rest is literally history. The Old South Meeting House has been a forum for spirited debate, and history-making outcomes, ever since. Today, as a National Historic Landmark, it continues to host regular discussions and lectures on the events that shape our world today, just as it did over 200 years ago. Check the Web site for a calendar of upcoming events.

{SECTION 2:
LIVING}
IN BOSTON

{ CHEAP TRICKS: CHAMPAGNE LIFE ON A BEER BUDGET }

"The wealthy man is not he who
has money, but he who has the
means to live in the luxurious state
of early spring."

—*Anton Chekhov, 1892*

It is one of the enduring ironies of Boston that those with the most money get the most free stuff. Dinner parties, grand openings, gift bags—you name it, they get it, often with not so much as a penny changing hands. Free parties and other events are the lifeblood of the social scene in Boston, and the best-kept secret in the city is that you don't have to be rich to get invited (although it helps). It's all about who you know. And who knows you.

The good news is that Boston's social world isn't nearly as tough to crack as it was about fifty years ago, when all the good stuff was reserved for Brahmins with names like Cabot and Lodge. Our newly meritocratic society has thrown open those previously closed doors, and today you'll find people from all walks of life and economic strata rubbing elbows at the same house parties, private club openings, debut shindigs, and networking events with their free canapés and champagne all aswirl. The high-society parties that the public sees are all $1,000 fund-raisers and impossible-to-score tickets, but the really fun *free* parties are invisible to the public. And that's just how the party givers want it.

The trick to scoring an invite to one of these free shindigs is getting on the social radar. Once you do, all sorts of unpublicized entertainment and party opportunities will begin to drift your way (provided you're not a self-important jerk—Bostonians have limited patience for these individuals, unless they're very, very, very rich). The key to tapping into the mother lode of Boston freebies can be summed up in one word: networking.

NETWORKING

Everyone has a "cohort," a group of people with whom they are naturally affiliated. You probably are already familiar with the common affinity groups, like your alumni club or your professional organization. And I assume that if you're interested in increasing your social network, you already belong to one or more of these organizations. But you may not be aware of another social phenomenon that has emerged in Boston in recent years—the networking group. These make no pretense of charity or fund-raising (although they occasionally hold benefits). Their only point is to help you meet and greet your way to fun. There is a near turf war raging between the city's networking organizations, each vying to increase its membership (which allows it to sell access to marketers and advertisers at top dollar—which is how they all fund the free and cheap parties they run). Events hosted by these organizations are either free or very inexpensive or offer a significant discount off regular prices. Plus, you'll meet lots of new people, and that's when the serious networking begins!

Boston Ski & Sports Club

(617) 789–4070
www.bssc.com

THE CATCH

Membership is $60 a year. }

With 30,000 members, this organization hosts every type of sports and outdoor adventure imaginable. The group also hosts a number of social events, including everything from private wine-tasting parties to weekends on the Vineyard. Many evening social events are free to members, and events with a fee are often marked way down from the retail cost charged to the public. The crowd tends to be in their late twenties to mid-thirties, and single, although their organized sports leagues bring out a little bit of every demographic.

Boston Young Professionals Association

www.bostonypa.com

Boston Professionals Association

www.bostonpa.com
(617) 591–1400

Basic membership in these two groups is free, and premium membership is $50 and up, but a premium membership gets you into up to twenty-four networking events and parties for free. The BYPA limits membership to those between twenty-one and forty, and there is no age limit with the BPA. Both groups offer parties, trips at home and abroad, special opening events, sports packages featuring pregame cocktail parties, and at least one big annual party.

Downtown Women's Club

www.downtownwomensclub.com
marthaslaight@gmail.com (Boston contact: Martha Slaight)

This nationwide women's networking organization, started here in Boston by Diane Danielson, boasts of members who are generally age thirty-five and older, earn over $75,000, live in urban areas, and are actively pursuing a career. The DWC sponsors free networking events throughout the month, usually with a cash bar, as well as some larger educational and social events that charge a small fee.

The Society of Young Professionals
(781) 444–7771
www.bostoneventguide.com/events/syp.htm

With over 25,000 members, this organization, which is affiliated with the *Boston Events Guide,* sponsors trips, parties, and charity events. Membership is free. Most of the group's social networking events carry a small fee—most also have complimentary appetizers (but a cash bar). You must be twenty-one to join. The crowd trends to twenty-five- to thirty-five-year-olds, people who would prefer to mingle over cocktails than to jam into a crowded nightclub (although they like to do some of that once in a while, too). A favorite is the weekly mixer, which costs $5.00 for members and features $2.00 martinis. (The entrance fee is occasionally waived.)

DO GOOD

For the more philanthropically oriented, nearly every museum, house of worship, hospital, and cultural organization in the city has a volunteer fund-raising organization attached to it, and it is around these that the city's charity event scene revolves. The major cultural institutions in the city, like the Boston Symphony, the Boston Ballet, the Museum of Fine Arts, and most of the biggest hospitals, have in-house fund-raising groups, and they staff their fund-raising committees and boards with big-money donors and other connected movers and shakers who are privately invited to participate. Still, there are a few organizations that allow Cheap Bastards like you and me to participate in boards, committees, and fund-raising event planning, just because we want to help.

The galas these groups plan are very expensive affairs—some top out at over $1,500 a ticket—but you don't have to go to the main event to get the benefits of your involvement. Just helping out will get you networked with great people, who, in turn, throw lots of private parties that most people never hear about. Plus, these volunteer organizations usually throw a number of smaller parties that lead up to the big event, usually held for members of the fund-raising committee and friends (as a thank-you, for networking, and often just to boost enthusiasm for the big party to come). There will be plenty of work involved if you join one of these fund-raising committees, and a membership is usually required (where applicable), but the networking benefits, not to mention the satisfaction of working for a very worthy cause, are unparalleled.

Listed below are some of the philanthropic organizations in town that will let you take part in their fund-raising committees without requiring you to make a major donation, be a mover or shaker, or have a personal invitation from the board of directors.

Boston Public Library

Associates of the Boston Public Library
700 Boylston Street
(617) 536–3886
www.bpl.org

THE CATCH

} You must be a member in order to participate. Annual membership is $55 for an individual and $100 for a family.

The Associates and their various fund-raising committees host three major fund-raising gala events per year, as well as monthly events at the library, most of which are free or have a small fee. The only requirements are that you have paid your membership fee and that you have convinced the committee members that you're going to work hard for the library.

The Boston Public Library Foundation's Young Professionals Group

700 Boylston Street
(617) 247–8980
www.bplf.com

The Young Professionals Group of the BPLF doesn't have a specific age requirement (they take the young and young at heart). It's free to join, and all you have to do is call the BPLF and get on their mailing list. They sponsor many free networking events throughout the year as well as several parties leading up to the two major fund-raising galas they host annually. The group is very involved in a variety of philanthropic activities in the city, including literacy, mentoring programs, and two big fund-raisers each year sponsored by the Young Professionals Group. Benefit committee volunteers are expected to sell tickets to the fund-raisers and buy at least a couple for the big shindig, but as long as you are a productive volunteer, you probably won't get kicked out if you don't go to the big bashes.

Brattle Theatre Foundation

50 Brattle Street
Cambridge
(617) 876–8021
www.brattlefilm.org

This nonprofit group is spearheading the fund-raising campaign for the Brattle Theatre, which for over 115 years has sought to elevate film to its rightful place as a fine art. The Brattle has faced near financial death several times in the past few years but has managed to raise the funds necessary to stay open each time. It eagerly welcomes those who want to join the foundation as a member and take part in the many fund-raising committees that are working hard to keep this treasured theater alive and vital for many years to come. Call the Foundation directly for information on how you can become involved.

IT'S WHO YOU KNOW

If you live in the city of Boston, you probably already have frequent contact with some of the most connected people in town: hairdressers, waitresses, bartenders, maître d's, concierges, artists, interior designers, art gallery owners, personal trainers, and other wealth intermediaries, as they are called by sociologists. Maybe you use their services, or maybe they're personal friends, but either way, they are the people who help the wealthy spend their money, and they are the best social networking resources you have.

Now I know what you're thinking: It is crass and heartless to befriend people just because of what they can do for you—and I am certainly not suggesting that you do that. Nor will these people let you do that: They can spot a brown-nosing hanger-on a mile away. I seek only to inform you that these people, who some view only as "service industry" folk, have a better lock on what is happening in Boston than nearly anyone realizes. It is worth your while to get to know them. The really nice folks you meet in this "wealth intermediary" world are people you'd want to be friends with anyway, and they, in turn, will probably know lots of other nice people, some of whom will throw great events and parties. Life is like a spider's web—your job is to be the spider.

Courageous Sailing Center

1 First Avenue (Charlestown Navy Yard)
Charlestown
(617) 242–3821
www.courageoussailing.org

If you like to sail, this is a great organization to meet like-minded people and help a great cause. This nonprofit provides free sailing instructions to kids, as well as paid memberships and classes to adults. It sponsors a number of fund-raising events throughout the year and is always looking for volunteer committee members who want to help with the planning. You don't have to be a member of Courageous to get involved. In fact, joining the events committees, and doing a good job, is a great way to get invited to join the high-powered board of directors of Courageous, one of the city's great philanthropic organizations.

The Esplanade Association

10 Derne Street
(617) 227–0365
www.esplanadeassociation.org

THE CATCH — Membership starts at $45 for an individual and goes up from there, but membership isn't a precondition of volunteering.

This organization is the caretaker of one of the city's most precious resources, the Esplanade, a manicured park that runs for over 2 miles on the Boston side of the Charles River. Members and volunteers are a vital part of this organization, and they not only get their hands dirty helping to keep the Esplanade looking good but also help plan the big fund-raising events that pay for all the upkeep. If you're interested in participating, call the association directly and let them know what you're interested in doing. They're eager to have new faces. The membership runs the gamut from students to longtime Back Bay residents and everything in between.

The Institute of Contemporary Art

The New Group
100 Northern Avenue
(617) 478–3100
www.icaboston.org

THE CATCH — Annual membership is $165 for an individual and $235 for a couple.

The ICA moved into its provocative and roomy new headquarters in December 2006 after years of fund-raising efforts, and the New Group was an important player in that effort. The New Group is an affiliate group within the ICA membership that seeks to introduce members to new artists through seminars and lectures. Its members are a vibrant collection of Boston professionals, age thirty and older, who are passionate about art. They're not just about art, though. The group is known to have some of the best parties in the city. The New Group hosts a variety of free networking and educational seminars for members throughout the year. And volunteering for the New Group events committee will give you the chance to help plan the two major fund-raising benefits that the group sponsors each year. This is one of the most inclusive cultural organizations in the city.

{ **FOOD:** }
FREE LUNCH

"Eat breakfast like a king, lunch like
a prince, and dinner like a pauper."

—*Adelle Davis*

Boston is such a foodie town that it's almost embarrassing: Our biggest celebrities aren't movie stars or sports heroes, but chefs, like Ming Tsai, Todd English, and Barbara Lynch. In many areas of pop culture, Boston still lags the leading edge, but not when it comes to cuisine. We're setting the bar for gourmet dining around the country, and it seems there's a new edgy restaurant opening up nearly every weekend. All this haute cuisine usually comes at a steep price, except for us intrepid Cheap Bastards. There are plenty of places to eat for free or cheap at the area's best restaurants, markets, stores, and food events. Whether you want an entire free meal, or a taste of something sweet, Boston is happy to share its culinary wealth with Cheap Bastards like us.

HAPPY HOURS

In a fit of Puritan madness in the mid-1980s, Massachusetts legislators banned the traditional happy hour, at which thirsty Bostonians could drink cheap or free at their favorite bar for two precious hours after work. Sadly, the Boston bar scene hasn't exactly embraced the next obvious thing, happy-hour free appetizers. A few places have dipped their toe in—some more than others. It's a lot more common to find half-price appetizers, and there are some great deals to be had on full meals. If you do partake of free chow at one of the fine establishments listed below, you'll be expected to buy a drink. If you're eating at half-price, you don't have to buy a beverage, but remember to figure your tip based on the full price of whatever you ordered. Cheap Bastards love to find new ways to save a few bucks, but cheaping out on the waitress is not one of them.

Bukowski's Tavern

1281 Cambridge Street, Cambridge; (617) 497–7077

50 Dalton Street; (617) 437–9999

THE CATCH

Bukowski's takes cash only.

What is there not to love about a bar that is named after a poet who wrote some of his best work while sloshed? This bar, named to honor Charles Bukowski, has one of the most awe-inspiring beer menus we've ever seen (and that's saying something) and is famous for its incredible burgers. You can sample said burger, or a footlong dog, for a paltry $1.69 each and every weekday before 8:00 P.M.

Cactus Club
939 Boylston Street
(617) 236–0200
www.cactusclubboston.com

THE CATCH

}

Must buy a drink to get the free deals.

Cactus Club, a hoppin' Mexican restaurant and lounge that fills up with twenty-somethings every night of the week, has some pretty sweet freebies and cheapies, even if it will set you back the cost of a margarita. First, the free stuff—there's an All You Can Eat Taco Bar on Sunday from 10:00 P.M. to midnight. On Wednesday from 6:00 to 8:00 P.M., if you buy a Sauza margarita, you get a free five-minute massage. Cactus Club also offers half-price appetizers Monday through Thursday from 4:00 to 7:00 P.M. at the bar.

Fritz Lounge
26 Chandler Street (South End)
(617) 482–4428

Fritz Lounge is a sports bar popular with the South End gay community. Patrons from all walks of life enjoy free happy-hour appetizers weekdays from 6:30 to 7:30 P.M. These aren't just chips and salsa—expect to find quiches, pizza, chicken wings, and other hearty fare.

McCormick and Schmick's
34 Columbus Avenue (Park Square)
(617) 482–3999

Half-price appetizers pack this high-end seafood place with hungry patrons every night from 3:30 to 6:30 P.M. and again from 10:00 P.M. to midnight. The menu changes nightly, but you can't lose with their thick, juicy $1.95 cheeseburger, which is available most nights.

News Café
150 Kneeland Street
(617) 426–6397
www.newsboston.com/events.html

Sometimes it pays to be a girl. The News Café, one of the trendier boîtes in downtown Boston, has dubbed Wednesday night Ladies Night. Women dine free on a three-course meal—salad, entree, and dessert—from 5:00 to 10:00 P.M. in the lounge. There's also a vegetarian entree. You may even see one of the local sports stars who frequent this joint.

Noir at the Charles Hotel

1 Bennett Street (Harvard Square)
Cambridge
(617) 661–8010

Every weekday from 5:00 to 7:00 P.M., this sultry bar offers Noir Nibbles, featuring $5.00 sandwiches, $4.00 flatbreads, $3.00 skewers, $2.00 salads, $1.00 desserts, and free nuts. (See what they did there? Cute idea—tasty, too.)

Prairie Star Southwestern Grill & Bar

111 Dartmouth Street
(617) 262–7575
www.prairiestarboston.com

Stop by on weekdays between 5:00 and 7:00 P.M. for half-price appetizers at the bar, which include chili, crab cakes, taquitos, and nachos.

Redbones

55 Chester Street (Porter Square)
Somerville
(617) 628–2200

THE CATCH

You'll be expected to buy a drink.

Some of the best barbecue in New England can be had here. They offer free appetizers Monday through Thursday from 4:00 to 6:00 P.M. in the upstairs and downstairs bars. The BBQ pit master decides what will be served for appetizers—they often feature chicken fingers, catfish fingers, or BBQ hash.

Ristorante Marino

2465 Massachusetts Avenue
Cambridge
(617) 868–5454
www.marinoristorante.com

THE CATCH

You'll be expected to buy a drink.

Italian appetizers are available in the bar area every night during dinner hours until 10:30 P.M. (9:30 P.M. on Sunday).

Swan's Cafe

64 Arlington Street (Park Plaza Hotel)
(617) 457–2357
www.bostonparkplaza.com

THE CATCH

You'll be expected to buy a drink.

}

Free appetizers are available during happy hour every night from 5:00 to 7:00 P.M., including nachos and cheese, cheese and crackers, and a variety of dips.

Whiskey's Food & Spirits

885 Boylston Street
(617) 262–5551

THE CATCH

To get the free appetizers, you have to buy a specialty drink.

}

Ladies enjoy free appetizers on Sunday nights when they order a specialty drink from 7:00 to 11:00 P.M. Whiskey's offers things like buffalo wings, chicken fingers, and mozzarella sticks.

HALF PRICE HOOK-UP

Half Price Hook-Up

http://bos-cc.boston-deals.com

Half Price Hook-Up sells $50 gift certificates to some of the best restaurants in the city for just $25 dollars (plus a $3.50 shipping and handling fee per certificate). Each Friday at 9:45 A.M., the Web site begins selling that week's featured restaurant certificate, and once the allotted certificates have been purchased (online through a secure server), they're gone. The number of certificates varies from week to week. Some go very fast—especially certificates to Dunkin' Donuts, which are snatched up in just minutes. The Hook-Up is a service marketed to listeners of three Boston radio stations owned by Clear Channel Entertainment, Kiss 108, Jamn 94.5, and Progressive Talk AM 1200 and AM 1430. But that doesn't mean you can't take advantage of it. And you should, because it's one of the few ways that you can get half off a meal at restaurants like Meze, West Street Grille, and 5 North Square, to name just a few. The Web site listed above lets you know what restaurant is on tap for the following two weeks, so mark your calendar and set your alarm to get in on this great deal.

FREE SAMPLES

Boston is packed with bakeries, coffee shops, farmers' markets, and other purveyors of delectable treats, and most are more than happy to offer free samples. All they ask is that you don't abuse the privilege. If you don't want to become rapidly known (it's a small town) as "that guy who eats our samples all the time but never buys any-thing," please keep things in proportion, patronize these shops with your cash when you taste something you like, and help keep them in business so they can live on to offer free samples for another day.

Big Sky Bread Co.

105 Union Street
Newton
(617) 332–4242
www.panoramabakery.com

This small bakery offers samples of some of their delicious artisanal breads.

Faneuil Hall Marketplace

(between State Street and Atlantic Avenue across from Government Center)
(617) 523–1300
www.faneuilhallmarketplace.com

Where once colonial revolutionaries fomented rebellion, today there stands a gour-mand's paradise. Faneuil Hall, built in 1742, anchors the general area now known as Faneuil Hall Marketplace, which also includes three long stone warehouses used for centuries as merchant markets—now transformed into one of the most vis-ited tourist attractions in the city of Boston. The warehouses house dozens of pubs, restaurants, shops, and small storefronts selling every food known to man. It is also Cheap Bastard paradise. Most of the food storefronts have samples available during normal business hours, but on the first Wednesday of every month, you'll find "A Taste of Quincy Market" (the historic name for the merchants' warehouses), in which food stores showcase their signature cuisine from 5:00 to 7:00 P.M. This Cheap Bastard's favorites include Boston Chipyard, Boston Chowda, Boston & Maine Fish Co., Carol Ann's Bake Shop, and Steve's Ice Cream.

Flour Bakery

1595 Washington Street (South End)
(617) 267–4300
www.flourbakery.com

One of the best bakeries in the city, Flour always has some samples on display for you to try.

Formaggio Kitchen

244 Huron Avenue
Cambridge
(617) 354–4750
www.formaggio-kitchen.com

South End Formaggio

268 Shawmut Avenue
(617) 350–6996
www.southendformaggio.com

These stores have been serving up the finest in gourmet and artisanal cheese, meats, and other delicacies for over twenty years. There are always cheeses and other nibbly things displayed for your sampling pleasure. The store hosts wine tastings as well, often paired with an appropriate cheese selection. Call the store for more info on tasting times, dates, and products scheduled to be tasted.

JP Licks

352 Newbury Street; (617) 236–1666

311 Harvard Street (Coolidge Corner), Brookline; (617) 738–8252

4A College Avenue (Davis Square), Somerville; (617) 666–5079

46 Langley Road, Newton Centre; (617) 244–0666

One Brigham Circle, 1618 Tremont Street (Mission Hill); (617) 566–6676

661 VFW Parkway (West Roxbury); (617) 325–1516

www.jplicks.com

JP Licks has some of the most intriguing ice cream flavor combinations going—potato pie, mint Irish lace, Bailey's cheesecake—and they're happy to let you sample.

New England Soup Factory

2-4 Brookline Place, Brookline; (617) 739–1899 (soupline), (617) 739–1695

244 Needham Street, Newton; (617) 558–9988 (soupline), (617) 558–9966

www.newenglandsoupfactory.com/index.html

As you might guess, these shops are all about the soup. Small samples are available for tasting.

Peet's Coffee & Tea

176 Federal Street; (617) 439–3177

100 Mount Auburn Street, Cambridge; (617) 492–1844

285 Harvard Street, Brookline; (617) 734–4725

776 Beacon Street, Newton Centre; (617) 244–1577

www.peets.com

Peet's wants you to love coffee as much as they do, and they're out to convert the world, one coffee drinker at a time. Most stores will offer sample cups of their coffees, and they often have samples of pastries or candies.

Trader Joe's

899 Boylston Street; (617) 262–6505

1317 Beacon Street, Brookline; (617) 278–9997

748 Memorial Drive, Cambridge; (617) 491–8582

www.traderjoes.com/about/index.asp

This unique grocery store specializes in wholesome offerings for people with discerning palates, including organics, kosher, vegetarian, vegan, gluten-free, and sugar-free. Samples are on offer throughout the store.

Whole Foods Markets

Charles River Plaza, 181 Cambridge Street; (617) 723–0004

15 Westland Avenue; (617) 375–1010

15 Washington Street, Brighton; (617) 738–8187

115 Prospect Street, Cambridge; (617) 492–0070

200 Alewife Brook Parkway, Cambridge; (617) 491–0040

340 River Street, Cambridge; (617) 876–6990

www.wholefoodsmarket.com

All stores are open 8:00 A.M. to 10:00 P.M. daily.

This high-end grocery store, which specializes in organic and chemical-free foods, knows that discerning shoppers want to try before they buy (especially at these prices). That's why there are sampling events at every local branch of Whole Foods Markets. Each store has an in-store demo coordinator whose job is to offer tastings of various products throughout the store. You can try everything from tofu hotdogs, gourmet pastries and cookies, and artisanal cheese to wholesome packaged foods.

FOOD FESTIVALS

Bostonians love to get together and eat, and the more the merrier. Food festivals are legendary in Boston, at which tens of thousands of people strap on the old feedbag, sometimes for a charity, sometimes just 'cause it's so yummy. The rule of thumb for all of these festivals is to get there early—it's no fun standing around in the hot sun (or the rain) with several thousand hungry Bostonians, especially when you're one of them. Some of these events charge a fee to get in—they're listed here because I think they're worth it, especially if you bring a big appetite.

Boston Vegetarian Food Festival

Reggie Lewis Athletic Center
1350 Tremont Street
(617) 424–8846 (organization's office)
www.bostonveg.org

The Boston Vegetarian Food Festival is a completely free event that brings together exhibitors of vegetarian natural foods from across the country. The festival offers the opportunity to talk to food producers, see and taste the latest vegetarian products being introduced to the marketplace, and hear from a variety of national experts on health and nutrition, who lecture throughout the day. There's even a children's activity area. It is the longest-running event of its kind in the country.

Chowderfest

City Hall Plaza
(617) 227–1528
www.bostonharborfest.com/chowderfest

THE CATCH } Admission is $7.00 and worth it.

Who makes Boston's best clam chowder? Wars have been waged over lesser questions. Finding the city's best chowder is the sole focus of the 10,000 people who swarm City Hall Plaza for one day in the summer for Chowderfest, part of the city's Fourth of July Harborfest celebration. Dozens of the city's top restaurants vie for the honor, as determined by the masses who stand in line for hours to taste as many chowders as they can. Between tastings, musical performances, jugglers, and all manner of distraction, the Plaza resembles a clam-besotted Woodstock, but it is one of the defining events of our fair city. Get there early to avoid the huge lines. Wear comfortable shoes and bring a hat and bottled water. City Hall Plaza is a mass of concrete and can get very hot in the middle of July.

The Jimmy Fund Scooper Bowl

City Hall Plaza
(617) 632–4215 (volunteer line)
www.jimmyfund.org/eve/event/scooper-bowl

THE CATCH

Volunteer to get in free. Tickets are regularly $7.00 for adults, $3.00 for kids ages three to ten, and free for kids under three.

The Jimmy Fund Scooper Bowl, the nation's largest all-you-can-eat ice-cream festival, is held in City Hall Plaza every June. Here you can taste ice cream from ten of the nation's leading ice-cream companies while raising money for the Jimmy Fund, which supports cancer research and treatment at Dana-Farber Cancer Institute. To get in free, call the volunteer line. Volunteer shifts are about three hours long. You'll be asked to collect tickets, scoop ice cream, and sell T-shirts—but then you'll be free to eat ice cream to your heart's content (although I'm not sure you'll want to after scooping it out for three hours).

The Taste of Boston

City Hall Plaza
(617) 779–3496
www.tasteofboston.com

THE CATCH

It's free to get in, and the entertainment is excellent, but tastings will cost you.

Every September, City Hall Plaza resembles a huge party (complete with a main stage featuring live, nationally known bands like the Goo Goo Dolls) as over fifty local restaurants and food vendors set up temporary shop to serve samples to the tens of thousands of visitors who come to the Taste of Boston. The event also features a celebrity-chef kitchen demonstration area and a children's play area. Although admission to the event is free, you have to buy "Taste Tickets" at $1.00 a pop in order to sample the foods. Each sample costs between one and five tickets, with most costing three to four tickets. That could make for a pricey night, unless you can pace yourself. Even if you don't taste a thing, there are plenty of things to see and do, and it's always a great time if you don't mind the crowds. A portion of the proceeds and all the leftover food go to the Greater Boston Food Bank, which is the largest hunger relief organization in the country and distributes free food directly to those in need.

{ WINE AND BEER TASTINGS: FREE SPIRITS }

"Good wine warms people's faces;
good money warms their hearts."

—*Chinese proverb*

Boston is packed with wine and liquor stores (could it be the long, cold winters?), and most of the best wine shops in town have been around for generations. The proprietors know the ins and outs of plonk, Châteaux Petrus, and everything in between, and they are eager to share it with sophisticated and neophyte wine lovers alike. Wine tastings can be formal affairs, presented by the vintners who actually produced the wines, or more informal tastings in which a shop puts out a variety of wines for you to try, without much fanfare or discussion. In either case, most shops will open wines that share a theme (Italian, Burgundies, ice wine) so that you can educate your palate. Boston is also home to two breweries making some of the finest specialty beers in the world (and they have the awards to prove it). Maybe we should thank those long winters after all.

WINE TASTINGS

Bauer Wine and Spirits
330 Newbury Street
(617) 262–0363
www.bauerwines.com

Wine tastings: Saturday, 4:00 to 6:30 P.M.

Beer tastings: twice a month; dates and times vary, so check the Web site.

Bauer wine buyer Howie Rubin made wine accessible to a whole generation of college students when he started doing wine commentary for local alternative radio station WFNX back in the 1980s, and the education continues today. This shop prides itself on its knowledgeable staff, and customers sometimes come here just to hang out and talk wine. They're also known for their excellent selection of exotic beers.

WINE AND BEER TASTINGS BY THE WEEK

SHOP	MONDAY	TUESDAY	WEDNESDAY	THURSDAY	FRIDAY	SATURDAY	SUNDAY
Auburndale Wine and Spirits						noon–4:00 P.M.	
Bauer Wine and Spirits						4:00–6:30 P.M.	
Beacon Hill Wine and Spirits				5:00–7:00 P.M.	5:00–7:00 P.M.	noon–3:00 P.M.	
Best Cellars	5:00–8:00 P.M.	5:00–8:00 P.M.	5:00–8:00 P.M.	5:00–8:00 P.M.	5:00–8:00 P.M.	2:00–5:00 P.M.	2:00–5:00 P.M.
Blanchards Wine and Spirits						2:00–5:00 P.M.	
Boston Beer Company (tour/tasting)			2:00 P.M. (May 1–August 31)	2:00 P.M.	2:00 and 5:30 P.M.	noon, 1:00 P.M., and 2:00 P.M.	
Brix					6:00–8:00 P.M.	6:00–8:00 P.M.	
Brookline Liquor Mart						1:00–5:00 P.M.	
Federal Wine and Spirits			5:00–7:00 P.M.				
Fine Wine Cellars						3:00–7:00 P.M.	
Gary's Liquors					4:00–7:00 P.M.	1:00–4:00 P.M.	
Gimbel's Discount Liquors				6:00–9:00 P.M.	6:00–9:00 P.M.	10:00 A.M.–5:00 P.M.	
Gordon's Fine Wine and Liquors Main Street				5:00–8:00 P.M.	5:00–8:00 P.M.	1:00–4:00 P.M.	
Watertown Street					5:00–8:00 P.M.		
Harpoon Brewery (tour/tasting)		3:00 P.M.	3:00 P.M.	3:00 P.M.	1:00 P.M. and 3:00 P.M.	1:00 and 3:00 P.M.	
(5:30 Club)		5:30–7:00 P.M.	5:30–7:00 P.M.	5:30–7:00 P.M.	5:30–7:00 P.M.		
Huntington Wine and Spirits				5:30–7:00 P.M.	5:30–7:00 P.M.		
Lower Falls Wine Company						noon–4:00 P.M.	
Martignetti Liquors					5:00–8:00 P.M.	5:00–8:00 P.M.	
Marty's Fine Wines and Gourmet Foods Allston						noon–2:00 P.M.	
Newton						3:00–5:00 P.M.	
Merchants Wine and Spirits				5:00–7:00 P.M. (selected)			
Reservoir Wine and Spirits				5:30–7:00 P.M.			
University Wine Shop (except July–August)						2:30–5:30 P.M.	
Upper Falls Liquors						noon–4:00 P.M.	
V. Cirace and Sons Inc.					4:00–7:00 P.M.	4:00–7:00 P.M.	
Wine Bottega					5:00–8:00 P.M.		
Wine Emporium (Tremont and Columbus)					afternoons (times vary)	afternoons (times vary)	
Wine Gallery (Brookline)				5:00–7:00 P.M.	5:00–7:00 P.M.	3:00–6:00 P.M.	
(Kenmore)				6:00–8:00 P.M.	6:00–8:00 P.M.	6:00–8:00 P.M.	
Wine Press						noon–6:00 P.M.	

Beacon Hill Wine and Spirits

63 Charles Street
(617) 742–8571
www.beaconhillwine.com

Thursday and Friday, 5:00 to 7:00 P.M.; Saturday, noon to 3:00 P.M.

In addition to the regular tastings, this wine shop has one or two bottles open every night of the week for you to sample. The owner has a policy of tasting every wine before he'll stock it, and he puts copious tasting notes up on all the shelves to help you make your selection. Visit the Web site to read tasting notes contributed by their many loyal customers.

Best Cellars

745 Boylston Street (Copley Square); (617) 266–2900
1327 Beacon Street (at Harvard Street), Brookline; (617) 232–4100
www.bestcellars.com

Every weekday, 5:00 to 8:00 P.M.; weekends, 2:00 to 5:00 P.M.

This unique chain of wine stores categorizes its wines based on each one's dominant aspect: luscious, smooth, fizzy, big, or sweet. They pour about four wines at their tastings. The shop has over a hundred bottles at $15 and under and has become one of the most popular wine stores in town because its owners have made wine affordable and understandable. They occasionally do a grand tasting, so check the Web site or sign up for the e-mail newsletter for updates.

Blanchards Wine and Spirits

741 Centre Street, Jamaica Plain; (617) 522–9300
286 American Legion Highway, Revere; (781) 289–5888
418 LaGrange Street, West Roxbury; (617) 327–1400
www.blanchardsliquor.com

All locations: Saturday, 2:00 to 5:00 P.M.

This liquor store chain has regular tastings as well as additional tastings throughout the week. They also feature a monthly grand tasting at one or more locations. Sign up for their newsletter to get the latest schedule and tasting notes on newly stocked products from the staff.

Brix

1284 Washington Street
(617) 542–2749
www.brixwineshop.com

Friday and Saturday, 6:00 to 8:00 P.M., unless otherwise noted on the Web site.

This wine and liquor store is sleek and modern, filled with frosted glass and an easy-to-navigate selection. It could be mistaken for a bar (which is what it will become once the state agrees to allow wine stores to sell wines by the glass). Wines for tasting are poured into crystal stemware along a beautiful 10-foot granite tasting table, presented by one of the knowledgeable owners. It's a great local gathering place.

Brookline Liquor Mart

1354 Commonwealth Avenue
Brookline
(617) 734–7700
www.blmwine.com

Saturday, 1:00 to 5:00 P.M.

This local treasure has been in the Miller family for seventy-six years, and they've passed their love of the grape down through the generations. Wine tastings here are an educational affair. They open seven bottles, usually on a theme (similar grape, style, or region), but the real fun is the periodic blind tastings, when they cover the bottles and let the customers figure out which wine is which (they give the answers at the end). Sign up on their Web site for their weekly newsletter, which includes tasting notes for new offerings. It will also keep you up-to-date on the grand tastings they host three or four times a year—seven tables with seven wines at each. *À votre santé,* indeed!

Federal Wine and Spirits

29 State Street
(617) 367–8605
www.federalwine.com

Wine tastings: Wednesday, 5:00 to 7:00 P.M.

Scotch tastings: check the Web site.

Tastings take place in the store's wine cellar. In addition to its regular tastings, this shop hosts eclectic tastings (a recent one showcased wines that go well with moose—and even had roast moose for tasters to try). Check the Web site for additional tasting events and scotch tastings—they specialize in single malts—in addition to the scheduled events.

Fine Wine Cellars

7 Boylston Street (Route 9)
Chestnut Hill
(617) 232–1020

Saturday, 3:00 to 7:00 P.M.

Gary's Liquors

655 VFW Parkway (Route 1)
Chestnut Hill
(617) 323–1122
www.garysliquors.com

Friday, 4:00 to 7:00 P.M.; Saturday, 1:00 to 4:00 P.M.

This award-winning wine shop has a mailing list to keep customers updated on coming events in addition to their regular wine tastings.

Gimbel's Discount Liquors

1637 Beacon Street (Washington Square)
Brookline
(617) 566–1672

Thursday and Friday, 6:00 to 9:00 P.M.; Saturday, 10:00 A.M. to 5:00 P.M.

Gordon's Fine Wine and Liquors

894 Main Street, Waltham; (781) 893–1900
Thursday and Friday, 5:00 to 8:00 P.M.; Saturday, 1:00 to 4:00 P.M.

599 Moody Street, Waltham; (781) 894–2771
Beer tastings twice a month; call or see the Web site for dates and times.

51 Watertown Street, Watertown; (617) 926–1119
Friday, 5:00 to 8:00 P.M.

www.gordonswine.com

In addition to its frequent regular tastings, Gordon's—an award-winning wine, liquor, and beer store now owned by the fourth generation of Gordons—has grand tastings throughout the year featuring 150 wines with twenty different suppliers. Through their Web site, they offer an e-mail newsletter, *The Daily Flash,* which updates their many happy customers on specials, wine dinners, and those not-to-be-missed grand tastings. Gordon's also boasts one of the area's only personal wine shoppers, just in case you can't tell your Zinfandels from your Bordeaux.

Huntington Wine and Spirits

301 Huntington Avenue (near Symphony Hall)

(617) 536–0164

www.hungtingtonwineandspirits.com

Thursday and Friday, 5:00 to 7:00 P.M.

This local shop offers four to six wines at all of its tastings and also presents grand tastings, the dates of which are posted on the Web site. Also look for their occasional beer-tasting events.

Lower Falls Wine Co.

2366 Washington Street

Newton Lower Falls

(617) 332–3000

www.lowerfallswine.com

Saturday, noon to 4:00 P.M.

Martignetti Liquors

64 Cross Street (North End)

(617) 227–4343

www.martignettiretail.com

Friday and Saturday, 5:00 to 8:00 P.M.

This chain of giant wine and liquor stores was founded the year Prohibition was lifted, and they've been going strong ever since. They now have some of the largest wine stores in New England. Check their Web site for their periodic grand tastings.

Marty's Fine Wines and Gourmet Foods

193 Harvard Avenue, Allston; (617) 782–3250

Saturday, noon to 2:00 P.M.

675 Washington Street, Newton; (617) 332–1230

Saturday, 3:00 to 5:00 P.M.

www.martyswine.com

A fixture on the tastings scene since it opened in 1948, and known for its outstanding selection of high-end wines, Marty's tastings feature wines from a single region. They also tend to pour wines in the $20–$60 range, so if you normally don't drink wines that good, Marty's is a great place to learn what you've been missing. Marty's boasts an exceptional gourmet foods section, so expect one heck of a cheese and snack platter during their tastings. Their wine events get very busy, so go early.

THE WINE GALLERY

The Wine Gallery
375 Boylston Street, Brookline; (617) 277–5522
*Hours of operation: Monday through Saturday, 9:00 A.M. to 9:00
P.M.; Sunday, noon to 6:00 P.M.*

516 Commonwealth Avenue (Hotel Commonwealth, Kenmore
Square); (617) 266–9300
*Hours of operation: Monday through Thursday, noon to 9:00 P.M.;
Friday and Saturday, noon to 10:00 P.M.; Sunday, noon to 6:00 P.M.*

www.wine-gallery.com

*This is heaven for Boston wine lovers: a store that has a self-service wine-
tasting machine that lets you select from sixteen whites and thirty-two reds—
all free. This miracle of science is called an Enomatic, but it's affectionately
known as the Wine Jukebox by its owners at the Wine Gallery.*

*Massachusetts liquor laws prohibit wine stores from giving tasters any more
than six to eight ounces of wine in one sitting, so the folks at the Wine Gallery
have devised a smart method to keep track. Each wine in the jukebox is
assigned a point value based on its price ($10 wines are 1 point, $20-$30
wines are 2 points, $30-$40 wines are 3 points, and so on). Each taster is
assigned a free card with twelve "credits" on it that you use to "pay" the
jukebox for each half-ounce taste. The more expensive the wine, the fewer
tastes you'll get. The most anyone can get is a nice, legal six ounces.*

*In addition to the Jukebox, the Gallery also hosts "traditional" wine, beer, and
liquor tastings. At the Brookline location, tastings are conducted in the specially designed tasting room, where you can sip samples from real glasses
while you sit at the wood tasting table, which accommodates up to thirty
people. In Brookline, beer tastings are on Thursday from 5:00 to 7:00 P.M.;
wine and spirits are tasted on Friday from 5:00 to 7:00 P.M. and on Saturday
from 3:00 to 6:00 P.M. Tastings at the Kenmore Square location (where free
valet parking is available) are held on Thursday from 6:00 to 8:00 P.M. for
beer, and on Friday and Saturday from 6:00 to 8:00 P.M. for wine and spirits.
The stores also host a variety of free wine events.*

Merchants Wine and Spirits
6 Water Street
(617) 523–7425

Thursday, 5:00 to 7:00 P.M.; times can vary, so call ahead.

Reservoir Wine and Spirits
1922 Beacon Street (Cleveland Circle)
Brighton
(617) 566–5588
www.reservoirwines.com

Thursday, 5:30 to 7:00 P.M.

University Wine Shop
1739 Massachusetts Avenue
(617) 547–4258

Saturday, 2:30 or 3:00 to 5:30 P.M.; no tastings in July and August.

This local wine shop specializes in wines under $10 and Italian wines.

Upper Falls Liquors
150 Needham Street
Newton
(617) 969–9200

Auburndale Wine and Spirits
2102 Commonwealth Avenue
Newton
(617) 244–2772
www.thepostscript.com

Saturday, noon to 4:00 P.M.

Don't miss the big spring sale at these two sister wine shops. It's a big catered party where they open eighty to a hundred wines for your tasting pleasure. Find out more—and sign up for the newsletter—at their Web site.

V. Cirace and Sons Inc.

173 North Street (North End)

(617) 227–3193

www.vcirace.com

Friday and Saturday, 4:00 to 7:00 P.M.

The Cirace family has owned this location for over a hundred years. The current owners' grandfather was originally in the wholesale grocery biz, and he was the first store owner granted a liquor license after Prohibition was repealed. The grandkids upgraded the wholesale food selection to a gourmet food shop, featuring Italian specialties, and the wine selection at this North End landmark runs to similar tastes.

Wine Bottega

341 Hanover Street

(617) 227–6607

Friday, 5:00 to 8:00 P.M., except for religious holidays.

This tiny treasure is in Boston's North End, the Italian section, and it likes to plan its wine-tasting schedule in the summer around the festivals that take over this neighborhood to honor a different Catholic saint each week. If a saint is from Tuscany, they taste Tuscans. For the fisherman's festival, they taste Sicilian wines. This shop prides itself on finding good values for its customers, and the salespeople all proudly wear the title "wine geek."

Wine Emporium

607 Tremont Street

474 Columbus Avenue

(617) 262–0379

www.thewineemporiumboston.com

Friday and Saturday afternoons.

This local wine store chain—with two locations, just a block apart—offers wine tastings on Friday and Saturday afternoons. Start times vary, so call ahead.

Wine Press
1024 Beacon Street
(617) 277–7020

Saturday, noon to 6:00 P.M.

This local wine shop presents the monthly wine specials at its tasting events.

BEER TASTINGS

We Bostonians are lucky to have not one but two breweries to call our own. Both welcome visitors with open arms and icy-cold free samples, as long as you're over twenty-one and have the ID to prove it.

Harpoon Brewery
Mass Bay Brewing Company
306 Northern Avenue
(888) HARPOON (ext. 522 to schedule private tours)
www.harpoonbrewery.com

Tours/tastings held Tuesday through Saturday, 3:00 P.M.; additional tour/tastings on Friday and Saturday, 1:00 P.M.

Since the 1980s, the Harpoon Brewery has been creating award-winning custom-crafted beer for the discerning beer drinker. Their seasonal beers are eagerly awaited not just in Boston, but in every lucky city that gets a batch of this liquid gold. No reservations are necessary to attend the tour/tastings; just remember to bring your ID. The tours last approximately thirty to forty-five minutes. Groups of fifteen or more can make reservations.

Harpoon also hosts the 5:30 Club, a group tour of the brewery held Tuesday through Friday from 5:30 to 7:00 P.M. Group size can range from fifteen to eighty people, but it must be scheduled in advance (can you say "office happy hour"?). The brewery charges a nominal $1.00 per person (refundable if the tour is cancelled twenty-four hours ahead) for these events. Call the private tour phone line to make 5:30 Club reservations.

The Samuel Adams® Brewery

Boston Beer Company
30 Germania Street
Jamaica Plain
(617) 368–5080

*Thursday, 2:00 P.M.; Friday, 2:00 and 5:30 P.M.; Saturday, noon, 1:00 P.M., and 2:00 P.M.;
additional tours held on Wednesday at 2:00 P.M. from May 1 through August 31.*

THE CATCH

Suggested donation is $2.00,
but it goes to charity.

}

Sure, their television ads are a little bit lame, and we feel bad for the guy who has to dress up as famous New England Patriot Sam Adams, but the beers are some of the best you'll ever taste. Be sure to bring an ID.

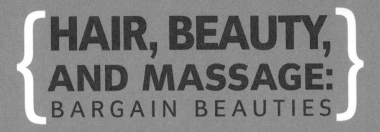

{ HAIR, BEAUTY, AND MASSAGE: }
BARGAIN BEAUTIES

"Sex appeal is 50% what you've
got and 50% what people
think you've got."

—*Sophia Loren*

Beauty may be skin deep, but that broke feeling you get after a trip to a high-priced salon goes right to the bone. Cheap Bastard to the rescue! You don't have to pay through the nose ever again to get styled, made up, or massaged—you just have to know when and where to book your appointments. Some of the top stylists on Newbury Street give their cuts away, pedicures and manicures can be had for a song, and massages? Well, the best massage I ever had cost me just $20. I like to think that Cheap also goes right to the bone.

HAIR SALONS

Some of the top salons in the city—salons that charge up to $200 for a cut and blow-dry—actually give away their services once or twice a week. Although newly hired salon stylists have met basic training and licensing requirements, they must still be taught the salon's signature techniques and styles—and even experienced stylists need ongoing training. They have to practice on someone's hair, and if you volunteer to be a hair model, that someone could be you—and you'll get your cut free or dirt cheap. If that sounds a bit risky, don't fret: The salon's senior stylists supervise the trainee every step of the way. So you won't leave in shock (leaving in shock is for people who pay full price!). You might be required to stay for an entire trainee class, which could be two or more hours, and women volunteers are generally in higher demand than men. You also won't get a whole lot of say in the style—you'll get whatever is being taught that day. But if you're open to new things, this is definitely the way to go. Unless otherwise stated, services are free. If you don't see your favorite salon listed, call them directly and ask—most have training nights from time to time.

Dellaria Salon
623 Commonwealth Avenue (Kenmore Square)
(617) 262–8750

Dellaria Day Spa
1148 Centre Street (Newton Centre)
Newton
(617) 527–8155
www.dellaria.com

This salon dynasty began in Boston, and they actively train their stylists at both their Kenmore Square and Newton Centre locations. Training happens in Kenmore Square on Monday nights at 5:30 P.M. (cut and blow-dry for longer hair) and 6:30 P.M. (for short-hair barbering). Get your name on the list by calling the salon. Coloring is available at the Newton Centre location on Monday nights, but models must be there by 2:00 P.M. to be evaluated for that night's class. Call the Newton location to get your name on the list.

Highlights Salon
286 Newbury Street
(617) 247–8200

This friendly salon uses lots of volunteers, so call and let them know what you're looking for. They'll match you with a stylist, who will call you to get more information about your hair. Salon training takes place on Wednesday nights at 7:00 P.M.

I Soci
8 Newbury Street, third floor
(617) 867–9484
www.isocisalon.com
anne@isocisalon.com

I Soci is an edgy salon that isn't afraid to push the envelope. It holds its employee education sessions every Tuesday at 5:00 P.M., and they need volunteers for both cuts and color. E-mail the salon if you're interested; include your name, phone number, a description of your hair (color; short or long), and the services you want. Models are chosen on a first-come, first-served basis. The salon will contact you when an opening becomes available.

James Joseph Salon

30 Newbury Street
(617) 266–7222
www.jamesjosephsalon.com

James Joseph Studio

168 Newbury Street
(617) 266–6600
www.jamesjosephstudio.com

THE CATCH

Cuts are $10, coloring is $25, and a blowout is $5.00.

}

Cut and color apprentice training takes place at this award-winning salon twice a week, on Tuesday and Wednesday at around 6:00 P.M. Cuts, including blow-dry, are $10, and coloring is $25. There's also a special blowout training session on Monday, which costs models $5.00 and takes place at the 168 Newbury Street studio location. Call the salon a week ahead, ask for Julie or Rebecca, and find out what their needs are for the upcoming class.

Jerel Roberts Stylists

138 Newbury Street
(617) 536–4443
www.jerelroberts.com

THE CATCH

Coloring can cost up to $15.

}

This salon holds its training sessions on Tuesday nights beginning around 4:00 P.M. Cuts are free, and coloring is never more than $15. Call Darla Kossack at the salon to let them know you and your hair are available.

LIQUID Hair Studios

640 Tremont Street
(617) 425–4848
www.liquidhairstudios.com

THE CATCH

Cuts only.

}

This salon, one of the funkiest in town, is renowned for its edgy style and its friendly, funny, welcoming staff. In-salon training happens on Wednesday nights at 7:00 P.M. Call ahead and tell them all about your hair to get on the list.

Runway Salon

11 Newbury Street, third floor
(617) 375–0002
www.runwaysalon.com

THE CATCH
}
Cuts are $15. Coloring
is $20 and up.

Runway uses lots of hair models and schedules training appointments on Monday and Tuesday at 10:00 A.M., noon, 2:00 P.M., and 4:00 P.M. You'll pay $15 for a cut and $20 or more for a color treatment. Sign up online or call the salon and voice your interest. The Web site sign-up form also lists the types of hair models they're looking for that week.

Super Cuts Training Center

24 Mystic View Road
Everett
(617) 381–5102
www.supercuts.com

It's a bit of a haul out of central Boston, but Super Cuts holds training throughout the week, and it is in need of lots of models. Just call them, leave your contact info, and they will schedule you sometime Monday through Friday.

Umi Salon

75 Newbury Street
(617) 247–0770
www.umisite.com

THE CATCH
}
Coloring
is $30.

In-salon training is held on Tuesday nights beginning at 5:00 P.M. at this salon, which caters to some of the city's grandest dames. There are a few ways to sign up to be a hair model—sign up on their Web site (click on "model call"), go in person to the salon on Tuesday at 4:30 P.M., or call Chrisinda Wain at the salon ahead of time. They'll want as much info as possible about your current hair style and what you're looking for. They'll give you a thorough description of what they are planning to do in the training session before you agree to come. Training sessions last about one to two hours. Cuts are free; coloring is $30.

Vidal Sassoon

14 Newbury Street
(617) 536–5496 (main number)
(617) 536–0254 (hair model line)

THE CATCH
}
Cuts are $16,
and coloring
is $25 to $30.

Vidal Sassoon salons hold their training workshops every Friday at 5:45 P.M. The best way to take part is to schedule a free consultation in the week before the workshop. They'll evaluate your hair, tell you about what they're working on in that week's workshop, and schedule you into a training session if it's a good match. Call the special hair model hotline to schedule your consultation.

HAIR TODAY, GONE (TO A GOOD CAUSE) TOMORROW

Locks of Love
2925 10th Avenue North
Lake Worth, FL 33461
(888) 896–1588
www.locksoflove.org

Locks of Love is a nonprofit organization that provides hairpieces to finan-cially disadvantaged children suffering from medical hair loss. Salons around the country offer free haircuts to anyone who is willing to donate their hair to the program. The children receive the hairpieces free of charge. You must have at least 10 inches of hair to donate, from tip to tip. You can pull curly hair straight to measure the minimum 10 inches. They need hair from men and women, young and old, all colors and races. Hair may be colored or permed, but not bleached or chemically damaged. Call your favorite salon if you want to make a donation. Once they know it's for a good cause, they may be willing to offer a free or discounted cut and send the donation to the organ-ization. If they're game, salon requirements can be found on the group's Web site. Here's one salon that offers free cuts to those who are donating to Locks of Love.

DeKwa Elements of Hair
132 Newbury Street, fourth floor
(617) 236–8082
www.dekwa.com

DeKwa takes walk-in appointments for donations to Locks of Love during reg-ular business hours, and they'll send the hair to Locks of Love for you. They'll shape the remaining hair into a blunt cut for free, but the service will not include a wash, style, or blow-dry. If you make an appointment ahead of time on Wednesday, not only will you get a cut, but a junior stylist will also wash, style, and blow-dry it for $25. On Tuesday afternoons from 4:00 to 5:00 P.M., DeKwa offers clients who want to donate their hair a free full-service appoint-ment with a junior stylist, but these appointments book up far in advance, so call at least a month beforehand. Some of the stylists at DeKwa also offer dis-counts to anyone who will donate hair, and those appointments are available during all regular business hours. All appointments must be held with a credit card, which is charged $25 if you fail to show up.

BEAUTY SCHOOLS

A number of local beauty schools offer dramatically reduced prices on all sorts of services—haircuts, colors, manicures, pedicures, facials, and other fabulously exotic treatments that normally cost an arm and a leg. The treatments are all performed by students after they have achieved a certain number of training hours, and their work is overseen by teachers. All of these schools charge a fee for student services, and some offer slightly more expensive services by instructors. The beauty of going to one of these schools is that you can book a reservation in advance and tell them what you want them to do (rather than waiting for a training class at a regular salon, where you may have to wait for an opening and you get whatever they're working on).

Aesthetic Institute of Boston
47 Spring Street
West Roxbury
(617) 327–4550
www.aestheticsinstituteofboston.com

Bojack Academy of Beauty Culture
47 Spring Street
West Roxbury
(617) 323–0844
www.bojackacademy.com

These two training schools are affiliated and offer a variety of services, ranging from cuts and colors to massages, facials, and even advanced microdermabrasion. All fees charged are dramatically lower than those charged in salons elsewhere in Boston. You can choose to have services done by students for a fraction of retail, or by a teacher for a few dollars more than that (but still way under what you'd pay elsewhere). All fees are listed on the schools' Web sites.

Blaine Beauty Schools
30 West Street (Downtown Crossing)
(617) 266–2661
www.blainebeautyschools.com

How does a $10 facial sound? Or a $45 foil? Call ahead to book your reservation at this school, one of the most respected in the industry. Many services require instructor consultation in advance, and prices for the same service may vary depending on instructor involvement.

Cali for Nails Academy
204 Adams Street, Suite 2
Dorchester
(617) 436–6766

Manicures for $3.00 are on offer here, provided by students, on a walk-in basis from 10:00 A.M. to 7:00 P.M. Monday through Friday.

Elizabeth Grady
222 Boston Avenue
Medford
(781) 391–9380

This is a little off the beaten path, but I think it's worth whatever effort you need to make to get here. Elizabeth Grady is one of the finest spa and salon chains in the country, and they have a training center right in our very own backyard that offers, at half price, all the services available at the Elizabeth Grady Salon. We can feel our skin getting better already. Needless to say, reservations go very quickly. And they're not easy to get, even when you know how. The aesthetic clinics run for only a couple of months once that year's students have completed the course work that the school requires before they can work on the public. Call the school directly and ask to be put on the mailing list. Three months before the next clinic is about to begin, you'll get mail or e-mail notifying you of the clinic dates. (You can also call to find out when they'll be running.) As soon as they're announced, start dialing for a reservation! The massage clinics run fairly consistently, about twice a week throughout the year, so those appointments are easier to get.

Empire Beauty Schools
867 Boylston Street
(617) 424–6565

Empire students see customers at fixed hours during the week—Monday through Friday, 9:30 A.M. to 2:30 P.M. and 5:30 to 7:30 P.M. They don't have a Web site, but they'd be happy to fax you a list of service prices upon request.

La Newton
636 Warren Street
Dorchester
(617) 427–6886

La Newton makes appointments with the public on a walk-in basis on weekdays from 10:00 to 10:30 A.M., 1:30 to 2:30 P.M., and 5:30 to 6:00 P.M. Students specialize in hair and manicure services.

New England Hair Academy

110 Florence Street
Malden
(781) 324–6799

This beauty school offers $8.00 haircuts, $15.00 color processes, and other similarly priced goodies. The academy prefers walk-ins during regular business hours, which vary with the season. Call ahead to learn more about their services and hours.

MASSAGE

The absolutely, hands-down best massage I ever had in my life was by a student at a massage school. I'm not sure if it was the massage or the amazing deal I got on it that made me so relaxed—but what does it matter, really? It did the trick, and, fortunately for you, there are local massage schools where you can re-create that magic. You can also reserve an instructor massage for slightly more than the student massage if you want someone with more experience. All of these schools charge a fee for the massages, but it's as little as one-quarter of what you'd pay in a downtown spa.

Massage Institute of New England

22 McGrath Highway
Somerville
(617) 666–3700
www.mine-massageinstitute.com

Student massages here run from $35 to $45, and professional massages are available for $50. Doctors, nurses, students, police officers, firefighters, teachers, and seniors get a $5.00 discount off student massages. Call the school for hours and to make reservations. Current hours are also listed on the Web site.

Muscular Therapy Institute

103 Morse Street
Watertown
(617) 668–1000 (student reservation line)
(617) 668–2000 (professional reservation line)

You can book a massage through the Student Therapy Center, which costs $30 an hour, or through the Professional Therapy Center, which costs $60 an hour. The students do massages during the school year, so call ahead for current appointment hours. Professional massages are available year-round.

Salter School

2 Florence Street
Malden
(781) 324–5454

This school accepts walk-ins or appointments on weekdays from 9:00 A.M. to 1:30 P.M. and specializes in Swedish-style massages. A massage costs $25.00, and a further $5.00 discount is available for seniors, active military personnel, firefighters, or police officers.

MAKEUP

There's nothing like a free professional makeover to leave you feeling like a goddess. Most of the cosmetics stores in the city offer makeovers for free, but the expectation is that you'll buy something when you're done. Some are a harder sell than others.

The Beauty Mark

33 Charles Street
(617) 720–1555

This quaint store is small, so they've chosen their product lines very carefully. If you're looking to sample top-of-the-line items, this is the place. If you want a full makeup application done by the makeup artist, however, it'll cost you big—$75.

MAC

The Atrium Mall
300 Boylston Street
Chestnut Hill
(617) 244–9501
www.maccosmetics.com

The salespeople in this store absolutely love makeup, and they love playing with it on their customers, so don't be shy about asking for help. The sales pressure is low, and the quality of the service is excellent.

ARE YOU BEING SERVED?

Most salespeople in department stores work on commission, so be aware that you're stepping into a bit of a lion's den when you ask for a makeover. If you're a regular buyer of a particular brand at a particular store, and you have a relationship with the salespeople, you'll often find that they're happy to provide a free makeover for the big night—some will even let you book an appointment. But if you don't already have a relationship, expect the very hard sell. Most of these stores host visiting "celebrity" makeup artists who schedule free makeover appointments with customers from time to time throughout the year, but, again, the assumption is that you'll buy. (Call the stores directly for a calendar of upcoming makeover events.) The following stores have extensive cosmetics departments.

Barneys New York

100 Huntington Avenue (Copley Place); (617) 385–3300

The Mall at Chestnut Hill, 199 Boylston Street, Chestnut Hill; (617) 969–5354

Bloomingdales

55 Boylston Street (Route 9)
Chestnut Hill
(617) 630–6000

Lord & Taylor

760 Boylston Street
(617) 262–6000
www.LordandTaylor.com

Macy's

450 Washington Street (Downtown Crossing)
(617) 357–3000
www.macys.com

Neiman Marcus

100 Huntington Avenue (Copley Place)
(617) 536–3660
www.neimanmarcus.com

Saks Fifth Avenue

800 Boylston Street (Prudential Center)
(617) 262–8500
www.saksfifthavenue.com

Sephora

800 Boylston Street (Prudential Center)
(617) 262–4200
www.sephora.com

This is a makeover nirvana for Cheap Bastards. There are always hordes of professionally trained makeup artists wandering the store, showing customers how to use the dizzying array of product choices here. These men and women know their stuff, and they're happy to share it with you. I love this place because, of all the cosmetics retailers in the city, this is the most laid-back about selling you something. Plus, they have a multitude of brands to choose from when making you over. The shop is open Monday through Saturday from 10:00 A.M. to 8:00 P.M. and Sunday from 11:00 A.M. to 6:00 P.M.

Shu Uemura

130 Newbury Street
(617) 247–3500

If you love the look of Madonna's crystal-flecked mink false eyelashes, this is the store that stocks them. They'll let you try on makeup to your heart's content, but if you want a full makeover, it'll cost you $75. They will let you apply it toward your purchases.

{ R E A L } ESTATE: } LIVE FREE OR DIE

"The house came to be haunted
by the unspoken phrase:
There must be more money!
There must be more money!"

—*D. H. Lawrence*

With real estate prices in metro-Boston among the highest in the continental United States, it can be as hard to find affordable housing as it is to find a local who properly pronounces his r's. The elimination of rent control and eviction protections for most city residents at the end of 1996 has also put a real crimp in the budgets of middle- and lower-income people, or anyone who hates paying three-quarters of their annual income for a Boston address. Many people have simply moved out of town, exchanging high housing costs for a commute from the suburbs, which brings its very own challenges (some consider the Southeast Expressway the manifestation of hell here on earth). Others have found creative ways to realize their dreams of home ownership (or even rentership) by staking their claim in the less desirable parts of the city. With rents for studio apartments running about $1,000 a month, and the median price for a 1,000-square-foot condo cresting above $400,000, creativity and patience seem like a small price to pay.

Fortunately, the city of Boston and the Commonwealth of Massachusetts are keenly aware of the difficulty that working people have when settling in the metro area. A host of agencies has been developed specifically to help people like you find a little slice of Boston to call your own.

LOW-COST APARTMENTS AND MORTGAGE PROGRAMS

Boston Fair Housing Commission—Metrolist
1 City Hall Plaza, Room 966
(617) 635–3321

The Commission keeps an updated list of below-market-rate and subsidized rentals and homes for sale at discounted rates. All residents of Boston can search the list, but some listings may have a waiting list or income qualifications. Contact the BFHC directly to learn about gaining access to the list.

The Boston Home Center
Department of Neighborhood Development
(617) 635–HOME
www.cityofboston.gov/dnd/default.asp

This department administers a number of assistance programs for home buyers, including educational programs, financial assistance, grants, and help in finding city-subsidized real estate. If you qualify, you can even get money for a down payment and closing costs. To qualify for some of the DND's loan programs, assets must not exceed $75,000, and total income can't be more than 120 percent of the area's median household income. If you qualify, however, the program can get you into your first Boston home with a far smaller up-front investment, and at lower total cost, than would have been possible otherwise.

Boston Housing Authority
52 Chauncy Street
(617) 988–3400
www.bostonhousing.org

THE CATCH } Income limits apply based on the type of housing you want.

The city of Boston, through the Boston Housing Authority, is the largest landlord in the city, responsible for housing more than 10 percent of the city's residents. It administers all sixty-four of the city's public housing projects. The BHA also provides rent subsidies (through the Section 8 voucher program). As of press time, the city's rental voucher program was closed to new applicants; however, the housing developments—which include facilities for the elderly, people with disabilities, and families—are accepting applications. Income limits apply, and residents are still expected to pay 30 percent of their household income for rent. The turnaround time from application to approval can be long, from eight to ten weeks, so it's important to apply as early as possible.

MassHousing (Massachusetts Housing Finance Agency)
1 Beacon Street
(617) 854–1000
www.masshousing.com

THE CATCH } To qualify for reduced-rate mortgages through this program, your household income can't exceed 135 percent of the median household salary for the area in which you want to buy.

MassHousing is the state's affordable housing bank. Founded in 1966, MassHousing has funded the construction of over 60,000 units of mixed-use rental housing throughout the state. MassHousing also makes construction loans to developers as long as they agree to offer at least 25 percent of the construction units for sale to lower-income households. Finally, it provides these households with mortgages that are far below conventional mortgage rates. Income and asset limits apply and vary with the specific program.

MassHousing also offers reduced-rate mortgage programs for people holding full-time jobs as employees of nonprofit organizations, the state, or the county. Applicants must work in one of the following fields: public safety, law enforcement, education, social services, or health care. Employees in these fields are eligible if they earn 135 percent or less of the area's median average wage (which translates to a household income of $108,000 for most of metro Boston).

In another innovative program that it sponsors in conjunction with the Massachusetts Bay Transportation Authority (the T), anyone who regularly uses public transportation to get to work (or who is a member of ZipCar, the car time-share service) is eligible for a no-down-payment, no-points, adjustable rate loan through the MassAdvantage program. The only catch is that you have to buy a home near public transportation, prove that you take the T to work regularly (such as ten previous months' worth of monthly T passes or a note from your employer stating that you participate in an employer-sponsored transportation program), and meet the 135-percent income requirement cited above.

UP-AND-COMING (AND CHEAP)

One of the best ways to find a cheap place to live is to work the laws of supply and demand. The most desirable neighborhoods are nearly untouchable by the workaday masses who didn't inherit Brahmin wealth. If you make too much to qualify for a low- or moderate-income rental program, but not enough to pay full price in one of the city's swank neighborhoods, you need to focus your search on one of the less-swank parts of town. Here's a list of up-and-coming neighborhoods, and why you should check them out. Two-bedroom apartments can still be had in all of these neighborhoods for around $1,000 a month, which is virtually unheard of in other sections of the city. All are accessible by public transportation and are convenient to major highways.

CHINATOWN: This area's high-rises and factory buildings are being converted to condos and lofts, but there are still bargains to be had in this oasis of Asian food, culture, and unexpectedly rockin' nightlife, all located just a stone's throw from the city's downtown core. It's better yet if you speak Mandarin. Students and artists are the trailblazers scooping up cheap rentals in this area, which has long had an almost exclusively Asian population.

SOUTH BOSTON: Southie, as it's known in these parts, is a literal island jutting in the sea southeast of downtown. It's an isolated little spit of land that has been undergoing profound changes—more high-end nightlife and restaurants, fancy new condo developments, a more diverse population—ever since it made national headlines during the busing crisis there in the 1970s. Still, much remains the same in Southie, a predominantly Irish, working-class neighborhood. Despite a case of mild xenophobia among Southie's native sons and daughters, yuppification has finally begun to take hold. If you're looking for bargains, avoid stylish Telegraph Hill, and look for apartments that are close to the area's remarkably beautiful beaches or along any of the alphabetized streets between A and K or between 1st and 5th Streets—the rest of the neighborhood has started sporting stratospheric prices. Don't even bother with Fort Point Channel—high-end developers have gotten their grubby mitts on the place, and it's the latest trendy address for those who want to look like urban homesteaders settling into a gritty, urban address but who don't want to deal with any of the actual grit they're likely to find in Southie proper.

DORCHESTER/SAVIN HILL: They say you can tell when a neighborhood is on the verge of becoming the next big thing when the gay community starts buying property there—and that's just what started happening a couple of years ago in Dorchester and the Savin Hill area. Long a bastion of working-class and immigrant families, this area is experiencing a swing toward the trendy, with new restaurants opening up regularly (there's even a fabulous gay bar). Real estate prices and rents are slowly creeping up, but get in now if you want to take advantage of what is destined to be the new "It" neighborhood.

EAST BOSTON: This neighborhood, with a strong Italian history, has become a haven for immigrant families looking for a community to call their own. The rest of Boston is slowly catching on to the cultural diversity of this section of the city, which is most famous for its outstanding mom-and-pop restaurants, nearly indecipherable Boston accents, and proximity to Logan International Airport.

LIVING FOR FREE

If you are willing to work for your housing, then taking a job as a nanny, domestic worker, or household manager (the modern term for a butler) is a great way to get free housing and a tidy salary. High-end assignments often include health care, vacation, other perks, and, in some cases, housing for your immediate family. Full-time live-in nannies in Boston can expect to make anywhere between $400 and $750 a week, and household managers can make up to $100,000 for the really juicy, multi-estate assignments.

Word of mouth is a good way to land a job like this. Be aware that most agencies won't touch you if you are not a U.S. citizen and don't have some kind of a work visa. Also, the IRS gets mighty testy if you don't pay taxes on your salary, even if that salary is paid entirely in cash. Complex tax rules apply both to those who hire full-time domestic help and to those who offer themselves for this type of work. If you go through an agency, most of these details will be fleshed out with your employer—make sure this happens, or else you could be stuck with paying what's owed.

Note that a live-in service job isn't for everyone, and the standards for admission into this profession are high and getting higher. People who can afford to have live-in help will expect you to have previous experience, and most nanny or domestic-help agencies run exhaustive background and criminal checks and require numerous stellar references from previous employers. Some even require a certificate from a doctor attesting that you are in good health and not the possessor of any unpleasant communicable diseases. However, if you've got the service pedigree, here are a few local and national placement agencies, and other resources, that can help you on your way to rent-free living!

Household Management

Cass & Company
28 State Street, Suite 1100
(888) 453–2277
www.cassandcompany.com

Specializes in domestic help, household managers, and nannies.

International Butlers Guild
134 West 82nd Street, Suite 3b
New York, NY 10024
(212) 877–6962
www.butlersguild.com
butlersguild@butlersguild.com

The International Butlers Guild is the real deal, an association for those who have chosen a personal-service profession as a way of life. The Web site lists job openings and hosts a butler chat room, and there's even a cool napkin-folding tutorial page.

Starkey International Institute for Household Management, Inc.
1350 Logan Street
Denver, CO 80203
(800) 888–4904
www.starkeyintl.com

This high-end-placement household management school specializes in training the butlers of tomorrow. It also assists clients and students in finding appropriate placements.

Nanny Agencies

American Nanny Company P.O. Box 600765, Newtonville, MA 02460-0007; (800) 262–8771; www.americannannycompany.com

Beacon Hill Nannies, Inc. 825 Beacon Street, Suite 19, Newton; (617) 630–1577, (800) 736–3880; www.beaconhillnannies.com

Boston Nanny Centre 135 Selwyn Road, Newton; (617) 527–0114, (800) 456–2669; www.bostonnanny.com

Nannies' Nook P.O. Box 220, Accord, MA 02018-0220; (781) 749–8097; www.nanniesnook.com

Nanny Poppins Inc. 165 U New Boston Street, Suite 272, Woburn; (617) 227–KIDS (5437); www.nannypoppins.com

{ CHILDREN AND TEENS: }
FREE TO BE YOU AND ME

"Your children and grandchildren
will have their share of happiness;
there's no need to work like a
horse for them."

—Chinese proverb

Boston is a great city for kids—it's packed with history, beaches, playgrounds, tours, and interactive museums, much of it created specifically for our littlest residents and visitors. The city's cultural institutions are also keenly aware that today's kids are tomorrow's patrons, so they provide plenty of ways for children to get exposure to the arts in a child-friendly way. Most of these activities are within walking distance from downtown Boston, or a short ride on the subway. Here is a partial list of what's out there—there are many other activities not listed here that are administered through the Commonwealth of Massachusetts Department of Conservation and Recreation and through Boston's Parks and Recreation Department. Both organizations have searchable online databases that list all of their offerings.

AFTER-SCHOOL PROGRAMS

Boston Centers for Youth & Families (BCYF)
1483 Tremont Street
(617) 635–4920
www.cityofboston.gov/BCYF

BCYF is Boston's largest youth and human services agency, overseeing forty-six community facilities that provide a variety of activities geared to the city's young people and their families, including after-school programs, fitness programs, recreational facilities and pools, and educational programs for children, teens, and adults. You can find a complete list of community centers in Appendix C or in a searchable directory with contact information and programs on the BCYF Web site. Some of these community centers are free to residents of the communities they serve, but most have a small annual membership fee that rarely exceeds $50 a year for an entire family. You can download a complete listing of free or very inexpensive children's activities throughout the city sponsored in partnership with the BCYF at www.cityofboston.gov/bcyf/pdfs/bgys_06_07.pdf. The file is large.

Boston Community Learning Centers

(See Appendix D for the twenty-five locations)
Boston Public Schools
26 Court Street
(617) 635–9000
http://boston.k12.ma.us/

These programs operate in twenty-five public schools throughout Boston's neighborhoods. They provide after-school sports and educational activities, as well as adult and parenting classes, with a special focus on English as a Second Language. A complete list of locations of BCLCs can be found in Appendix D.

Boys and Girls Clubs of Boston

50 Congress Street, Suite 730
(617) 994–4700
www.bgcb.org

The Boys and Girls Clubs were founded in Boston over 110 years ago, and there are now five clubs throughout the Greater Boston and Chelsea area serving children and teens. The clubs provide a wide array of after-school activities for kids ages six to eighteen. Membership fees do apply and are based on ability to pay. Most clubs charge $25.00 for the school year, September through June, with decreased fees of $5.00 for teen members, since many are paying out of their own pockets. During the summer the clubs run a summer camp program (including field trips) from 8:00 A.M. to 5:00 P.M. The cost is $150 to $200 for the summer. The Boys and Girls Clubs have no income restrictions for members and welcome all children to participate.

ARTS, CRAFTS, DANCE, AND MUSIC

ArtBeat

212-A Massachusetts Avenue
Arlington
(781) 646–2200
www.artbeatonline.com

THE CATCH
} The course is free, but they charge for materials.

Try the ArtBeat drop-in open studio for kids' crafts projects. The hands-on art studio is open to the public every day and serves artists from four years old to adult. The instruction is free, but there is a charge for the materials you use. Depending on the medium, it could be as much as $10.

KNOWLEDGE IS FREE

Stumped on the definition of an isosceles triangle? The Boston Public Library and all of its branches offer Boston public school students free help with homework through its Homework Assistance Program. The Homework Assistance Program provides two services to students in Boston: a mentoring program serving third- through eighth-graders at every local branch and an online service, HAP Online, serving fourth- through twelfth-graders. The One-on-One Mentoring Program places ninety high-performing tenth-, eleventh-, and twelfth-graders into all the branch libraries throughout Boston. These mentors help third- through eighth-graders with homework and assist fourth- through twelfth-graders with using library resources. They also read with kids who are in pre-kindergarten and higher grades. The HAP Online service offers online help with tutors for students in grades 4 through 12 on subjects including math, science, social studies, and English. The service is provided every day from 2:00 to 10:00 P.M. and is available in Spanish Sunday through Thursday from 2:00 to 10:00 P.M. In-person Homework Assistance hours vary by branch. To get more information about either of these programs, contact the branch library nearest you. There's a complete list in Appendix B.

Artists for Humanity
100 West 2nd Street
(617) 268–7620
www.afhboston.com

AFH is an innovative art program that helps children and teens learn about art by producing artistic products that are then sold to fund the programs. AFH holds free painting workshops for kids between ten and thirteen years of age at their Saturday Blast program. Kids work with professional artists to learn about how art is created and to express their own creativity. Saturday Blast happens from 10:00 A.M. to 1:00 P.M. at the AFH EpiCenter. For middle and high school kids, AFH offers arts "entrepreneurship" programs in which they get to work alongside professional artists in a variety of media, including painting, screen print, photography, sculpture, and graphic design, to produce finished art that is sold through the AFH. There is even a small stipend available for participants. This program runs through the summer, mid-July to late August, and after school during the school year, Tuesday through Thursday from 3:00 to 6:00 P.M. (There's an April deadline to register for the summer program.) Contact AFH directly to register for either program.

Boston Ballet
(617) 456–6359
www.bostonballet.com

The Boston Ballet's free Taking Steps after-school program is a special twelve-week workshop that meets three times a week to introduce girls ages eleven through fourteen to a variety of dance and movement forms. It is held at the Roxbury Community College and the Reggie Lewis Athletic Center. Taking Healthy Steps, a weeklong program in August reserved for girls ages eleven through fourteen, helps develop basic movement awareness, leadership skills, and self-esteem. Call the Ballet directly to register.

Cloud Place
647 Boylston Street (Copley Square)
(617) 262–2949
www.cloudfoundation.org

This performance and exhibit space also houses a nonprofit organization that is committed to providing opportunities for young artists to showcase their work. Their Youth Fusion program is a year-round series of film screenings, exhibitions, and performances organized by their youth curators to highlight the exceptional art being done by kids in Boston. Check their Web site for current events and exhibitions.

Coop for Kids/Harvard Coop
1400 Massachusetts Avenue
Cambridge
(617) 499–2000
www.harvard.bkstore.com

The Coop offers arts and crafts after their Story Telling events, which take place every Tuesday and Saturday. Story Telling events begin at 11:00 A.M. and run for a little under thirty minutes. After the stories, children are offered the opportunity to make crafts for free. This activity is best for kids ages two through six.

FILMS

AMC Boston Common
175 Tremont Street
(617) 423–3499
www.amctheatres.com

This fun "summer movie camp" runs each Wednesday from mid-June to early August. The pre-movie activities run from 9:30 to 10:15 A.M. and include coloring contests, balloons, and special guests. Then the real fun starts: movies! They begin at 10:30 A.M. and are rated G or PG. Children are admitted on a first-come, first-served basis.

Boston Public Library
700 Boylston Street
(617) 536–5400
www.bpl.org

The BPL's Kids Cinema program occurs on the first Friday of each month at the Central Branch Library in Copley Square. The program features two or three short movies, geared to short attention spans, and they begin at 10:15 A.M. The program runs about fifty to sixty minutes and is appropriate for kids ages three through seven. The showings happen in the Rabb Lecture Hall, which seats 350, but arrive early as these shows do fill up. Occasionally, feature movies are presented on Sunday at 2:00 P.M. and are more appropriate for children who are slightly older. Check the Web site for the most up-to-date information. (See Appendix B and the Film chapter for a list of other metropolitan-area libraries that host periodic films.) Children's movies are also regularly shown at the following branch libraries throughout the city.

CHARLESTOWN
179 Main Street; (617) 242–1248; children's film on Tuesday at 10:30 A.M.

DORCHESTER
Lower Mills Branch, 27 Richmond Street; (617) 298–7841; children's film on Friday at 10:30 A.M. (schedule varies; consult Web site for details).

EAST BOSTON
276 Meridian Street; (617) 569–0271; children's film on Friday at 10:00 and 11:00 A.M.

JAMAICA PLAIN
Connolly Branch, 433 Centre Street; (617) 522–1960; children's film on Wednesday at 10:30 A.M.

MATTAPAN
10 Hazelton Street; (617) 298–9218; children's film on Thursday 10:30 A.M.

NORTH END
25 Parmenter Street; (617) 227–8135; children's film on Monday at 11:00 A.M.

ROSLINDALE
4238 Washington Street; (617) 323–2343; preschooler film on Monday at
10:30 A.M.

ROXBURY
Dudley Branch, 65 Warren Street; (617) 442–6186; preschooler film on Tuesday
at 10:30 A.M.

Egleston Square Branch, 2044 Columbus Avenue; (617) 445–4340; preschooler
film on Monday at 10:30 A.M.

Parker Hill Branch, 1497 Tremont Street; (617) 427–3820; preschooler film on
Tuesday at 10:30 A.M.

SOUTH BOSTON
646 East Broadway; (617) 268–0180; children's film every other Wednesday at
10:30 A.M. and noon.

SOUTH END
685 Tremont Street; (617) 536–8241; preschooler film on Monday at 10:30 A.M.;
monthly Tuesday-night film for teens and tweens at 6:00 P.M. (see Web site for
schedule).

WEST END
151 Cambridge Street; (617) 523–3957; children's film (schedule varies; consult
Web site for details).

Brookline Public Library

361 Washington Street
Brookline
(617) 730–2370
www.town.brookline.ma.us/Library/Children/programs.htm

The library hosts Friday Flicks, movies for preschoolers, every Friday at 10:30 A.M.

WATER SPORTS

Community Boating Inc.

21 David Mugar Way
(617) 523–1038
www.community-boating.org

THE CATCH

} Junior Program membership
is $1.00, and kids must be
able to swim 75 yards.

For over sixty years, Community Boating has
been teaching people how to sail, kayak, and
windsurf on the gentle waters of the Charles
River. Community Boating headquarters is
located in a historic boathouse to the east of the Hatch Shell on the Esplanade. For
$1.00, kids ages ten through eighteen can take part in the Junior Program, which
runs from mid-June to the end of August, Monday through Friday from 9:00 A.M. to
3:00 P.M. Participants must have parental permission. Classes in all water sports
are offered in a variety of skill levels.

Courageous Sailing Center

1 First Avenue (Charlestown Navy Yard)
Charlestown
(617) 242–3821
www.courageoussailing.org

THE CATCH

} Sign up by the first week of April to get in. Spots fill very fast.

For over two decades, Courageous Sailing has taught kids eight to eighteen years old how to sail. Classes are free and are held in Charlestown, Jamaica Plain, and Dorchester on a first-come, first-served basis. The sessions are eight weeks long, with classes held in the morning and afternoon.

G-ROW Boston

600 Pleasant Street
Watertown
(617) 923–7564
www.growboston.org

Started by Olympic rower Holly Metcalf, this rowing program is free to girls who are in the seventh through twelfth grades in the Boston public schools. The program helps girls learn a new sport, develop self-confidence, and learn the importance of teamwork and competition. There is an after-school program that runs from September through May and meets three afternoons per week. Registration begins in September and again in November. There's also a weeklong summer camp program, also for seventh- through twelfth-grade girls, that meets every day for one week from 9:00 A.M. to 2:00 P.M. Registration takes place near the end of the school year. All classes take place at the Community Rowing Boathouse, located on Nonantum Road on the Newton/Brighton line, and G-Row provides transportation from local subway stops for team members.

Piers Park Sailing Program

95 Marginal Street
East Boston
(617) 561–6677
www.piersparksailing.org

This program offers free sailing lessons throughout the year for Boston kids ages ten through seventeen. To participate, teens must have basic swimming skills and a health/immunization record. PPSP is also wheelchair accessible for kids with physical challenges. Programs run after school in the spring, all summer, and after school in early fall. In addition to sailing instruction, each summer program includes a full-day sailing field trip to some of the beautiful islands in Boston Harbor.

SPORTS/PARKS/PLAYGROUNDS

Boston Common Frog Pond

Boston Common
(617) 635–2120
www.bostoncommonfrogpond.org

THE CATCH

} Admission is $4.00 for kids over thirteen.

The Frog Pond is a privately funded facility that is jointly operated by the Parks Department and the private foundation created to build it. During the winter months, it's a skating rink; in the summer months, it's a wading pool and fountain. There's a warming hut and refreshment stand next to the pond, and it's one of the most popular spots in the city when the temperature dips. The skating rink is open from mid-November to mid-March and is free for children thirteen and under. (Skate rental is $8.00, $5.00 for kids under thirteen.) For children older than thirteen, admission is $4.00. It's open Monday from 10:00 A.M. to 5:00 P.M., Sunday through Thursday from 10:00 A.M. to 9:00 P.M., and Friday and Saturday from 10:00 A.M. to 10:00 P.M. There's no charge for use of the wading pool in the summer months.

Christopher Columbus Waterfront Park

Commercial Street next to Long Wharf
(617) 635–4505
www.bostonharborwalk.com

This is Boston's first waterfront park, and it features a magnificent view of the harbor and the sailboats moored along the nearby wharves. The park has grassy open space, a wisteria-covered trellis, spray showers for kids to play in (bring towels), a play lot, and a rose garden. It's a great relaxing place to sit down and cool off after a day of trotting the kids around town.

Feast of the East Festival

East Arlington Business District
Massachusetts Avenue
East Arlington
(781) 643–4600
www.feastoftheeast.com

This annual festival, organized by the Arlington Chamber of Commerce, happens in early June and offers free entertainment to children—pony rides, face painting, cotton candy and popcorn, clowns, and balloons. Come to hear the free musical entertainment and to enjoy free arts and crafts.

GREENS KEEPERS

Boston Parks and Recreation Department
1010 Massachusetts Avenue, third floor
(617) 635–4505
www.cityofboston.gov/parks
The Parks and Recreation Department administers and/or maintains dozens of playgrounds, tot lots, gardens, parks, cemeteries, and playing fields throughout metropolitan Boston. Their Web site provides a complete search-able list, as well as links to ongoing activities sponsored by the Department.

Massachusetts Department of Conservation and Recreation
251 Causeway Street, Suite 600
(617) 626–1250
www.mass.gov/dcr
The DCR is the state agency that administers much of the public space, state parks, and recreational facilities throughout the Commonwealth of Massachusetts. These facilities include ice-skating rinks, tennis courts, public pools, beaches, and playgrounds. The Web site features a searchable, com-prehensive, well-organized list of all the public recreation facilities and parks throughout the metro area and Massachusetts, including the Esplanade and the Paul Dudley White Bike Path. The site also includes an updated calendar of current events at DCR facilities, which includes the Hatch Memorial Band Shell on the Esplanade, as well as other popular outdoor event locations.

Memorial Drive Sundays
Cambridge
(617) 626–1250
www.mass.gov/dcr/parks/metroboston/charlesR-activities.htm

Memorial Drive from Eliot Bridge to Western Avenue is closed on Sunday from 11:00 A.M. to 7:00 P.M., beginning the last Sunday of April and ending the second Sunday of November. The road becomes a family park where you and the kids can walk, bike, and skate without worrying about traffic. Vendors, music, and skating lessons are often available along the route, and there are plenty of benches and grassy areas between Memorial Drive and the Charles River, which flows next to the road for the length of the closed area.

Minuteman Bike Path

www.minutemanbikeway.org

This 11-mile trail, which begins at Alewife Station in Cambridge and ends at Depot Park on South Street in Bedford, literally passes through New England's colonial heritage. In towns like Lexington, Arlington, and Bedford, the trail passes locations where our forebears fought for independence. The Minuteman Path, administered by a variety of local bike-oriented volunteer organizations, including MassBike, is one of the first and best bike path conversions in the country. It met with stiff community resistance when first proposed, but now it's a very popular weekend family destination and, as such, can get very crowded. It's mostly flat, so it's perfect for young bicyclists or in-line skaters. Markers pointing out areas of historic or natural significance add a nice educational element. It's also a popular bike commuter route, since it ends at a major subway station. The path is open from 5:00 A.M. to 9:00 P.M. every day.

Miriam & Sidney Stoneham Playground

Located on the Esplanade, between Fairfield Street and Massachusetts Avenue
(617) 227–0365
www.esplanadeassociation.org

This beautiful playground along the banks of the Charles River is owned by the state Department of Conservation and Recreation and was built with funds raised by the Esplanade Association. The play space has two areas. One is for kids under three and features climbing structures, slides, baby swings, and a toy car. Older kids can climb on the challenging jungle gym, which has a cool fire pole, monkey bars, swinging tire, and more. The playground is open daily from dawn to dusk. On Sunday afternoons during the summer, the volunteers with the Esplanade Association host a variety of fun events for kids, including model sailboat racing, fishing, and puppet shows. Check out the Web site for event details and times.

INDOOR PLAY SPACE

Guggies Art Center and Play Space

368 Boylston Street
Brookline
(617) 731–2388
www.guggies.com

Guggies is a play space featuring arts and crafts for kids from toddlers to school age. Art projects are ongoing. Art classes are an additional charge. It's open Monday through Friday from 10:00 A.M. to 5:00 P.M. Weekend hours vary, so call ahead.

Play Space at Atrium Mall

300 Boylston Street
Chestnut Hill
(617) 527–1400
www.simon.com

THE CATCH }
It's $40 for a four-week membership for unlimited use for an entire family.

This play space is free, but constant parental supervision is required. There are climbing structures for the kids and a seating area for parents, and the floor is padded with soft mats. The play area is located on the fourth floor of the mall, but keep in mind that the restrooms are located on the first level. The play area is open during mall hours Monday through Saturday 10:00 A.M. to 9:30 P.M. and Sunday 11:00 A.M. to 6:00 P.M.

MUSEUMS/HISTORIC SITES

Boston Children's Museum

300 Congress Street
(617) 426–8855
www.bostonkids.org

THE CATCH }
$1.00 admission on Friday from 4:00 to 9:00 P.M.; admission is steep at other times.

For over ninety years, this museum has featured interactive, educational exhibits that keep kids occupied and enthralled. Exhibits include Black Boston (celebrating Boston's diversity), the science workshop, a turtle-viewing area, and historical toys. There are ongoing special events, and everything at this award-winning museum is hands-on. Admission is steep on most days, but only $1.00 on Friday nights.

Castle Island and Fort Independence
William Day Boulevard
South Boston
(617) 727–5290
www.bostonharborwalk.org

This outdoor space is historic and eclectic and can provide more than enough activities to keep your family occupied all day. Part of the Harborwalk system of walking trails throughout Boston, Castle Island is a peninsula that juts into Boston Harbor, providing spectacular views of the airport, harbor shipping activity, and the Harbor Islands. On one end of Castle Island is an enclosed lagoon that boasts a beautiful beach. The walking path that surrounds the lagoon is great for cycling, walking, and in-line skating. Castle Island is also home to Fort Independence, a stone armory that dates back to 1851. It's open during the summer, and walking tours are free on Saturday and Sunday between Memorial Day weekend and Labor Day weekend, from noon to 3:30 P.M. The tours last about thirty minutes. The fort and the island are on the State and National Registers of Historic Places, and Fort Independence is a National Historic Landmark. There is a clam shack near the large parking lot (the lot fills up early in the summer), and there's even a place to rent little sailboats to use in the lagoon. Picnic tables and grills are located throughout the area, and the entire place is swarming with families on nice summer days.

Faneuil Hall
State Street across from City Hall
(617) 523–1300
www.faneuilhallmarketplace.com/entertainment2.html

This shopping and dining paradise is also a bonanza for kids—entertainers of all stripes fill the walkways and courtyards throughout the day to make you laugh, sing, or marvel at their magic. Several musicians, storytellers, acrobats, and clowns are usually strolling around on any given summer weekend day. Check the Web site to see who is performing, but it's best to simply show up and see who's around. Just walk toward the big, clapping crowd.

John Fitzgerald Kennedy National Historical Site
83 Beals Street
Brookline
(617) 566–7937
www.townofbrooklinemass.com/TownInformation/JFKNationalHistoricSite

This is the renovated birthplace and first home of President John F. Kennedy. It's open Wednesday through Sunday from 10:00 A.M. to 4:30 P.M., with guided tours occurring every thirty minutes. The home, where JFK was born in 1917, was purchased back by the family after his 1963 assassination. His mother, Rose Kennedy, painstakingly decorated the home and chose the mementos and photographs that commemorate the president's life. Student learning and activity materials are available. National Park Service rangers also lead tours in the neighborhood to point out places that played an important role in JFK's childhood.

Massachusetts State House
Beacon Street at Park Street
(617) 727–3676
www.sec.state.ma.us/trs/trsidx.htm

Designed by renowned architect Charles Bulfinch and completed in 1798, the Massachusetts State House is a fascinating walk through one of the earliest houses of democracy in the country. The State House is open to the public Monday through Friday from 10:00 A.M. to 4:00 P.M., and free tours are available throughout the day.

Museum of Afro-American History
46 Joy Street (Beacon Hill)
(617) 725–0022
www.afroammuseum.org

This not-for-profit cultural museum celebrates the contributions of African Americans. It's open Monday through Saturday 10:00 A.M. to 4:00 P.M. and is free. Learn about black film stars, scientists, politicians, movers and shakers, and more. Special events and lectures are also available. Check the Web site for updated info.

Museum of Science
O'Brien Highway (Science Park)
(617) 723–2500
(617) 589–0267 (observatory hotline)
www.mos.org

The Museum of Science charges a fee to get in, and it's not cheap. Fortunately for families, it also offers several participatory events that are free to all. The first, located in the lobby of the museum's Charles Hayden Planetarium, is called Welcome to the Universe. Its goal is to put into perspective the vast size of our universe and solar system. The exhibit includes the Community Solar System Trail, an interactive treasure hunt for bronze "planet" models that have been placed around the city at appropriate relative distances from the "sun" model in the Hayden Planetarium. Before you visit the Universe exhibit, go to the MoS Web site, and print out the Community Solar System Passport (www.mos.org/automedia/media/pdf/1893_passport.pdf). It includes directions to locations throughout the metro-Boston area where you can find each "planet." Take a rubbing of each planet to complete the passport. Then, mail the passport to the museum, and your child will get a special certificate commemorating his or her planet-finding prowess. Planets are located as far away as the Riverside T station in Newton. All planets are accessible by public transportation.

The museum lets all comers visit the Gillian Observatory and its Meade LX200 telescope for free on Friday nights from 8:30 to 10:00 P.M. The observatory is located on the top level of the museum's parking garage (parking is not free). Call the observatory hotline to find out what constellations are visible on a given night. Museum employees will be on hand to help you enjoy the stars.

USS *Constitution* and Museum
Charlestown Navy Yard
Charlestown
(617) 426–1812
www.ussconstitutionmuseum.org

This museum/ship, the oldest commissioned ship in the U.S. Navy, has free admission and offers a number of free child-oriented programs. Kids can explore the life of a sailor, discuss piracy, and look at nautical art. Tours are available. The museum is open May 1 through October 15 from 9:00 A.M. to 6:00 P.M. and October 16 through April 30 from 10:00 A.M. to 5:00 P.M.

STORES FOR FUN

These stores are a destination all to themselves—packed with the latest in fun toys and teeming with other kids. And while I think it's borderline cruel to take kids to a toy store if you're not going to buy them a toy, these stores make it worth your while to stop in. Each one has a fun space for kids to enjoy themselves, but don't be surprised if you hear that familiar, plaintive cry—"pleeeeeeez!"

The Construction Site
200 Moody Street
Waltham
(781) 899–7900
www.constructiontoys.com

Build it and they will come. This store has just about every building block or tool ever made for kids. Play spaces around the store are equipped with various types of building toys and blocks to help your child discover the budding architect within.

Curious George Goes to Wadsworth

1 JFK Street
Cambridge
(617) 498–0062
www.curiousg.com

This great bookstore features artisan toys. Although the store is centered around the theme of the beloved monkey, there are hundreds of other books and products that kids can peruse.

Henry Bear's Park

361 Huron Avenue, Cambridge; (617) 547–8424

19 Harvard Street, Brookline Village; (617) 264–2422

685 Massachusetts Avenue, Arlington; (781) 646–9400

www.henrybear.com

This store has repeatedly been named the best toy store in the Boston area by a variety of local publications. It has an amazing array of toys and a friendly, attentive staff. Kids can drive trains across the big train table, play house in the kitchen play space, and play with Legos and Duplos on the building-block table. Parental supervision is required.

Home Depot Kids' Workshops

5 Allstate Road, South Bay Plaza; (617) 442–6110

75 Mystic Avenue, Somerville; (617) 623–0001

1 Mystic View Road, Everett; (617) 389–2323

615 Arsenal Street, Watertown; (617) 926–0299

1100 Revere Beach Parkway, Chelsea; (617) 889–4258

1213 VFW Parkway, West Roxbury; (617) 327–5000

www.homedepotclinics.com

THE CATCH
For kids ages five to twelve. Children must be accompanied by an adult. Hours may vary due to unforeseen circumstances, so call ahead.

Give a kid a dollhouse, and she'll play for a day. Teach her to build her own, and one day she just might build you a new dining room set. Home Depot workshops help kids complete a small construction project—like a birdhouse or a picture frame. These workshops are taught at every Home Depot in the country and are designed to teach children do-it-yourself skills and tool safety. Plus nothing beats the feeling of building something yourself. Prefabricated kits help make the projects easy (or at least easier), and every kid receives the coveted orange Home Depot associate's apron and an achievement pin. The workshops are held the first Saturday of each month between 9:00 A.M. and noon.

Magic Beans

312 Harvard Avenue
Brookline
(617) 264–2326
www.mbeans.com

There's a fenced-off play space located in the back of the store that is perfect for babies just crawling or learning to walk. There's a restroom close by. Magic Beans also holds story hours for kids on Tuesday at 11:00 A.M. (for infants to three-year-olds) and on Thursday at 4:00 P.M. (for kids three and older).

Stella Bella Toys

1360 Cambridge Street
Cambridge
(617) 491–6290

THE CATCH } Play groups cost $5.00.

This is a great place for new moms and little tykes. It has a play space with a huge, colorful mural as the backdrop and lots of great books and games. A New Parent Coffee Hour is held on Friday mornings from 11:00 A.M. to noon; this event allows parents to socialize while babies play with a selection of toys that Stella Bella makes available for their teething pleasure. The store also offers play groups on Tuesday from 10:00 to 11:00 A.M. for infants seven to eighteen months old, and on Wednesday from 4:00 to 5:00 P.M. for toddlers eighteen to thirty months old. These staff-led play groups are $5.00.

STORYTELLING

Barefoot Books

1771 Massachusetts Avenue
Cambridge
(617) 349–1610
www.barefootbooks.com

Check the Web site for story-time events. The store sometimes offers concerts and creative activities sessions as well as readings.

FREE (STORY) TIME

The public library system in the metro-Boston area has made an enormous commitment to ensuring that children develop a love of reading as early as possible. That's why nearly every branch of the public libraries in Boston, Cambridge, Newton, Dedham, Needham, Milton, and other surrounding communities host frequent story hours for children from toddlers up to school age. For a complete listing of branches, and Web sites that list story hours, see Appendix B.

Barnes and Noble Bookstores

Downtown Crossing, 395 Washington Street; (617) 426–5184

Prudential Center, 800 Boylston Street, Suite 179; (617) 247–6959

325 Harvard Street, Brookline; (617) 232–0594

Arsenal Marketplace, 485 Arsenal Street, Watertown; (617) 923–4401

170 Boylston Street, Chestnut Hill; (617) 965–7621

www.bn.com

These bookstores offer free story hours (appropriate for two- through six-year-olds), and the story times come with other fun activities geared to further expanding kids' creativity. Call the store closest to you for updated schedules and times of story hours.

Brookline Music School

25 Kennard Road
Brookline
(617) 277–4593
www.bmsmusic.org

Story time takes place the first Friday of every month and is appropriate for children of preschool age and under. It starts at 10:00 A.M., it's free, and it runs for about an hour. There are both stories and music.

Coop for Kids/Harvard Coop

1400 Massachusetts Avenue
Cambridge
(617) 499–2000
www.harvard.bkstore.com

Story-time events happen on Tuesday and Saturday at 11:00 A.M. and run for a little under thirty minutes.

Newtonville Books, The Lizard's Tale

296 Walnut Street
Newton
(617) 244–6619
www.newtonvillebooks.com

There are no formal story hours here, but there are monthly readings and signings by young adult and children's book authors. Some of these events are free. Some charge for admittance. For others, buying the book will get two people in free.

CHILDREN'S THEATER PROGRAMS

Boston City Lights Performing Arts School

1154 Washington Street
(617) 451–9034
www.bostoncitylights.org

Since 1979 this South End performing arts training center has offered classes for kids in underserved communities in such disciplines as acting, singing, dancing, recording, set building, photography, mime, and everything else to do with a career in the entertainment field. Funded by local philanthropist Duggan Hill, who also serves as executive director, the school offers all of its courses for free "in exchange for a lot of hard work," says Hill. Most of the students are ten to twenty years old, but City Lights has a policy of never turning anyone away. Students are required to study all three disciplines of singing, dancing, and acting. Students train with professional instructors, whose classes also include paying students who register separately from the City Lights program.

City Stage Co. of Boston

539 Tremont Street
(617) 542–2291 (classes)

This theater company offers two free after-school theater-arts programs for kids. The first is geared for kids ten to fourteen years old and takes place after school twice a week. There's also a more intensive Saturday program for teenagers. Both programs encourage kids to write and perform their own material. The performances take place in locations throughout the city. Call to register.

Dorchester Nazarene Compassionate Center

Youth in Action Theatre Arts Program
Second Church of Dorchester
44 Moultrie Street (Codman Square)
Dorchester
(617) 288–2289, ext. 210

THE CATCH

There is a one-time application fee of $25 to $50.

This program hosts an after-school theater-arts program that teaches kids ages fifteen to seventeen about scriptwriting and staging theatrical productions. The program also includes an educational component that teaches the history of theater arts. Admission takes place throughout the school year. Most sessions take place on Fridays after school and on weekends. Hours vary.

Huntington Theatre Company

264 Huntington Avenue
(617) 273–1558
www.huntingtontheatre.org

THE CATCH

These workshops cost $150 per year, but scholarships are available that knock the cost down to $25.

One of the best theater companies in the city, Boston University's Huntington Theatre offers after-school programs during the school year for kids from grades 6 through 12. For younger kids, ages eleven to fifteen, the Acting Class provides a comprehensive introduction to theater. For older or more experienced thespians, the Acting Class Too offers more in-depth instruction for kids ages thirteen to seventeen. There's also Scene Study and Playwriting workshops overseen by theater professionals. All programs meet once a week from 4:00 to 6:00 P.M. during the school year (the day of week varies by semester and program). The programs normally cost $150 per year, but if the student writes and submits an essay to the theater education director that outlines why he or she wants to take part in the program, the fee is reduced to $25 for the school year. Everyone who applies for the scholarship gets one. And here's the best part: After completing one of these programs, the kids get a special Huntington Student Club card that entitles them to two free tickets to every Huntington Theatre production every year until they turn twenty-one!

PARK IT

ParkARTS
www.cityofboston.gov/parks/parkarts

Boston is a city of parks, and ever since 1997 the mayor's office has sponsored a celebration of the arts, known as ParkARTS, that makes full use of those glorious green spaces. The program features over eighty free, participatory, performing and visual arts programs in parks and common spaces throughout the city all summer long. The performances include theater (such as Shakespeare in local parks and mobile stages on which small local theater groups showcase their talents) and musical groups. There are Monday Night Movies, family-friendly movies shown in a different neighborhood park each week, as well as hands-on arts workshops throughout the summer to teach kids and adults how to express themselves through arts and crafts.

Since 1998 the Parks Department has also worked with Boston's Institute of Contemporary Art (ICA) to present contemporary works of art in Boston's open spaces through the ICA's Vita Brevis program. ParkARTS is responsible for almost half of the programs offered throughout the park system, and they are all free and open to the public. For more information on events coming to a park near you, check out the schedule on the Parks Department Web site.

Strand Youth Theatre Project
543 Columbia Road (Upham's Corner)
Dorchester
(617) 388–5628
www.cityofboston.gov/arts/strand.asp

THE CATCH } Open to Boston residents only, and an audition or interview is required.

These beginning and advanced theater classes, designed for kids ages fourteen through nineteen, stress scene study, monologue, and group performance. Classes take place in the newly renovated, 1,400-seat Strand Theatre, which is owned and managed by the city of Boston. As part of the program, enrolled students are required to attend plays and concerts throughout the city, for which they get free admission. Transportation to outside events is often provided.

True Colors Out Youth Theater

43 Thorndike Street
Cambridge
(617) 621–6090
www.thetheateroffensive.org

THE CATCH } An audition is required.

This program is free of charge and geared toward gay, lesbian, or bisexual youth, or youth who are allies of this community. Auditions are usually held in the beginning of September and February. The rehearsals are held on Tuesday and Thursday from 6:00 to 9:00 P.M., at the Cloud Place at 647 Boylston Street in Boston. If accepted into the program, a youth (between the ages of fourteen and twenty-two) can receive a stipend of around $100 per month.

MEDICAL INSURANCE

MassHealth

Commonwealth of Massachusetts Executive Office of Health and Human Services
One Ashburton Place, eleventh floor
(800) 841–2900 (MassHealth general information)
www.mass.gov

MassHealth is the program in the Massachusetts Department of Health and Human Services that provides free and reduced-cost health insurance coverage, through private providers, Medicaid, and other sources. There are a number of different plans depending on your circumstances. Coverage type is based on your age, health, and family and employment circumstances. If you are not eligible under those criteria, you may qualify based on income alone—many of these programs are geared to people who are living within 150 to 200 percent of the federal poverty level (which for a family of four is around $40,000). Call the information line for more details about the specific programs that may suit your needs.

{CLOTHING AND HOUSEHOLD GOODS: CHEAP AND CHIC}

"One man's trash is another man's treasure."

— *Anonymous*

In a city as affluent as Boston, there are some real treasures hiding in our thrift stores—some are so good you feel like you're stealing. It's not unusual to find couture from last year on the racks next to the beat-up sweatshirts and scratched lamps. Nothing this good comes easy though. You will pay with sweat, elbows in the ribs from other aggressive shoppers, and, likely, a headache from sifting through the haystack to get to that fashionable little needle (in the right size) buried somewhere within. Some of our thrift stores sell such high-end stuff that although items are marked way, way down, they're far from what you'd call cheap. It's all about value: What would you pay for last season's Versace? If "nothing" is still your preferred price point, and you're in need of some household goods, there's still no better place to go shopping than curbside on trash day. If you hit the right part of town, you could potentially furnish your home with high-quality stuff that might be in need of only a little fluffing and buffing.

THRIFT, CONSIGNMENT, AND SECONDHAND

This is by no means a comprehensive list of every thrift, consignment, or second-hand store in the Boston area, but these are widely regarded as having the best selection, the best turnover of product, and the best prices.

Boomerang's
716 Centre Street
Jamaica Plain
(617) 524–5120
www.aac.org/boomerangs

Boomerangs is the Boston AIDS Action Committee's award-winning resale store, stocking new and used clothes for men, women, and children. It'll be tough to find many items over $10, unless you want a new men's suit—which would cost you about $20. A portion of the sales goes to support the AAC's outreach to people living with AIDS.

Children's Orchard

807 Boylston Street
Brookline
(617) 277–3006
www.childrensorchard.com/store.cfm?StoreNum=75

This store is one of the many Children's Orchard franchise stores in Massachusetts, but quantity doesn't mean poor quality. If you're looking for children's toys, furniture, books, or accessories—you name it—you can find it at a Children's Orchard, which features gently used children's items. If you don't see what you want the first time you visit, come back in a week, as the merchandise turns over frequently. You can also call the main Children's Orchard service number, (800) 999-KIDS, and the home office can probably track it down.

Christ Church Thrift Shop

17 Farwell Place
Cambridge
(617) 492–3335
www.cccambridge.org/ThriftShop.html

THE CATCH }
Open
September to
May.

The Church Lady has never looked this chic. Started in Christ Church back in the 1960s, the Thrift Shop now occupies three large rooms in a building behind the church, and proceeds fund the 240-year-old church's preservation. Those three rooms are just packed with what the Thrift Store likes to call "experienced" clothing, preread books, tested knickknacks, and small home goods. You'll find designer dresses, costume jewelry, and fine men's suits, shirts, and sweaters. The Thrift Shop is a favorite with the college crowd—and Cheap Bastards, too.

The Closet

175 Newbury Street
(617) 536–1919

This store falls into the category of "you get what you pay for." The items are a bit north of your basic "thrift" or "secondhand" store price point, but the quality and selection are so high that some shoppers refuse to tell their friends they buy their couture here, all in the vain hope that word will not get out. Their ploy has not worked, and the Closet is one of the most popular, and well-stocked, secondhand stores on Newbury Street—it may be one of the best stores on Newbury Street, period. Furniture is either antique or no older than five years. Clothing is usually not older than two years, or else it's clearly vintage.

Garment District

200 Broadway
Cambridge
(617) 876–5230
www.garment-district.com

Take a deep breath and wear your elbow pads. Go to the Garment District, which sells a great variety of jeans, fun costumes, wigs, vintage, accessories, housewares, jewelry, and makeup on its second floor. Save the second floor for later—for now, hit the first floor, also known as "Buck a Pound," which is exactly what it sounds like. All the clothing in the warehouse-size room is $1.50 a pound—there's all manner of clothes, young and old, ripped and perfect, stained and clean as a whistle. On Friday all the Buck a Pound stuff is 75 cents a pound. Wear a mouth guard if you venture in on these days. The competition can be fierce.

Karma Designer Consignment Boutique

26 Prince Street
(617) 723–8338

Enter this store and be transfixed. Gorgeous high-end consignment items—Versace, Chanel, even some new items—await. Nothing here is exactly cheap, but it's a bargain basement compared to what you would have paid when these little gems were new. Besides, they're new to you.

Morgan Memorial Goodwill Inc.

1010 Harrison Avenue; (617) 541–1270

520 Massachusetts Avenue, Cambridge; (617) 868–6330

230 Elm Street, Somerville; (617) 628–3618

470 West Broadway, South Boston; (617) 307–6367

www.goodwillmass.org

Shop in the stores that started the secondhand craze. From vintage and retro to designer brands and popular household items, you'll find it all—and you'll be funding a good cause—at these Boston Goodwill locations.

Oona's

1210 Massachusetts Avenue
Cambridge
(617) 491–2654

Looking for just the right item to wear to that '70s disco party? Halloween? A fancy cocktail party? Tiny Oona's is legendary for its costumes, crazy vintage items (like garish fake furs), leather coats, and peacoats. It's the place to go for vintage and retro clothing. You could spend an entire afternoon playing dress-up with all the wigs and gloves they have in stock.

Poor Little Rich Girl

416 Highland Avenue
Somerville
(617) 684–0157
www.poorlittlerichgirlstore.com

THE CATCH

} No men's clothing.

There's barely room to move at Poor Little Rich Girl, but everywhere you look is a designer label, no more than two or three years old (unless it's clearly vintage) and in perfect condition. Want a suede jacket for under $50? A Saks brocade cocktail dress for $40? This is the place. The staff is super picky about what they take on consignment, so you'll be sure to find the best. There's a $5.00 rack at the front of the store for those who think any price with two digits in it is too much.

Savers

1600 VFW Parkway
West Roxbury
(617) 323–8231
www.savers.com

Savers is a chain of thrift stores across the country, and they get shipments frequently from their nonprofit partners. They stock designer and vintage clothing, home decor, books, toys, electronics—it's like the Wal-Mart of thrift stores. Go early and go often, as they replenish their stock several times a week.

Second Time Around

176 Newbury Street; (617) 247–3504
219 Newbury Street; (617) 266–1113
99 Charles Street; (617) 227–0049
8 Eliot Street, Cambridge; (617) 491–7185
1169 Walnut Street, Newton; (617) 964–4481
www.secondtimearound.net

For over thirty-five years, Second Time Around has been selling just barely used designer and couture items, and now they have a whole chain of stores. If you set up an account on their Web site, you can even search their stock and see which store is hiding a particularly perfect Chanel cocktail dress or pair of Blahnik pumps.

Urban Renewals

122 Brighton Avenue
Allston
(617) 783–8387

Cash
only.

It's big, it's hugely popular with the college kids, and it's in "Rock City"—as Allstonians like to call their town. With all that going for it, how can you help but find the perfect shirt, dress, shoes, necklace, chair—and more—at rock-bottom prices? It gets packed here on the weekends, so head over on a weeknight.

THE SHRINE OF CHEAP

Filene's Basement

426 Washington Street
(617) 542–2011
www.filenesbasement.com

If you have anything even approaching attention deficit disorder, you'll want to avoid Filene's Basement. This mammoth place, which for a hundred years has sold overstock and out-of-season apparel and accessories for men and women from brand-name retailers and designers, invented the term "chaos," and it is not for the faint of heart. Lucky for us Cheap Bastards, its founders also invented the term "automatic markdowns." The longer an item is on the shop floor, the less it costs—the reduced price is already printed right on the price tag, right next to the date on which that price will take effect. It's like eBay, but in slow motion, and in person.

Be warned. The store extends two stories under what used to be Filene's, and it's sadly the only thing left of that historic department store chain, which closed in 2006. Unlike its high-end deceased parent, the Basement presents its merchandise in great piles in what look like boxes in the middle of the aisles, although most designer clothing, dresses, and lingerie are hung on racks. Waiting lines for the communal dressing rooms are long, so seasoned Basement shoppers—who might shop there every day—will simply change while standing in the aisles. They dress accordingly (leggings or large flowy skirts, tight tank tops, slip-on shoes). Every August, the Basement becomes a lace and satin scrum when the store holds its world-famous bridal gown sale (imagine 1,000 brides trying to grab a $3,000 dress marked down to $300, and you get a pretty good mental picture). "The Vault" section in the back of the women's department is a little less manic. It's a sectioned-off enclave of higher-priced (but still mega-bargain) items that are unsold, end-of-season merchandise from very high-end Boston couturiers like Louis Boston. For Boston's Cheap Bastards, Filene's Basement is a shrine.

TRASHY TREASURES

Bostonians are big consumers of stuff. When it's time to upgrade that stuff, many of them can't be bothered to go through the hassle of selling their old stuff in consignment stores or through an online auction site. For them, the most effort they're willing to put into getting rid of all their stuff is dragging it down to the curb on trash day. That's where you come in. If you are open to the idea of picking up someone else's "trash"—and I use the term loosely—you are in for a treat. It's not only furniture that you'll find out there, but lamps, filing cabinets, rugs, all manner of housewares, televisions, even computers. It may or may not work, but it's there for the taking. There are some commonsense rules you'll want to follow if you want a piece of all this free treasure.

Rules of Trash Day Etiquette

Only "shop" the best neighborhoods. The general rule of thumb about trash picking is this: The more expensive the real estate, the higher the quality of the trash. The hot spots are Back Bay, Beacon Hill, South End, the waterfront of the North End, and Cambridge near Harvard. From mid-May to early June, the best stuff can be found near any college or university in greater Boston—especially Commonwealth Avenue around Kenmore Square near Boston University, Beacon Street in Chestnut Hill near Boston College, and anywhere near Harvard Square, and particularly the Harvard Business School graduate housing near Western Avenue—as the students clear out and head home.

Get there early. Trash haulers come early in the morning of the specified trash day. Boston rules stipulate that you can't put anything out on the curb any earlier than 5:00 P.M. on the day before. Begin your hunt at about 7:00 P.M. the day before the scheduled trash pickup. This is when most people have come home from work, and they're likely to lug the big items down to the curb before they settle down for dinner. Rarely will people put out the good stuff in the morning of trash day—the trucks usually come too early, and who wants to lug bulky furniture out of the house before they've even had a cup of coffee?

Bring a hand truck. If you don't mind being clearly identified as a trash picker, bring a hand truck, or a small rolling grocery cart (the ones that you can pull behind you on two wheels). When you see something good, it won't be there for long, so you'll want to cart it away immediately.

Be polite. Don't open up trash bags looking for stuff, but if you do, tie them back up again. Less considerate trash pickers think nothing of opening up bags, strewing the contents hither and yon, and just walking away. These people give trash pickers a very bad name. Expect some fierce competition out there. There are hordes of individuals trolling the street along with you, and they've been doing it for longer than you have (sometimes out of necessity). There's no hierarchy involved among trash pickers, but if you find yourself in a standoff with one of the more experienced members of the fellowship (and you'll know who they are), best to back down and live to trash-pick another day.

Be discreet. Wait until the person putting out the trash has gone back inside before pouncing. For some reason, people don't want to see their former items being hauled off by people who are clearly going to reuse them. It destroys the illusion that the item is simply disappearing into the Big Dump in the Sky. I've seen people haul stuff back inside if they think there's a feeding frenzy brewing—if it's that valuable, they figure they'll just keep it. Discretion is the better part of trash picking.

Trash-Hauling Schedule

Here is a partial list of the trash-hauling schedule for Boston proper. Some of the neighborhoods are divided up for trash hauling on different days. Use the city of Boston's Web site to search for specific street addresses to find out when the trash pickup is for that street.

City of Boston Public Works Department
Sanitation Division
Boston City Hall, Room 714
(617) 635-7575
www.cityofboston.gov/whoami

Back Bay: Trash and recycling on Monday; trash on Thursday.

Beacon Hill: Trash on Monday and Wednesday; trash and recycling on Friday.

Charlestown: Trash and recycling on Wednesday.

Chinatown/Bay Village: Trash on Monday and Wednesday; recycling on Friday.

Financial/Leather District: Trash on Monday and Wednesday; recycling on Friday.

North End: Trash on Monday and Wednesday; trash and recycling on Friday.

Roxbury: Trash and recycling on Monday; trash on Thursday.

Roxbury/Mission Hill: Trash and recycling on Tuesday; trash on Friday.

South End: Trash and recycling on Tuesday; trash on Friday.

For Mattapan, Jamaica Plain, West Roxbury, Dorchester, Hyde Park, East Boston, Allston/Brighton, Roslindale, and South Boston, you can look up the trash-hauling day for specific streets (you must use a street number) on the city of Boston's information Web site.

{ **HEALTH** }
AND MEDICAL:
CHEAP CHECKUPS

"The first wealth is health."

—*Ralph Waldo Emerson*

Boston is the undisputed medical capital of the world, with more hospitals located here than in some cities twice its size. As the cost of medical care continues to skyrocket, here and everywhere, there are dozens of hospitals and clinics in Boston where you can get free or reduced-cost care. The Massachusetts legislature is in the process of implementing new rules that require all residents of Massachusetts to purchase some kind of health insurance, so, at press time, there was no way to know what effect these new rules would have on the availability of free or reduced-cost care at the various medical facilities listed here. But these rules likely won't affect either the surfeit of free clinical trials available to anyone who meets certain criteria or Boston's community health clinic system, the first in the country.

CLINICAL TRIALS AND RESEARCH

Not only is Boston the medical capital of the country, but it has one of the most active medical research communities in the country as well—grants flow to our many researchers, fellows, and medical universities to test out techniques and drugs through clinical trials conducted at almost every hospital in town. This is good news for whatever ails us Cheap Bastards. If you meet the requirement of a particular clinical trial, you can get treatment for free, as well as follow-up care. Some of the trials offer stipends to participate. Almost all of these databases and hospitals list or conduct psychiatric clinical trials and research as well.

There are always risks associated with clinical trials, so make sure to balance your need for care with the potential risks of being a human guinea pig before agreeing to participate. Consult the Center for Information and Study on Clinical Research Participation at www.ciscrp.org for a comprehensive overview of what it means to be part of a clinical trial.

Beth Israel Deaconness Medical Center
300 Brookline Avenue
(617) 667–7000
www.bidmc.harvard.edu

To access a list of clinical trials, go to the home page and type "clinical trial" in the search engine. The search results page will display links to information about all of the current clinical trials available for enrollment. Trials are available in all clinical areas.

Boston Clinical Trials and Medical Research, Inc.
18 Shepard Street
Brighton
(617) 202–6322
www.bostontrials.com

This company coordinates trials of various medications for a wide variety of ailments for various sponsors, including hospitals and pharmaceutical companies.

Boston Medical Center
One Boston Medical Center Place (Massachusetts Avenue at Harrison Avenue)
(800) 841–4325 (Health Connection hotline)
www.bmc.org/patients/healthconnection.html

Call the Health Connection hotline to find out about all available clinical trials. The hotline is operated from 8:30 A.M. to 5:00 P.M. Trials are available in all clinical areas.

Boston Shriners Hospital
51 Blossom Street (at Cambridge Street)
(617) 722–3000

This hospital conducts clinical trials and research relating to the treatment of burns and pain management in children. Call the hospital directly for information about current trials.

Caritas Christi Hospitals
www.caritaschristi.org/clinical.asp?s=536

This clinical trials database lists all trials for the Caritas Christi hospitals in Massachusetts. Boston Caritas hospitals include Caritas St. Elizabeth's Medical Center (at 736 Cambridge Street) and Caritas Carney Hospital (at 2100 Dorchester Avenue in Dorchester). Trials are available in all clinical areas.

Children's Hospital

300 Longwood Avenue
(617) 355–6000
www.childrenshospital.org/research/clinical/Search.cfm

This hospital conducts clinical trials in all clinical areas relating to children's health and disease.

CRNet

www.crnet.mgh.harvard.edu/clinical_trials/view_areas.asp

This Web site serves as a clearinghouse for all the clinical trials currently being run at Massachusetts General Hospital (along Cambridge Street near Charles Street), Brigham and Women's Hospital (75 Francis Street in the Longwood area), Spaulding Rehabilitation Hospital (125 Nashua Street in the West End), and McLean Hospital (psychiatric hospital at 115 Mill Street in Belmont). Trials are available in all clinical areas.

Dana Farber Cancer Institute

44 Binney Street
(866) 408–DFCI (3324)
www.dfci.harvard.edu/res/clinical/

This hospital conducts numerous clinical trials on new cancer treatments and drugs, as well as psychiatric trials relating to the impact of cancer on patients and their families.

Massachusetts Eye and Ear Infirmary

243 Charles Street
(617) 523–7900
www.meei.harvard.edu/research/trialstudies.php

The Massachusetts Eye and Ear Infirmary conducts clinical trials relating to conditions and diseases of the eye, ear, nose, and throat.

Mount Auburn Hospital

330 Mount Auburn Street
Cambridge
(617) 492–3500
(617) 499–5774 (clinical trial center line)
www.mtauburn.caregroup.org/body.cfm?id=37

This hospital conducts clinical trials in all clinical areas. Call the hotline for a complete listing of current clinical trials.

STUDY HALL

Several national online databases keep track of all clinical trials and studies in the country or specialize in a particular medical area.

AIDS Clinical Trials Information Service
www.actis.org
This site provides information on federally and privately sponsored clinical trials for people with AIDS and HIV infection.

Center Watch
www.CenterWatch.com
This site is an open resource listing over 40,000 active industry- and government-sponsored clinical trials, as well as new drug therapies in research and those recently approved by the FDA.

Coalition of National Cancer Cooperative Groups
www.cancertrialshelp.org
This database lists current clinical trials relating to cancer.

EmergingMed.com
This database of cancer-related clinical trials connects participants directly with the doctors who are conducting the trials.

National Cancer Institute
(800) 4–CANCER
www.cancer.gov/clinicaltrials
This site provides a nationwide listing of cancer-related clinical trials.

U.S. National Institutes of Health
www.clinicaltrials.gov
This large database lists clinical trials in all clinical areas.

Veritas Medicine
www.veritasmedicine.com
This site provides a comprehensive, searchable listing of ongoing clinical trials in all clinical areas.

New England Baptist Hospital
125 Parker Hill Avenue (off Huntington Avenue)
Roxbury
(617) 754–5800
(617) 754–5616 (clinical research line)
www.nebh.caregroup.org/display.asp?node_id=4063

This hospital conducts clinical trials and research on diseases and conditions of the musculoskeletal systems.

Tufts–New England Medical Center Hospitals
750 Washington Street (at Kneeland Street)
(617) 636–5000
www.nemc.org/resadmin/

There are several hospital divisions in the NEMC hospital area, including the Floating Hospital for Children. The hospitals conduct trials in all clinical areas.

FREE/LOW-COST MEDICAL CARE

Technically speaking, we could all get some free medical care if we wanted. Every hospital in the state is required by law to provide emergency medical care regardless of ability to pay, and some hospitals, like Boston Medical Center, which was founded as a public hospital, give away hundreds of millions of dollars of free care of all types each year. Of course, somebody really is paying for all that care—and that somebody is you and me and everyone else who has medical insurance, which helps reimburse hospitals for giving free care. For that reason, as well as the extremely long waiting times one finds in emergency rooms, and the impact it would have on people with genuine emergencies, it's probably best to avoid the emergency room unless you are faced with a true emergency. That said, there are dozens of low-cost insurance plans available to Bostonians who fall within certain income, demographic, or family parameters. More details on plans administered through the city of Boston and its partners, like CareNet and CenterCare (available at local community centers), are available at the Boston Public Health Commission's Web site at www.bphc.org/howto/access_adultcare.asp or through the Mayor's Health Line at (617) 534–5050. Information on state and federal insurance programs (like MassHealth, the state's Medicaid insurance program) are available through the Commonwealth of Massachusetts Department of Health and Human Services, at www.mass.gov or by calling the Health Access and Resource line at (800) 531–2229.

Hospitals

Boston Medical Center
One Boston Medical Center Place (Massachusetts Avenue at Harrison Avenue)
(617) 638–8000
www.bmc.org

The BMC is the result of the merger of its predecessor hospital, the Boston City Hospital (the first public hospital in Boston), with Boston University School of Medicine. Despite the merger, the BMC has maintained its commitment to serving low- and middle-income families and underserved communities and is still considered by many as Boston's "safety net" hospital because it gives away more free care than any other hospital in the city. The BMC administers low-cost insurance HealthNet, a managed care organization, in cooperation with fifteen community health centers in Boston.

Boston Shriners Hospital

51 Blossom Street

(617) 722–3000

www.shrinershq.org/shc/boston/index.html

This hospital is one of twenty-two around the country that offers free care for children under eighteen. The Shriners Hospital in Boston specializes in burn care and rehabilitation.

Boston Community Health Centers

Boston is home to more than two dozen community health centers. In fact, the very first health center in the country opened in Boston's Dorchester neighborhood in 1965. Community health centers provide low-cost care geared to the needs of each neighborhood. The staff at community health centers deliver primary care, mental health, pediatrics, obstetrics and gynecology, dental care, and social services.

Allston/Brighton

Joseph M. Smith Community Health Center 287 Western Avenue, Allston; (617) 783–0500; www.josephsmith.org

St. Elizabeth's Health Care at Brighton Marine 77 Warren Street, Brighton; (617) 562–5200; www.caritas-semc.org

Boston

Fenway Community Health Center 7 Haviland Street; (617) 267–0900; www.fenwayhealth.org

Health Care for the Homeless Program 729 Massachusetts Avenue; (617) 414–7779

MGH Back Bay Healthcare Center 388 Commonwealth Avenue; (617) 267–7171

North End Community Health Center 332 Hanover Street; (617) 742–9570

Sidney Borum Jr. Health Center 130 Boylston Street; (617) 457–8140; www.jri.org/jrihealth.htm#sidney

Charlestown

MGH Charlestown Healthcare Center 73 High Street, Charlestown; (617) 724–8167

Chinatown

South Cove Community Health Center 885 Washington Street; (617) 482–7555; www.scchc.org

Dorchester

Bowdoin Street Community Health Center 230 Bowdoin Street, Dorchester; (617) 754–0100; www.bowdoinstreethealth.org

Codman Square Health Center 637 Washington Street, Dorchester; (617) 825–9660; www.codman.org

Dorchester House Multi-Service Center 1353 Dorchester Avenue, Dorchester; (617) 288–3230; www.dorchesterhouse.org

Geiger-Gibson Community Health Center, Harbor Health Services, Inc. 250 Mount Vernon Street, Dorchester; (617) 288–1140

Harvard Street Neighborhood Health Center 632 Blue Hill Avenue, Dorchester; (617) 825–3400; www.harvardstreet.org

Neponset Health Center, Harbor Health Services, Inc. 398 Neponset Avenue, Dorchester; (617) 282–3200

Upham's Corner Health Center 415 Columbia Road, Dorchester; (617) 287–8000; www.uphamscornerhealthctr.com

East Boston

East Boston Neighborhood Health Center 10 Gove Street, East Boston; (617) 569–5800

Jamaica Plain

Brookside Community Health Center 3297 Washington Street, Jamaica Plain; (617) 522–4700

Martha Eliot Health Center 75 Bickford Street, Jamaica Plain; (617) 971–2100

Southern Jamaica Plain Health Center 640 Center Street, Jamaica Plain; (617) 278–0710

Mattapan

Mattapan Community Health Center 1425 Blue Hill Avenue, Mattapan; (617) 296–0061

Roslindale

Greater Roslindale Medical & Dental Center 4199 Washington Street, Roslindale; (617) 323–4440; www.roslindale.org

Roxbury

Dimock Community Health Center 55 Dimock Street, Roxbury; (617) 442–8800; www.dimock.org

Roxbury Comprehensive Community Health Center 435 Warren Street, Roxbury; (617) 442–7400

Whittier Street Health Center 1125 Tremont Street, Roxbury; (617) 427–1000; www.wshc.org

South Boston

Harbor Family Health Center 37 Devine Way, South Boston; (617) 269–0312

Mary Ellen McCormack Health Center, Harbor Health Services, Inc. 10 Logan Way, South Boston; (617) 288–3119

South Boston Community Health Center 409 West Broadway, South Boston; (617) 269–7500

South End

South End Community Health Center 1601 Washington Street, South End; (617) 425–2000; www.sechc.org

LOW-COST STD CLINICS

In addition to the clinics listed above, many of which offer free, confidential testing for sexually transmitted diseases, there are additional low-cost clinics available. All clinics are first-come, first-served, so go early, bring a book, and be prepared to wait. Before you go, check out the Massachusetts Department of Public Health's Web site on STD clinics (www.mass.gov/dph/cdc/std/services/clivis.htm). It's a good overview of what to expect, and the site lists the rules regarding confidentiality.

Boston Medical Center
One Boston Medical Center Place (at Harrison and Massachusetts Avenues, South End)
(617) 414–4290

Hours: Monday, 8:00 to 11:00 A.M. and 1:00 to 3:00 P.M.; Tuesday, 8:00 to 11:00 A.M. and 1:00 to 3:30 P.M.; Wednesday, 1:00 to 3:00 P.M. and 5:00 to 6:00 P.M.; Thursday, 1:00 to 3:00 P.M.; Friday, 8:30 to 11:00 P.M.

Massachusetts General GID Clinic
55 Fruit Street (off Cambridge Street, near Charles Street)
Cox Building, fifth floor
(617) 726–2748
www.mgh.harvard.edu/id/clinical_practice/std_clinic/

Hours: Monday through Friday, 8:30 to 11:00 A.M.; Monday and Wednesday, 1:00 to 3:00 P.M.; Monday, 5:00 to 7:00 P.M. by appointment only.

MGH Chelsea Health Center
151 Everett Avenue
(617) 887–4600
www.mgh.harvard.edu/id/clinical_practice/std_clinic

Hours: Tuesday, 1:00 to 3:00 P.M.; Thursday, 3:00 to 5:00 P.M.

Planned Parenthood Express Center

Davis Square Plaza
260 Elm Street
Somerville
(617) 616–1600
www.pplm.org

Hours: Monday through Friday, 11:00 A.M. to 7:00 P.M.; Saturday, 10:00 A.M. to 5:00 P.M.

The Center offers walk-in screenings during regular business hours for all sexually transmitted diseases, or you can call to make an appointment.

Planned Parenthood Greater Boston Center

1055 Commonwealth Avenue
(617) 616–1600
www.pplm.org

Hours: Monday, 8:00 A.M. to 7:00 P.M.; Tuesday through Friday, 7:30 A.M. to 7:00 P.M.; Saturday, 7:30 A.M. to 2:00 P.M.

The Center offers STD testing and HIV testing by appointment. You can also walk in for HIV testing on Tuesday from 3:00 to 6:00 P.M. High school students and low-income people can get services and testing at a very low fee.

{ FITNESS, FUN, AND GAMES: FREE TIME }

"The word *aerobics* came about
when the gym instructors got
together and said, 'If we're going to
charge $10 an hour, we can't call it
jumping up and down.'"

—Rita Rudner

It happens every April. After five months of nearly continuous bad weather, the air temperature rises, the trees begin to bud, and staying late at work no longer seems a viable option. Bostonians burst from their homes and offices to soak up as much of the glorious daylight as they can, and they head straight for the beaches, parks, and playgrounds of our city. The founding fathers of Boston recognized how important it is for Bostonians to have open green space in which to frolic and play (and walk the dog). They established the Boston Common in 1634, and our politicians have been designating public spaces ever since. As a result, the city of Boston is literally surrounded with playgrounds, skating rinks, tennis courts, ball fields, gardens, and beaches, all created for the most important job of all: having fun.

Even in the depth of winter, there are plenty of places to keep fit until the weather turns agreeable again. Boston has a vast infrastructure of community centers that provide affordable fitness and recreation opportunities for everyone year-round. Most of it is free, or so inexpensive that there's no excuse for anyone to hibernate during the bleak season.

PARKS

City of Boston Parks and Recreation Department
(617) 635–4505
www.cityofboston.gov/parks

Commonwealth of Massachusetts Department of Conservation and Recreation
(617) 626–1250
www.mass.gov/dcr

These two organizations control almost all of the public space in the city of Boston, including playgrounds, skating rinks, pools, tennis courts, tot lots, and ball fields. The city Parks Department hosts ParkARTS, a summerlong program that brings arts, music, theater, festivals, and other interactive activities to parks throughout metropolitan Boston. For a complete schedule of ParkARTS events, visit www.city ofboston.gov/parks/ParkArts/. All events are free.

In addition to parks and recreational facilities, the Department of Conservation and Recreation oversees state parks and wildlife refuges and also helps to administer the Boston Harbor Islands. The Web sites of both organizations have online databases of all their properties and facilities, and both allow you to narrow your search to specific areas, neighborhoods, or facility types. Many of the parks listed below are overseen by one of these two organizations, but they're so noteworthy that they deserve a closer look.

Blue Hills Reservation
Reservation Headquarters
695 Hillside Street
Milton
(617) 698–1802
www.mass.gov/dcr/parks/metroboston/blue.htm

Named for the hills that dominate the interior of this wilderness park, the Blue Hills Reservation is just minutes from downtown Boston. The reservation hosts hiking and biking trails, an educational museum, historic Native American artifacts, Ponkapoag and Houghton Ponds, ball fields, fishing, camping, an observatory, and horseback riding—there's even a ski hill. Reservations are required for some activities, like camping or using the ball fields, so call ahead.

Boston Nature Center and Wildlife Sanctuary
500 Walk Hill Street
Mattapan
(617) 983–8500
www.massaudubon.org/Nature_Connection/Sanctuaries/Boston/index.php

Hours (Nature Center): Monday through Friday, 9:00 A.M. to 5:00 P.M.; Saturday, Sunday, and Monday holidays, 10:00 A.M. to 4:00 P.M.

Hours (trails): Open every day, dawn to dusk.

THE CATCH

There is a $2.00 suggested donation for nonmembers. No pets are allowed on the site.

This sixty-seven-acre sanctuary, run jointly by the Massachusetts Audubon Society and the city of Boston, is located in the heart of the city, on the grounds of the former Boston State Hospital. Two miles of wheelchair-accessible trails and boardwalks traverse meadows and wetlands that coyotes, pheasants, and many species of migratory birds now call home. The George Robert White Environmental Conservation Center hosts a variety of educational programs designed to teach children and adults the impact that humans have on nature. The sanctuary also includes the Clark-Cooper Community Gardens, one of Boston's oldest and largest community gardens.

Charles River Reservation
Along the Charles River from Boston University Bridge to Brighton

This park offers 17 miles of pedestrian/bicycle trails as well as recreational facilities, skating, baseball, boating, and canoeing.

The Emerald Necklace
www.emeraldnecklace.org

In 1896 the city of Boston christened an interconnected chain of parks and gardens, called the Emerald Necklace, that form a necklace of green surrounding the perimeter of the city. Each park within it was designed by renowned landscape architect Frederick Law Olmsted, who also designed Central Park in New York City. The Emerald Necklace is now listed in the National Register of Historic Places. Here are some of the beautiful parks that make up this local treasure.

Arnold Arboretum
125 Arborway
Jamaica Plain
(617) 524–1718
www.arboretum.harvard.edu
www.emeraldnecklace.org/arboretu.htm

Hours: open from sunrise to sunset.

The Arnold Arboretum was created from funds generated by the Arnold estate when it was bequeathed to Harvard University in 1872. Today, this 265-acre park, owned by Harvard University but leased for 1,000 years to the city of Boston for use as a public park, is a riot of colors, ponds, forests, and hidden treats, like the Larz Anderson Bonsai Collection, which includes bonsai trees dating back to the mid-1700s. As the oldest arboretum in the country, the Arnold Arboretum contains trees and shrubs from around the world, with special emphasis on plants native to Asia and New England. Lilac Day happens every Mother's Day, and it is the only day that picnicking is allowed in the Arboretum. The Hunnewell Building houses the Arboretum's permanent collection, library, and archives. Restrooms are available here as well.

Back Bay Fens
Along Boylston Street in the Fenway area

The Fens still retains remnants of its beginnings as a freshwater marsh, and it's a place best avoided at night due to crime. But during the day, it is one of the most beautiful parks in the city. It is home to the Kelleher Rose Garden, ball fields, and the city's oldest remaining original Victory Garden, where families grew fresh fruits and vegetables during the rationing of World War II. Trails meander along the ponds and marshes that dot the area.

Boston Common
Located between Park, Beacon, Boylston, Charles, and Tremont Streets

Boston Public Garden
Located between Arlington, Beacon, Charles, and Boylston Streets

America's oldest public park, the Boston Common was first used in 1634 as a grazing ground for cattle for the fledgling city's residents. It then became a military training ground, and today its forty-eight acres are filled with monuments, music performances, picnics, and outdoor activities. It hosts the annual Shakespeare on the Common series, as well as fund-raising events nearly every weekend from Memorial Day to Columbus Day. The Public Garden, the first botanical garden in the United States, is located across Charles Street to the west. Here, Swan Boats glide across a twenty-four-acre lagoon, and the meticulously tended rose gardens spring to life each spring. Gardeners plant an ever-changing rotation of seasonal flowering plants. It's a popular spot for wedding photos, reading, picnicking, or just relaxing on a sunny bench.

Franklin Park
Walnut Street
Jamaica Plain
(617) 635–4505

At over 500 acres, Franklin Park is the largest park in the Emerald Necklace. Olmsted designed this as a "country park" similar to New York's Central Park, which he also designed. Distinct areas within the park include a zoo, a golf course, a stadium, playing fields, and wooded areas laced with trails, picnic areas, tennis courts, ponds, streams, and historic ruins.

Jamaica Park
507 Jamaicaway
Jamaica Plain
(617) 522–6258

The main attraction of this park is Jamaica Pond, a sixty-acre kettle hole formed by an ancient glacier. Natural springs feed the 90-foot-deep pond, which is the largest naturally occurring body of water within Boston. Prior to being acquired as a park in 1894, an ice-cutting industry flourished here. Fishing (trout, which is stocked by Boston, as well as pickerel, bass, hornpout, salmon, and perch), rowing, sailing, and walking/jogging are the primary activities today.

Olmsted Park
Pond Avenue
Brookline

This park, originally named Leverett Park but renamed in the 1900s to honor the designer of the Emerald Necklace, has woodlands, meadows, and three ponds and sits on the Boston and Brookline line. There are plenty of places to sit down and contemplate or get up and move. Footbridges and pedestrian paths are located around Wards Pond, at the center of the park. A bike/pedestrian path system on the Brookline side from Jamaica Pond to Boylston Street (Route 9) was recently completed.

Riverway Park
Along the Muddy River from Landmark Center in the Fenway area to Route 9

This narrow little park is hidden away behind a thick bank of trees along the Muddy River. Even though you're next to a busy roadway, the well groomed trail, footbridges, and thick stand of beech trees lining the riverbank make you feel like you're a thousand miles away from anything urban.

The Esplanade
South side of the Charles River from the Museum of Science to the Boston University Bridge
The Esplanade Association
10 Derne Street (administrative offices)
(617) 227–0365

Created in stages beginning in 1910, the Esplanade is a 3-mile-long ribbon along the Charles River filled with green space, gardens, forests, fountains, lagoons, the stage known as the Hatch Memorial Band Shell, a boathouse and docks, a playground, and memorials to those who helped bring this lovely oasis to fruition. It is a great place to read, sunbathe, sail toy sailboats, or listen to a concert. During the summer months there is a free concert nearly every weekend day, including the world-famous Fourth of July Concert by the Boston Pops. The concert and the accompanying fireworks display are televised internationally. (For more information on the Fourth of July Concert, see page 16 of the Music chapter.) For a complete schedule of Hatch Shell concerts, visit the DCR's events guide at www.mass.gov/dcr/events/hatch.pdf.

SLEEP WITH THE FISHES

Boston Harbor Islands

(617) 223–8666

www.bostonislands.org

Boston may not be at the top of your list as a good camping destination for the family, what with all the noise, traffic, and concrete (makes it hard to put

THE CATCH } Campsites are $8.00, plus transaction fee, for Massachusetts residents. No loud music or alcohol are allowed at campsites.

tent stakes in). But turn your eyes east and behold the beautiful Boston Harbor Islands. The Boston Harbor Islands are thirty islands of dramatically varying sizes and types located off the city's coast, and many have picnic or camping facilities at little or no cost. A $10 ferry ride (adults, per person) from Long Wharf in Boston gets you to Georges Island, and free ferries shuttle you to the other islands from there. On four of the islands—Grape, Bumpkin, Peddocks, and Lovells—camping is available, but you must have a reservation (available at ReserveAmerica.com or call toll-free 877-422-6762; your camping reservation is not site-specific). Peddocks Island has one central camping area (no individual sites), and the other islands have ten to twenty individual campsites and one group campsite. The cost to rent a campsite is $8.00 for a family site (one to four people) for Massachusetts residents, $10.00 for nonresidents, plus a $9.50 transaction charge.

Stonybrook Reservation

Turtle Pond Parkway

West Roxbury, Hyde Park

(617) 698–1802

This peaceful 476-acre woodland area is filled with trails for hiking and biking, ponds teeming with fish, soccer and baseball fields, tennis courts, picnic areas, an ice-skating rink, and a pool. Here you can find the John F. Thompson Center, New England's first recreational facility designed specifically to accommodate visitors with physical impairments. You can make reservations for the Thompson Center by calling (617) 361-6161.

RECREATION CENTERS

Boston Centers for Youth & Families (BCYF)
(617) 635–4920
www.cityofboston.gov/BCYF

BCYF is Boston's largest youth and human services agency, overseeing forty-four community facilities that provide a variety of activities geared to the city's young people and their families, including after-school programs, fitness programs, recreational facilities and pools, and educational programs for children, teens, and adults. See Appendix C for a complete listing of locations, or you can find a searchable directory with contact information and programs on the BCYF Web site. Some of these community centers are free to residents of the communities they serve, but most have a small annual membership fee, which rarely exceeds $50 a year for an entire family.

GROUP SKATES

Inline Club of Boston
Kendall Square, P.O. Box 426185
Cambridge, MA 02142-0021
www.sk8net.com
membership@sk8net.com

THE CATCH

} You must wear a helmet and wrist guards to participate in group skates.

The ICB has been teaching people how to skate right since 1992. Their weekly group skates are a great way to learn the best routes with the best surfaces, pick up some good urban skating skills, and meet like-minded athletes. Novice skaters can join the group skate on Sunday mornings at 10:15 A.M. at JFK Park at the corner of Memorial Drive and North Harvard Street for an easy urban skate tour. Advanced skaters meet at the Hatch Shell on the Esplanade on Tuesday nights at 7:00 P.M. for a 12-mile advanced urban skate tour. More advanced skaters interested in racing should contact the club directly; the ICB is happy to give instructor referrals to newbies. The club also hosts an annual two-day skating event in August, SkateBoston, but it costs $75 to participate in those events. For more information about SkateBoston, visit www.skate-boston.com.

BIKE PATHS

Biking is a really popular sport in Boston, thanks to the relatively flat terrain and the commitment to bike paths made by our local pols. But, in true Boston tradition, some of these paths aren't well signed, many have dangerous intersections, they're not all in great condition all the time, and they can get extremely crowded on the weekends. Despite all that, they're definitely a nice alternative to Boston drivers (although on the weekends, I prefer to take my chances with the cars). Here are some of the best.

Dr. Paul Dudley White Bike Path
Along the Charles River, through Boston, Cambridge, Newton, Watertown, and Waltham
www.mass.gov/dcr/parks/metroboston/maps/bikepaths_dudley.gif

This 17-mile paved and gravel trail begins at the Museum of Science in Boston, follows the Esplanade, then Charles River Park, and ends officially in Watertown Square. But new extensions are constantly adding more miles of trail, and today, with a little hunting for the next leg (since some parts of it aren't well marked), you can follow this bike path to Waltham and beyond. It's a very popular bike commuter route during the week, and it's packed with walkers, in-line skaters, and strollers on the weekends. In the summer, charity "walk-a-thons" take over the Esplanade section of the path at least one day each weekend, so check out the schedule at www.mass.gov/dcr/events/hatch.pdf before spending any weekend time here.

Minuteman Bikeway
From Alewife MBTA station to Bedford
www.minutemanbikeway.org

This 11-mile asphalt path, administered by a variety of local biking organizations, has become a major thoroughfare for bike commuters living in communities west of the city into the Cambridge area. The path, formerly a rail bed with a very gradual uphill grade as you proceed west, is very well maintained. The scenery—marshes, forests, gardens, and ponds—is breathtaking in places. The path attracts hundreds of families and young bicyclists on the weekends, so it's best to avoid it if you're a more advanced rider. It's perfect for in-line skating. In the winter the trail is not plowed, so it makes a great cross-country skiing trail. The bike path is open year-round from 5:00 A.M. to 9:00 P.M.

Mystic River Bike Path

Mystic River Reservation
Medford, Somerville, Everett
(617) 727–5380
www.mass.gov/dcr/parks/metroboston/mystic.htm

The Mystic River bike path can be a little tricky to follow, as it sometimes involves confusing road crossings and some dead ends at major highways, but a map provided by the DCR will help you find your way. You can access the paths in Somerville near the Assembly Square Mall and Route 28, and ride them along the Mystic River to Medford. You can download the map at the DCR Web site listed above. The bike path is open year-round from dawn to dusk.

Neponset River Trail

(617) 727–5290
www.mass.gov/dcr/parks/metroboston/lnrt.htm

The Lower Neponset River Trail, a former railroad bed along the shore of the Neponset River, is like taking a ride through the industrial history of the area. The 2.4-mile path links the Neponset area to the larger network of DCR trails. The trail currently stretches from the historic Port Norfolk neighborhood in Dorchester, through Pope John Paul II Park, across Granite Avenue through the Neponset Marshes, and through the Lower Mills area, where it crosses several old railroad bridges and passes next to old converted mills. It terminates at Central Avenue in Milton. Busy roads currently link the Neponset River Trail from Port Norfolk to the Harborwalk Trail along the Boston shore, which travels past the JFK Museum and up to Castle Island. Intrepid riders with a local map can navigate to the Harborwalk and turn this ride into a round-trip route of 20 miles or more.

Pierre Lallement Bike Path

Southwest Corridor Park
From Melnea Cass Boulevard to Forest Hills
www.mass.gov/dcr/parks/metroboston/southwestCorr.htm

Named for the Parisian who is credited with patenting the first design for a bicycle and who lived out his final years in Roxbury, the Southwest Corridor Park is a 4.7-mile, fifty-two-acre, linear park stretching from the Back Bay to Forest Hills. It winds through the neighborhoods of the South End, Back Bay, Roxbury, and Jamaica Plain, mostly along the Amtrak and MBTA's Orange Line tracks. Along the way, there are eleven tot lot areas, two spray pools, seven basketball courts, five tennis courts, two street hockey rinks, two amphitheaters, and approximately 6 miles of biking, jogging, and walking paths.

BOATING

Community Boating

At the Charles River across Storrow Drive from the Charles Street pedestrian overpass
(617) 523–1038
www.community-boating.org/contact.html

THE CATCH

} Adult learn-to-sail
packages start at $80.

Community Boating, housed in the historic boat-house along the banks of the Charles River, teaches thousands of people to learn to sail every year. Kids can learn for $1.00 (see the Children and Teens chapter for details), and adults can purchase the thirty-day learn-to-sail package for $80. A sixty-day boating pass is $135. There are also kayaks available for rental.

Public Garden Swan Boats

(617) 522–1966
www.swanboats.com/new/welcome.shtml

Hours: April to mid-June, 10:00 A.M. to 4:00 P.M.; mid-June to Labor Day, 10:00 A.M. to 5:00 P.M.; after Labor Day, noon to 4:00 P.M. on weekdays and 10:00 A.M. to 4:00 P.M. on weekends.

You know it's spring when you see the Swan Boats gliding silently along the waters

THE CATCH

} Tickets are $2.75 for adults, $1.25
for children (ages two to fifteen),
and $2.00 for seniors.

of the lagoon in the Boston Public Garden. Immortalized in the children's book *Make Way for Ducklings*, the Swan Boats were launched by the Paget family in 1877, and the fourth generation of Pagets runs the Swan Boat concession today. A wooden likeness of a giant swan hides the driver/peddler at the back of these beautiful boats, and it takes him about fifteen minutes to pedal his passengers around the entire lagoon. It's a must-do adventure that children (including this one) love.

POOLS

Many of the city's recreation centers have pools available for their members, but free public pools administered by the DCR are also located throughout the metropolitan area, keeping Bostonians cool when the summer heat ramps up. The pools are usually open from mid-June until Labor Day weekend, 10:00 A.M. to 6:00 P.M., although the DCR sometimes opens them earlier in the year and keeps them open a couple of extra hours at night if we get a heat wave. For a full listing of opening dates, visit www.mass.gov/dcr/recreate/pools.htm.

BRIGHTON

Artesani Playground Wading Pool, 1255 Soldiers Field Road; (617) 626–4973

Brighton-Allston Swimming and Wading Pool, North Beacon Street; (617) 254–2965

BROOKLINE

Reilly Memorial Swimming Pool, 355 Chestnut Hill Avenue, Cleveland Circle; (617) 277–7822 or (617) 698–1802

CAMBRIDGE

McCrehan Memorial Swimming and Wading Pool, 359 Rindge Avenue; (617) 354–9154

Veterans Memorial Swimming and Wading Pool (Magazine Beach), 719 Memorial Drive; (617) 354–9381

HYDE PARK

Moynihan Wading Pool, 920 Truman Parkway; (617) 698–1802

Olsen Swimming and Wading Pool, 95 Turtle Pond Parkway; (617) 364–9524 or (617) 698–1802

JAMAICA PLAIN

Johnson Playground Spray Deck, corner of Lamartine and Green Streets, Southwest Corridor Park; (617) 727–0057

Stony Brook Spray Deck, corner of Lamartine and Boylston Streets, Southwest Corridor Park; (617) 727–0057

MATTAPAN

Ryan Wading Pool, 350 River Street; for info call (617) 727–5290

MISSION HILL

Mission Hill Spray Deck, behind Boston Police Headquarters, Southwest Corridor Park; (617) 727–0057

ROXBURY

Cass Memorial Swimming Pool, Washington Street; (617) 445–9519

SOMERVILLE

Dilboy Memorial Swimming and Wading Pool, Alewife Brook Parkway; (617) 623–9321

Latta Brothers Memorial Swimming and Wading Pool, McGrath Highway; (617) 666–9236

WATERTOWN

Dealtry Memorial Swimming and Wading Pool, Pleasant Street; (617) 923–0073

BEACHES

The idea of swimming in or near Boston Harbor has been a bit of a touchy subject ever since the harbor was determined to be one of the country's most polluted in the late 1980s. But a lot has happened since then. Although the water isn't yet pristine, it's getting there, and the beaches are beautiful, despite the fact that they're usually right next to reminders of the city (the airport, the highways, the gas tanks). Extended bouts of very hot weather or lots of rain can still dramatically affect water quality, so it's best to call the DCR water quality hotline (617–626–4972) before you hit the beach if either or both conditions arise. Most of these beaches open for Memorial Day weekend and close after Labor Day, and lifeguard service begins mid-June, unless hot weather comes early.

East Boston

Constitution Beach
799 Bennington Street

This half-mile-long, deep stretch of sand overlooking Logan Airport underwent a major renovation in the mid-1990s and has upgraded amenities and a new pedestrian overpass that gets visitors safely over the MBTA tracks that run next to it. You'll find parking, recreational fields for softball, seasonal skating and basketball, a bathhouse, boating, a large playground, a picnic area, tennis and handball courts, shade shelters, and foot showers. Take the Blue Line to the Orient Heights stop.

South Boston

Carson Beach
William J. Day Boulevard

This very popular beach offers some of the most stunning views of the harbor available anywhere. There's some free parking, public restrooms, shade shelters, a cafe, the newly renovated Edward J. McCormack Bathhouse, and a walkway along the edge of the water from Castle Island to the Kennedy Library. Take the Red Line to the JFK/UMass stop.

L Street Beach
M Street Beach
Pleasant Bay/Castle Island
William J. Day Boulevard

The L and M Street Beaches are located along busy Day Boulevard, but they're separated from the road by a grassy strip of parkland with benches and shade trees that helps give you the feeling of being in the middle of nowhere. Pleasant Bay is completely enclosed by a causeway that extends from Day Boulevard to Castle Island, so the beach along Pleasant Bay is clean and the water is warm. It also abuts Castle Island, and from here you can look out into Boston Harbor. Castle Island also has plenty of free parking, picnic facilities, a beautiful boardwalk, a snack bar, and a pre–Civil War stone garrison, Fort Independence, which offers tours during summer months. It's one of the most popular beaches in the area. Take the #9 or #11 bus from the Red Line's South Station stop to City Point, and from there stroll along the boardwalk until you find your spot in the sun.

Dorchester

Savin Hill Beach
Playstead Road

Malibu Beach
Morrissey Boulevard

These two beaches, which are next to each other, have new sand, boardwalks, lighting, promenades, and bathhouses, but they're surrounded on both sides by very busy roads, so it can be a little noisy. There's a small parking lot for fifty cars. These beaches are accessible via the MBTA Red Line's Savin Hill station.

Tenean Beach
108 Tenean Street

Tucked away in the shadow of Interstate 93, Tenean Beach abuts an industrial area and the neighborhood of Port Norfolk. Still, it's a remarkably quiet and peaceful beach with great views of downtown Boston. There's a new playground, bathhouses, picnic shelters, new water fountains, bike areas, and shade shelters. Getting here by public transportation is tough—the closest MBTA Red Line stop is North Quincy station, and then it's a long walk from there along very busy roads. Fortunately, there's parking for approximately 150 cars, and this hidden little beach usually doesn't get too crowded.

Quincy

Wollaston Beach
Quincy Shore Drive

Wollaston Beach, at more than 1.5 miles long, is the largest Boston Harbor beach. It looks south toward Hull and into the Atlantic Ocean, rather than the harbor, so you get the feeling of being miles away from the city. A continuous walkway, a seawall, concession stands, outdoor showers, and enclosed changing areas are located all along the beach. There's plenty of beachside parking, but this beach gets packed in the summer, so if you're driving, go early. Take Wollaston Beach/Ashmont Bus #217 from the MBTA Red Line's Wollaston station, or walk along Beach Street from the Wollaston station.

Revere

Revere Beach
Revere Beach Boulevard
www.mass.gov/dcr/parks/metroboston/revere.htm

Revere Beach is the oldest public beach in America (designated as such in 1896). The beach is miles long, with a bandstand, shade shelters, and a bathhouse; the beach sand is gorgeous; and the views out over the Atlantic Ocean can almost make you feel like you're miles from the heart of the city. Almost. Across Revere Beach Boulevard you'll find a host of kitschy souvenir stores, world-famous Kelly's Roast Beef (makers of what are believed to be the largest roast beef sandwiches ever created), dive bars, restaurants, and all manner of flashy cars "cruising" up and down the boulevard. Throngs of people turn up here on hot days, thanks to its easy accessibility on public transportation. Take the Blue Line to the Revere Beach or Wonderland stations.

{ LIBRARIES: }
FREE ACCESS

"Books are the treasured wealth of
the world and the fit inheritance of
generations and nations."

—*Henry David Thoreau*

Boston practically invented the concept of the free municipal library. The first large library in the country to be funded by the public was our very own, built originally in 1854 with 16,000 volumes (the "new" Boston Public Library building was built in Copley Square in 1895). It was also the first library in the country that allowed the public to borrow materials. It was home to the first children's library as well as a treasure trove of history. It houses the personal books and papers collection of President John Adams. The Central branch in Copley Square is home to world-famous murals by John Singer Sargent and Pierre Puvis de Chavannes, and it has an exhaustive collection of rare books and manuscripts, including some first-edition folios by William Shakespeare and original scores from Mozart. The main branch and the neighborhood branches offer the public not just books; there are CDs and DVDs, Internet access, and hundreds of readings, performances, lectures, and films—all free. A complete listing of branches, as well as a listing of locations and branches of the public library systems for all the cities and towns immediately surrounding Boston, is found in Appendix B. In addition to the public library system, the city's long-standing history as an academic powerhouse has fostered the growth of a wonderful selection of cultural, ethnic, research, and historical libraries, many of which are open to the public.

RESEARCH LIBRARIES

Harvard University Libraries

There are many fine universities in Boston with many fine libraries, but for sheer depth, historical significance, and public access, you really can't beat the libraries of Harvard University. Indeed, Harvard University, the oldest institution of higher learning in the United States, largely exists thanks to the bequest by a Charlestown minister named John Harvard. Upon his death in 1638, half of his estate and his private library of 400 books were bequeathed to the fledgling college, which was formed by a vote of the Great and General Court of the Massachusetts Bay Colony in 1636. Nearly 400 years later, that small collection has grown into a phenomenal repository of world knowledge and history. There are over ninety libraries on or near school grounds (for the full list, visit www.lib.harvard.edu/libraries), but only a few allow public access. Those that do are worth at least one visit. Most require that you have one or more forms of picture ID with you, and none will allow the general public to check out materials. Check the library's hours and admittance policies before venturing out. These libraries hold frequent events and exhibitions, including materials rarely seen by the outside world. For a complete listing of happenings at Harvard's libraries, visit www.hcl.harvard.edu/info/exhibitions.

Andover-Harvard Theological Library 45 Francis Avenue, Cambridge; (617) 495–5788; www.hds.harvard.edu/library

Arnold Arboretum/Horticulture Library 125 Arborway, Jamaica Plain; (617) 522-1086; www.arboretum.harvard.edu/library/library.html

Arthur and Elizabeth Schlesinger Library on the History of Women in America 3 James Street, Cambridge; (617) 495–8647

Blue Hill Meteorological Observatory Library Pierce Hall, 29 Oxford Street, Cambridge; (617) 495–2836; www.deas.harvard.edu/~library/bluehill.htm

Davis Center for Russian and Eurasian Studies Library 1737 Cambridge Street, Cambridge; (617) 495–4030; www.daviscenter.fas.harvard.edu

Houghton Library Harvard Yard, Cambridge; (617) 495–2441; www.hcl.harvard.edu/libraries/#houghton
Houghton has one of the largest and most exhaustive rare book and manuscript collections in the world, including the collections of Dr. Samuel Johnson (who wrote the first dictionary).

John G. Wolbach Library (aka Harvard-Smithsonian Center for Astrophysics Library), 60 Garden Street, Cambridge; (617) 495–7289; www.cfa.harvard.edu/library

John K. Fairbank Center for East Asian Research Library 625 Massachusetts Avenue, first floor, Cambridge; (617) 495–5753; www.fas.harvard.edu/~fairbank/library.htm

Library at Minda de Gunzburg Center for European Studies 27 Kirkland Street, Cambridge; (617) 495–4303, ext. 246

Ukrainian Research Institute Reference Library 1583 Massachusetts Avenue, Cambridge; (617) 496–5891; www.huri.harvard.edu/library.html

Massachusetts Historical Society
1154 Boylston Street
(617) 536–1608
www.masshist.org/welcome

Hours: Monday, Wednesday, and Friday, 9:00 A.M. to 4:30 P.M.; Tuesday and Thursday, 9:00 A.M. to 7:30 P.M.

THE CATCH
You must bring a photo ID.

This 200-year-old library has a vast collection composed of manuscripts, books and pamphlets, newspapers, maps, works of art, photographs, and historical artifacts that track the evolution of early American history. Special collections include letters between Abigail and President John Adams, the pen that Abraham Lincoln used to sign the Emancipation Proclamation, and life casts of Lincoln's face and hands. The library welcomes researchers, but since the library book stacks are closed to everyone but library staff, you'll need to fill out call slips for any books you want to view. You'll also have to fill out a registration form and present a current form of photo identification just to get in. All materials must be used in the reading room. You'll also need an appointment with the curator if you'd like to see the artifacts—again, the library welcomes requests from those with a genuine research interest.

New England Historic Genealogical Society

101 Newbury Street
(617) 536–5740
www.newenglandancestors.org

Hours: Tuesday, Thursday, Friday, and Saturday, 9:00 A.M. to 5:00 P.M.; Wednesday, 9:00 A.M. to 9:00 P.M.; closed on Sunday and Monday.

THE CATCH
}
Membership is $75, and day passes are $15.

The NEHGS Research Library offers a comprehensive glimpse into the family tree of nearly everyone who lives in New England. Its collection includes over 200,000 books, periodicals, and microform materials, as well as over one million manuscripts. Its book holdings include nearly all published New England genealogies, local histories, and related periodicals.

PRIVATE LIBRARIES

Boston Athenæum

10½ Beacon Street
(617) 227–0270
www.bostonathenaeum.org

Hours: Monday through Friday, 9:00 A.M. to 5:00 P.M.; Saturday, 9:00 A.M. to 4:00 P.M.

The Boston Athenæum, a National Historic Landmark, is the heart and soul of Boston's literary and artistic history. Founded in 1807 by a group of fourteen Boston literati, the Athenæum became the repository of the private libraries of George Washington and Henry Knox and the private papers of hundreds of authors. The library houses rare manuscripts and books, and its art collection was the genesis of the Museum of Fine Arts, which vacated the Athenæum for its own building in 1876. Membership is required to visit the Athenæum, but the public is welcome to visit the first-floor art gallery during regular business hours. Make sure to take the half-hour Art and Architecture tour, which will give you a glimpse into the rest of this historic building; it departs from the front desk on Tuesday and Thursday at 3:00 P.M.

Congregational Library

14 Beacon Street
(617) 523–0470
www.14beacon.org

Hours: Monday through Friday, 8:30 A.M. to 4:30 P.M.

The Congregational Library houses an extensive closed-stack collection of printed church histories, town histories, sermons, annual reports of religious and charitable associations, Boston city directories, and contemporary religious studies material. Books may be borrowed in person or by mail. Members of the public may borrow books for up to four weeks as long as you provide a valid address.

The French Library and Cultural Center/Alliance Française

53 Marlborough Street
(617) 912–0400
www.frenchlib.org

Hours: Monday, Tuesday, and Thursday, 10:00 A.M. to 6:00 P.M.; Wednesday, 10:00 A.M. to 8:00 P.M.; Friday and Saturday, 10:00 A.M. to 5:00 P.M.; closed on Sunday.

THE CATCH

The library is free to the public, but membership, which is $60 for individuals, is required to borrow books or other materials.

The French Library and Cultural Center is located in two adjacent, historic mansions on Marlborough Street, and its mahogany-paneled periodical room is as pleasant a place for quiet reading and contemplation as you're likely to find in the city—regardless of the language. Members of the public may use the library for free and can browse its thousands of French-language books, newspapers, magazines, films, videos, and CDs. To borrow, however, you must be a member. Your membership buys you reduced-price admission to its cultural education programs, film series, special events (like its show-stopping Bastille Day party, which takes over a block of Marlborough Street each July), and borrowing privileges.

Goethe Institut—Boston

170 Beacon Steet
(617) 262–6050

Hours: Monday through Thursday, 9:00 A.M. to 1:00 P.M. and 2:00 to 5:00 P.M.; Friday, 9:00 A.M. to 1:00 P.M. and 2:00 to 4:30 P.M.

This library dedicated to all things German has a reading room with a magnificent view of the Charles River and is open to the public at all times (but it only lends materials to educational organizations). Its library collection includes German books, newspapers, periodicals, and DVDs. It hosts a variety of free events throughout the year, such as parties, lectures, films, and visual arts.

The Mary Baker Eddy Library for the Betterment of Humanity
200 Massachusetts Avenue
(617) 450–7000

Exhibit and shop hours: Tuesday through Sunday, 10:00 A.M. to 4:00 P.M.; closed on Monday.

Reference Room hours: Tuesday through Saturday, 10:00 A.M. to 4:00 P.M.

Research Room hours: Tuesday through Friday, 10:00 A.M. to 4:00 P.M.; Saturday by appointment.

THE CATCH } It's free to read, but you'll need a $25 membership to borrow books.

You might be drawn to the Christian Science Church area at the corner of Huntington and Massachusetts Avenues for its mammoth reflecting pool, a peaceful yet powerful landmark in the Symphony Hall section of Boston. But once there, you'll want to stay for the fascinating Mary Baker Eddy Library, which houses two collections that are open to the public. At its core are works relating to the life, work, and ideas of Mary Baker Eddy, founder of the Church of Christ, Scientist; women's rights activist; and founder of the *Christian Science Monitor,* a Pulitzer Prize–winning newspaper. The library's materials include collections emphasizing American history, women, religion, the history of science, and the relationship of science and religion. You can research and read the holdings in both the Reference and the Research Rooms for free, but to borrow you must have a membership card, which costs $25. Access to the Mapparium, a 30-foot stained-glass globe built in 1935 that you view from the inside, costs $6.00.

Scandinavian Library
206 Waltham Street
West Newton
(617) 965–0621
www.scandinavianlibrary.org

Hours: Saturday, 11:00 A.M. to 3:00 P.M.

This library, founded in 1994, has more than 6,000 books by Nordic authors or about the Nordic countries (Sweden, Norway, Denmark, Finland, and Iceland) and their cultures. The library has subscriptions to the newspapers from these countries as well as Scandinavian-language CDs, audio books, and videos. The library has a well-stocked travel, business, and Nordic organization reference area. Check its calendar to learn about ongoing events, parties, and other activities of interest to Scandinavians and those with an interest in the region.

100 FOR THE PRICE OF 1

There are dozens of libraries throughout the metropolitan Boston area encompassing public, university, and private collections. Thanks to an active consortium program in Massachusetts, you may have free access to many of them with the library card you already possess. Nearly every library in the area is a member of one or another of the library consortia that have organized to give greater access to the wide variety of educational resources that are spread throughout Massachusetts and New England. Holding a card in a consortium member library will get you borrowing privileges at most, but not all, member locations. Many have private and specialized research facilities that are not open to the public at any time. Others restrict borrowing privileges. Visit each consortium's Web site for details on which libraries will honor your consortium membership. Here's a list of local consortia, and the libraries that are members.

The Boston Library Consortium
www.blc.org

Boston College

Boston Public Library

Boston University

Brandeis University

Brown University

Marine Biological Laboratory & Woods Hole Oceanographic Institution

Massachusetts Institute of Technology

Northeastern University

State Library of Massachusetts

Tufts University

University of Connecticut

University of Massachusetts–Amherst

University of Massachusetts–Boston

University of Massachusetts–Dartmouth

University of Massachusetts–Lowell

University of Massachusetts Medical Center

University of New Hampshire

Wellesley College

Williams College

Fenway Library Consortium
www.fenwaylibraries.org

Brookline Public Library

Emerson College

Emmanuel College Cardinal
Cushing Library

Hebrew College

Lesley University

Massachusetts College of Art

Massachusetts College of
Pharmacy & Health Sciences

Museum of Fine Arts

New England Conservatory of
Music

Roxbury Community College

Simmons College

Suffolk University

University of
Massachusetts–Boston

Wentworth Institute of
Technology

Old Colony Library Network
www.ocln.org

Abington Public Library

Avon Public Library

Braintree/Thayer Public Library

Brockton Public Libraries

Canton Public Library

Cohasett/Paul Pratt Memorial
Library

Duxbury Free Library

Hanover/John Curtis Free Library

Hingham Public Library

Holbrook Public Library

Hull Public Library

Marshfield/Ventress Memorial
Library

Massasoit Community College

Milton Public Library

Norwell Public Library

Plymouth Public Library

Quincy Libraries

Randolph/Turner Free Library

Rockland Memorial Library

Sandwich Public Library

Scituate Town Library

Sharon Public Library

Stoughton Public Library

Walpole Public Library

Weymouth Public Libraries

Whitman Public Library

Minuteman Library Network

www.mln.lib.ma.us

Acton Public Library

Arlington/Robbins Library

Ashland Public Library

Bedford Free Public Library

Belmont Public Library

Public Library of Brookline

Cambridge Public Library

Concord Free Public Library

Dedham Public Library

Dover Town Library

Framingham Public Library

Franklin Public Library

Holliston Public Library

Lexington/Cary Memorial
Library

Lincoln Public Library

Maynard Public Library

Medfield Public Library

Medford Public Library

Medway Public Library

Millis Public Library

Natick/Morse Institute Library

Needham Free Public Library

Newton Free Library

Norwood/Morrill Memorial
Library

Somerville Public Library

Stow/Randall Library

Sudbury/Goodnow Library

Waltham Public Library

Watertown Free Public Library

Wayland Public Library

Wellesley Free Library

Weston Public Library

Westwood Public Library

Winchester Public Library

Woburn Public Library

Dean College/E. Ross Anderson
Library

Framingham State
College/Henry Whittemore
Library

Lasell College/Brennan Library

MassBay Community College/
Perkins Library/Learning
Resource Center

Mount Ida College/Wadsworth
Learning Resource

Newbury College

Professional Arts Consortium/ProArts

www.proarts.org

Berklee College of Music

The Boston Architectural Center

The Boston Conservatory

Emerson College

Massachusetts College of Art

School of the Museum of Fine
Arts

Social Law Library
John Adams Courthouse
One Pemberton Square, Suite 4100
(617) 523–0018
www.sociallaw.com

Founded in 1804, this excellent resource for lawyers and those interested in the law is the oldest law library in the country. Although located in the Massachusetts Supreme Judicial Court courthouse, the library is largely funded through private sources and offers access to a vast collection of historic and contemporary legal documents for both the public and practicing lawyers. Public access is allowed, but borrowing is reserved for members. The library also hosts a variety of events and lectures that are open to the public; some require an RSVP, which can be completed on the library's Web site.

{NEWSPAPERS: FREE PRESS}

"Most of us probably feel we couldn't be free without newspapers, and that is the real reason we want the newspapers to be free."

—Edward R. Murrow, 1958

With so many newspapers giving away their content for free on the Internet, the idea of shelling out money for the daily news is so twenty minutes ago. Sometimes, though, holding a paper in your hands, browsing through photos, and not getting eyestrain from it all is a very welcome change of pace. That doesn't mean we're gonna pay for it, though. And in Boston, we don't have to. You can find all the news—local, regional, entertainment, specialty, and national—free at the corner of nearly every major intersection in the city. Just hunt down a news box—it's the metal thing that looks like a filing cabinet with windows. Please don't grab more papers than you need. Leave enough for all the other Cheap Bastards!

Barstool Sports

www.barstoolsports.com

Even a feminist who hates sports has to give it up to the guys who put out this entertainment, sports, and gambling magazine every Friday. Their edgy, guy-centric humor makes *Barstool Sports* one of the funniest reads in town. (I confess that *Barstool Sports* has become one of my guilty pleasures.) They write smart commentary on sports with a nod toward the over-under, they cover pop culture without a smidgen of political correctness, and as for women . . . well, every issue features a different bikini-clad chick on the cover and a "Ms. Barstool Sports" competition inside. Pick one up at news boxes throughout the city, but mainly downtown.

Bay Windows

(617) 266–6670
www.baywindows.com

This newspaper, distributed weekly throughout the state, is the largest gay and lesbian publication in the region. It covers national, state, and regional news with a gay and lesbian perspective. Pick it up for the outstanding entertainment section and informed local political coverage. It is available in news boxes, bookstores, and convenience stores throughout Massachusetts, but especially in downtown Boston. Visit their Web site for a complete listing of distribution locations.

FREE NEWS YOU CAN USE

Free neighborhood weeklies flourish in Boston. We are a city made up of clearly defined neighborhoods, and the needs of each one are as unique as the mix of people you'll find there. I read my local paper, the Boston Courant, for its coverage of condo conversion hearings and crime, but especially for the impassioned editorials about the importance of curbing your dog. Across the highway, the South Boston Tribune's editorials cover such pressing topics as preservation of the inalienable right to save an on-street parking spot with your lawn chair if you've shoveled it out after a snowstorm. Most of these papers are weekly and are distributed directly to all the homes in the neighborhood; they're also available at local stores. These newspapers show that even residents of a sophisticated metropolis like ours are really just myopic, self-interested villagers at heart. Here's a list.

Back Bay Sun
(617) 523–9490

This weekly is distributed to all homes in Back Bay and is available in Back Bay shops.

Beacon Hill Times
(617) 523–9490
www.beaconhilltimes.com

A weekly distributed to all homes in Beacon Hill and available in local stores.

Boston Courant
(617) 267–2700

This weekly paper covers all things dealing with the Back Bay, South End, Beacon Hill, and Fenway neighborhoods. Distributed through news boxes and free home delivery.

Bulletin Newspapers
(617) 325–1500

These small local weeklies—*West Roxbury Bulletin, Roslindale Bulletin, Hyde Park Bulletin, Jamaica Plain Bulletin, Allston/ Brighton Bulletin,* and *Boston People's Voice*—are distributed through local stores in each of the neighborhoods they cover.

Charlestown Patriot Bridge
(617) 241–8500
www.charlestownbridge.com

Covering the town of Charlestown and the Navy Yard. Delivered free to all neighborhood homes, but it costs 25 cents in the local stores.

East Boston Times
(617) 567–9600
www.eastietimes.com

Delivered weekly to homes and available in local stores.

Everett Independent
(617) 567–9600
www.everettindependent.com

Delivered weekly to homes and available in local stores.

Jamaica Plain Gazette
(617) 524–2626
www.jamaicaplaingazette.com

Available every two weeks in stores throughout the neighborhood.

Lynn Journal
(617) 567–9600
www.lynnjournal.com

Delivered weekly to homes and available in local stores.

Mattapan Reporter
(617) 436–1222
www.mattapanreporter.com

Delivered monthly to all households in the 02126 zip code. Also available in local stores.

Mission Hill Gazette
(617) 524–2626
www.missionhillgazette.com

Available monthly in stores throughout the neighborhood.

South End News
(617) 266–6670

Weekly news and entertainment paper distributed through convenience stores and libraries exclusively in the South End.

DAY-OLD NEWS IS FREE NEWS

Almost all local papers are free online if you're willing to register. (Some premium content, mostly columnists, is available only to paid subscribers.) While the business logic of this arrangement eludes me, I'm more than happy to take advantage of it. There's another way to get one of the big metro dailies for nothing. When you're heading home from work after 5:00 P.M., keep your eyes peeled, especially outside major subway and bus terminals, for Boston Herald vendors handing out that day's paper for free. No news is good news, and old news is better ('cause it's free!).

Boston Haitian Reporter
www.bostonhaitian.com

This monthly, which focuses on local and national news of interest to Bostonians of Haitian descent or Haitian immigrants, is distributed to stores and health and community centers serving Haitian communities in Brockton, Milton, Dorchester, Roslindale, Mattapan, Hyde Park, Cambridge, and Somerville.

Boston Metro
(617) 210–7905
http://boston.metro.us

If you took a bus or subway recently, you probably sat on one of these papers. The ubiquitous little tabloid, available in news boxes absolutely everywhere, is one in a chain of regional weekday newspapers that distill the previous day's events into the written version of a sound bite. The news is a combination of stories from national and international wire services as well as local and national *Metro* reporters. The *Metro* is tops at what it does, which is keeping the commuter population busy in between stops on their chosen form of public transportation.

The Boston Parents' Paper
(617) 522–1515
www.boston.parenthood.com

Geared to today's moneyed parents, the *Boston Parents' Paper* (its holding company distributes similar regionally targeted *Parents' Papers* across the United States) has articles about parenting, extensive lists of parent resources, and plenty of advertisements to show you where to buy it all. But of course, that's why it's free and available wherever parents go: doctors' offices, toy stores, bookstores, and supermarkets. For a listing of locations, visit the Web site and click on "Find Our Magazine."

The Phoenix
(617) 536–5390
www.thephoenix.com

Stuff@Night
www.stuffatnight.com

The Phoenix, a full-color tabloid, is more than fifty years old, the undisputed granddaddy of local alternative newsweeklies. After a brief foray as a paid publication, it is free today and available in news boxes all over the city. The paper has won about every major journalism award available, including a Pulitzer Prize for Classical Music Criticism, and it continues to break news with its crack investigative reporters. It is best known for its lively coverage of Boston arts, nightlife, and music, as well as its provocative personals section (where fully half of Boston professes their love of "long walks on the beach"). The paper's success has helped its owner, Stephen Mindich, create a media empire that includes a radio station, WFNX; similar tabloids in Portland, Maine, and Providence, Rhode Island; as well as another free magazine, *Stuff@Night,* a sort of *Phoenix* lite (also available in news boxes citywide). The *Phoenix* has long been known as the proving ground for some of the country's finest writers, many of whom have gone on to fame and fortune, including authors Susan Orlean and Caroline Knapp, *Esquire* writer Charles Pierce, and former *New York Times* film critic Janet Maslin.

Boston's Weekly Dig
(617) 426–8942
www.weeklydig.com

If you don't want or need a weekly dose of angst and snark, steer clear of the *Weekly Dig.* This hip, edgy magazine, covering entertainment, pop culture, and local news, is authoritative, very funny, and geared to a young audience. It is written with all the ennui and world-weariness that its young editorial staff can muster up. They regularly give a glimpse into a side of the city that high-powered professionals with steady paychecks rarely see. Pick it up if you're young, youngish, or want to feel young for a few minutes. The listings section includes many excellent ways for college-age Cheap Bastards to make their monthly allowance stretch as far as possible. You'll find it in news boxes throughout the city.

NEWS OF THE WORLD

If you don't have Internet access but need your daily news fix, there's a way to get it for free. The Boston Public Library and its branches (listed in Appendix B) receive hundreds of local, regional, national, and international newspapers and magazines, which are available for you to read free. You won't be allowed to remove any of the periodicals from the library branch, but don't despair. Head to the Main Branch in Copley Square, and with a free library card you may check out newspapers for use in the beautiful Newspaper Room, located on the first floor in the McKim Library, the library's historic original wing. If you want magazines, head to the Periodical Desk on the second floor of the McKim Library, where you will also need a library card. You can't take magazines out of the building either, but you can read them in the grand reading room, Bates Hall. Built with a grant in 1852 from Joshua Bates, a self-educated senior partner at the banking firm Baring Brothers and Company, Bates Hall is a soaring but peaceful space with vaulted ceilings and fifteen arched and grilled windows that let in tons of natural light. It is the perfect place to sit and catch up on world events. You'd never guess that the bustle of Copley Square is just on the other side of those gracious windows.

Allston-Brighton Tab, Boston Tab, Brookline Tab, Newton Tab
(800) 982–4023
www.townonline.com

The *Tab* papers, part of Community Newspaper Group, service most of the communities in the Greater Boston area. The papers are locally oriented, with lots of good, heavy-hitting local reporting, entertainment news, and listings. These papers are available in news boxes at major intersections and stores in their respective towns. For a complete listing, call Community Newspaper Group. These papers are also available online.

The Improper Bostonian
(617) 859–1400
www.improper.com

While the cover of the *Improper* is all about the superlatives (Boston's Best [fill in the blank]!), smart, funny writing rules the rest of the publication (especially columnist Ezra Dyer, who just keeps figuring out ways to make me laugh). It's a witty, urbane, and helpful magazine to have when you're looking for something to see, hear, eat, date, or buy in the city of Boston. It's available in news boxes throughout the metro area.

La Semana Newspaper

(617) 541–2222

www.lasemanacuencavision.com

This Spanish-language newspaper has 17,000 readers all over New England and is distributed in the Boston area in news boxes and in stores. Call the newspaper directly to get a list of specific locations.

{ PETS: }
BORN FREE

"'Cause I'm as free as a bird, now."
—*Lynyrd Skynyrd*

Sometimes it feels as though there are more dogs in the city of Boston than there are people. While purebred pets can be extremely expensive, sometimes $1,000 or more, there are plenty of little buddies who can be adopted for considerably less than that. Most adoptions aren't free, especially for puppies and kittens, because almost all adoption agencies spay or neuter and vaccinate the animal before you can take it home. If you're feeling ready for a new little bundle of animal love in your family, here are some inexpensive resources to help you find him, care for him, and make his life in Boston more enjoyable.

GET A PET

Free pets are rare in Boston, but they're out there. The best way to locate a free pet adoption is to go through bulletin board postings at a veterinarian's office or check out Web site listings. Remember that free adoptions posted on bulletin boards (either paper or online) rarely include a medical report from a veterinarian. Many agencies also post on bulletin boards, but they'll charge you a fee to complete an adoption, so make sure you know exactly who you're adopting from to avoid any surprises. If you adopt from a different state, you'll often be liable for shipping; in addition, you won't have a chance to inspect the pet's condition before it arrives, and there's little recourse once it does if it's sick or injured.

Animal Rescue League of Boston

10 Chandler Street
(617) 426–9170
www.arlboston.org

THE CATCH

Adoption fees are $25 to $155. You must be twenty-one or older with Massachusettts ID with current address.

You must have proof of home ownership or landlord's contact info (to ensure there are no pet policies that will interfere with the adoption) and up-to-date vet records for your other pets, and you must complete an application and have an interview with adoption personnel to adopt a pet here. The adoption fee includes health screening, initial vaccinations, spaying or neutering, veterinary care for the first two weeks (up to $300) if the animal develops shelter-related illness, rabies vaccination, microchip ID and registration, heartworm test and preventative for dogs, feline leukemia test for cats, deworming, a tag and collar, and a leash or carrier. The center is open Tuesday through Thursday from noon to 8:00 P.M. and Friday and Saturday from noon to 5:00 P.M.; it is closed on Sunday and Monday.

Boston Animal Control

26 Mahler Road (pet adoption location)
Roslindale
(617) 635–1800 or (617) 635–1913
www.cityofboston.gov/animalcontrol/default.asp

THE CATCH } Adoption fees are $25 to $125. You must be twenty-one to adopt.

This office is the central adoption point for the Boston Animal Control department, which is responsible for enforcing animal laws in the city of Boston. The adoption fee includes neutering/ spaying, rabies vaccination, distemper vaccination, implantation of a microchip ID for dogs, deworming, and physical examination. Puppies and kittens adopted under the age of four months may return to the shelter for the remainder of their puppy and kitten shots, as well as a heartworm test and first heartworm pill (for dogs over six months of age) or a feline leukemia test for cats.

Craig's List

www.boston.craigslist.org

Many people who are moving to a place that won't take cats or whose dog Fred just came up pregnant are turning to Craig's List to find new homes for their pets. Always use discretion and your best judgment when using this site—it's best to ask for some references (like their vet) before arranging a meeting. You can also find tons of pet-related products and furniture posted here at low or no cost. Look under the "Pets" forum or in the "Free" section of the "For Sale" area.

Massachusetts Society for the Prevention of Cruelty to Animals

Animal Care and Adoption Center
350 South Huntington Avenue
(617) 522–5055
www.mspca.org

To adopt, you'll need a form of picture ID, something that shows your current address, and your landlord's name and contact info if you rent your home. If you own your own home, they'll ask to see verification, either through a tax, water, or mortgage bill. If you have other animals in the household, please bring information about your veterinarian (the clinic name and phone number are fine) to ensure everyone is up-to-date on vaccinations. Adoption fees are as follows: dogs, $155; cats, $100; rabbits, $75; other animals, $25–$50. These fees include a full exam, spaying/neutering, vaccinations, heartworm test and preventative, flea/tick preventative, ID tag and leash, and implantation of a microchip ID and registration where appropriate. The center's hours are Tuesday, Wednesday, Friday, and Saturday from noon to 5:00 P.M. and Thursday from 1:00 to 7:00 P.M.; it is closed on Sunday and Monday.

PETCO Stores

119 First Street, Cambridge; (617) 868–3474
Hours: Monday through Saturday, 9:00 A.M. to 9:00 P.M.; Sunday, 10:00 A.M. to 8:00 P.M.

304 Western Avenue, Brighton; (617) 254–8800
Hours: Monday through Saturday, 9:00 A.M. to 9:00 P.M.; Sunday, 10:00 A.M. to 8:00 P.M.

www.petco.com

PETCO locations hold adoption events throughout the year. Local adoption agencies bring pets or photos of pets, and adoption agency personnel are on hand to answer questions and schedule adoption interviews.

Saint Meow's

(617) 767–6294
www.saintmeows.com

THE CATCH
} There is a fee of $90 per cat.

Saint Meow's cat adoption service holds clinics at Animal Spirit (2348 Massachusetts Avenue, Cambridge; 617-876-9696) on Saturday from noon to 4:00 P.M. and at the Cambridge PETCO (119 First Street, Cambridge; 617-868-3474) on Wednesday from 5:30 to 7:30 P.M. Adoptions include a vet exam, spay/neuter surgery, rabies vaccine, feline leukemia and FIV blood test, deworming, full grooming, nail-trimming demonstration, and a discount coupon booklet.

SAVE ME

Dog rescue organizations help place dogs, often purebred, that are either abandoned by their owners or returned to breeders for a variety of reasons: medical issues, changing family circumstances, or a poor pet/family dynamic. Adopting a rescue dog is an excellent way to adopt a quality purebred dog for a fraction of the cost of going through a breeder.

The American Kennel Club (www.akc.org/breeds/rescue.cfm) has links to hundreds of breed-specific rescue groups throughout the United States. There is usually a fee (which will rise depending on the popularity of the breed) if you go through one of these organizations. You might have a long wait for especially popular breeds. Several other Internet sites list pets available through pet rescue programs. They include www.Petfinder.org, www.Petark .com, www.1-800-Save-A-Pet.com, and www.pets911.com.

LOW-COST PET CARE

Alliance for Animals Metro Action Clinic

232 Silver Street
South Boston
(617) 268–7800
www.afaboston.org/clinic.htm

THE CATCH

This clinic requires pre-payment by credit card.

} This clinic offers low-cost spaying, neutering, and vaccinations. It's open seven days a week from 9:00 A.M. to 5:00 P.M. A complete list of fees is available on their Web site.

Animal Rescue League Spay Waggin'

10 Chandler Street
(617) 426–9170 or (617) 426–3028
www.arlboston.org

The Spay Waggin' is a low-cost mobile spay/neuter program created by the Animal Rescue League to help clients in financial need. While they require no proof of financial need, they ask that those with adequate resources have the surgery performed at their local veterinarian. The Waggin' doesn't accept appointments. Everything is done on a first-come, first-served basis. The Spay Waggin' arrives at all surgery sites at around 9:30 A.M., but clients often start lining up as early as 7:00 A.M. You should expect to stay until at least 10:30 A.M. to fill out paperwork. Only pet owners may drop off pets for services—you'll need to sign a legal consent form and answer any questions the veterinarian may have. Call the ARL for a list of Waggin' surgery sites and times.

Massachusetts Society for the Prevention of Cruelty to Animals and Massachusetts Veterinary Medical Association

Spay/Neuter Assistance Program (SNAP)
Animal Care and Adoption Center
350 South Huntington Avenue
(617) 541–5007 (SNAP helpline)
www.mspca.org/site/pp.asp?c=gtIUK4OSG&b=126801

THE CATCH

You must apply to participate in this low-income program.

} This jointly administered program gives reduced-cost spay and neuter operations for low-income pet owners. By obtaining a discount certificate, you can take your pet to more than 200 veterinary hospitals or clinics throughout Massachusetts and pay a reduced charge for services. You will be notified as to your eligibility for the Spay/Neuter Assistance Program within two weeks of the time your application is received. Applications are available online at the MSCPA Web site listed above.

Merwin Memorial Animal Clinic

542 Cambridge Street
Allston
(617) 782–5420

This low-cost clinic is run by volunteer veterinarians and is open Monday through Saturday from noon to 3:00 P.M. Their only service is animal vaccines, and they cost around $30, more or less depending on the age and type of animal and the type of vaccine. This is a walk-in clinic, and clients are seen on a first-come, first-served basis.

STOP—Stop the Overpopulation of Pets

(617) 571–7151
www.thestopclinic.com

THE CATCH
Spaying/neutering is $50 to $60.

This organization uses a 21-foot-long custom mobile van to travel throughout the area performing spaying/neutering for cats. Clients drop off their cats in the morning for neutering surgery and vaccinations, then pick them up the same evening. Check the Web site for STOP locations and times.

LEASH-FREE DOG PARKS

For dog owners, one of the drawbacks of city living is a dearth of places for Fido to do what he does best—run and run and run. After years of skirmishes between city dog control officers and renegade owners who let their dogs off-leash (against state and local rules, which require that dogs be leashed at all times unless they're in your house or on your property), city officials have begun to designate special parks where dogs can roam free. When you visit them, always clean up after your dog, and do not let your dog off-leash unless it is well voice-trained. All dogs in the city of Boston must be registered with the Boston Animal Control Office (www.cityof boston.gov/animalcontrol).

Boston Common

For years, animal control officers ticketed anyone who let their dogs off-leash here. But a form of détente has settled since a pilot off-leash program was tested and found successful. Today, owners may officially unleash the hounds from 6:00 to 9:00 A.M. and from 4:00 to 8:00 P.M. daily. The place is crawling with walkers, bikers, and squirrels, so don't even think of unleashing your dog here unless it is extremely well voice-trained.

Cambridge Dog Park
Auburn Street at Hawthorne Street

Charlesgate Dog Run
Massachusetts Avenue at Beacon Street

The dog run is very small, but it's fenced in.

Danehy Park
99 Sherman Street at Garden and New Streets
North Cambridge
(617) 349–4800

This fifty-acre park is on a former landfill. There is an unfenced leash-free area located within this park.

Fort Washington Park
Waverly Street between Erie and Putnam Streets
Cambridge
(617) 349–4800

Minton Stable Gardens
Williams Street
Jamaica Plain

Peters Park Dog Run
Washington Street at East Berkeley Street
www.peterspark.org
info@peterspark.org

This beautiful park is tended by a very active community group, Friends of Peters Park. Check their Web site for rules and regulations.

{ SECTION 3: EXPLORING } BOSTON

{ WALKING
TOURS: }
FREEDOM TRAIL

"It is good to collect things; it is
better to take walks."

–*Anatole France*

Boston is one of the most walkable cities in the country, and it's also one of the most historic. The combination of those two factors means that Boston has an embarrassment of riches when it comes to free walking tours. Many highlight the proud history of our city, which is tied inextricably with the history of our country. Other tours focus on the art and architecture of our many churches, gardens, libraries—and even our breweries. Boston's miles of shoreline and our rich naval heritage provide water lovers with the opportunity to test their sea legs during free boat tours. In fact, you could spend a month taking tours of Boston and never spend a penny. Summertime offers the best selection of walking tour options, but many tours run in the winter months as well. Make sure to wear comfortable shoes, and bring an umbrella, because as Mark Twain famously observed, "If you don't like the weather in New England, wait a minute. It will change." And Cheap Bastards just hate getting caught in the rain.

HISTORIC WALKING TOURS

Many of Boston's historic sites are administered by the National Park Service. There are two NPS visitor centers in the greater Boston area, and they are co-located with two historic sites: the Old State House and the Charlestown Navy Yard. The NPS offices' hours are given with each attraction. All of the NPS tours listed below are free, but the NPS also administers several local historic sites that charge a small admission price for tours—which can add up quick if you're traveling with the family. A National Park Service Park Pass ($50 a year) gets you and your family into any national park in the United States where an admission fee is charged, as well as into all the NPS sites in Boston that charge a fee.

Boston African American National Historic Site

Museum of Afro-American History

46 Joy Street (Beacon Hill)

(617) 725–0022 (museum information)

(617) 742–5415 (National Park Service)

www.afroammuseum.org or www.nps.gov/boaf

Memorial Day to Labor Day, Monday through Saturday, 10:00 A.M., noon, and 2:00 P.M.

Labor Day to Memorial Day, Monday through Saturday, 2:00 P.M.

This historic site is actually a collection of fifteen sites that are part of the rich history of black America's fight for freedom, much of which occurred here in Boston. This tour, also called the Black Heritage Trail, leaves from the Shaw Memorial, which commemorates Robert Gould Shaw and the African-American Massachusetts 54th Regiment, the only all-black regiment in the Civil War. It's located across from the State House on Beacon Street on the edge of the Boston Common. The tour ends at the Museum of Afro-American History, which requests a donation of $5.00. There are tours of the museum, a short educational video, as well as interpretive exhibits. This area is called Beacon Hill for a reason, so be prepared to do some hill climbing.

Boston National Historic Park

NPS Downtown Visitor Center (across from Old State House)

15 State Street (at Washington Street)

(617) 242–5642

www.nps.gov/bost

Visitor Center hours: daily, 9:00 A.M. to 5:00 P.M.

Tours: daily from mid-June to Labor Day weekend, 10:00 A.M., 11:00 A.M., and 2:00 P.M.; from the day after Labor Day through Thanksgiving, on weekends at 10:00 A.M., 11:00 A.M., and 2:00 P.M. and on weekdays at 2:00 P.M.

THE CATCH: Tours take place weather permitting, so call ahead to make sure they're happening. Tours are first-come, first-served and limited to thirty people.

The Boston National Historic Park is composed of six different sites administered by the NPS, all of which are part of the world-famous Freedom Trail, a fifteen-site self-guided tour throughout Boston and Charlestown. The buildings and locations along the trail paint a vivid portrait of the crucial role that Boston and her patriots played in the American Revolution. The ranger tour begins at the Visitor Center, visits six sites (from the Old South Meeting House to the Old North Church), and takes ninety minutes. The Visitor Center also has maps and educational material about the Freedom Trail for those wishing to walk the whole thing in a self-guided tour. You won't really need a map, though. There's a thick red stripe painted on the sidewalk that guides visitors around to all the sites.

Boston Women's Heritage Trail
(617) 522–2872
www.bwht.org/tour.html

Self-guided tours are usually too much like work (and even when they're free, that's no bargain), but the Boston Women's Heritage Trail is worth the effort. It's also the only tour in Boston highlighting the long history of contribution and accomplishment by the city's great women. The Web site of the Boston Women's Heritage Trail allows you to download a variety of different tours, each high-lighting a different aspect of women's history or a different geographic region. Interested in women artists, activists, educators, or abolitionists? There's a tour for each, and they're all downloadable from the site, including maps. Some of the tours were researched and designed by Boston schoolchildren and their teachers.

HISTORIC SITES

Many of the sites listed below are located along the Freedom Trail (it will be noted in the description). The National Park Service tour does not go to all the Freedom Trail sites, nor does it go inside the historic buildings and sites that it visits, even though many offer free tours. If you plan on trying to incorporate any of these additional tours into your day on the Freedom Trail, you'll want to leave a minimum of five hours to complete the whole thing.

Bunker Hill Monument and Museum

Monument Square
Charlestown
(617) 242–5641
www.nps.gov/bost/Bunker_Hill.htm

Monument and lodge open daily year-round, 9:00 A.M. to 5:00 P.M.

Memorial Day to Labor Day, interpretive talks daily on the hour, 10:00 A.M. to 4:00 P.M. (except holidays).

THE CATCH

> The monument and museum were undergoing renovations at press time and were expected to reopen in June 2007. Call ahead to confirm hours.

It says a lot about Bostonians' capacity for optimism that one of our most notable and visible public monuments commemorates a Revolutionary War battle that we lost. The fact that we kicked a bunch of British butt in the process seemed ample reason to celebrate, and we do. This granite monument, erected in its present form in 1842, is 221 feet tall with 294 steps to the top and marks the site of the first major battle of the American Revolution. The monument and the "lodge" nearby, which houses an interpretive center, are stops on the Freedom Trail.

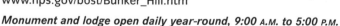

Faneuil Hall

State Street (across from City Hall)
(617) 242–5642
www.nps.gov/bost/Faneuil_Hall.htm

Informational talks daily every half hour, 9:30 A.M. to 5:00 P.M. (unless there is an event in the hall).

Wealthy merchant Peter Faneuil built Faneuil Hall, a stop on the Freedom Trail, in 1742 and gave it to Boston as a gift. It has served as an open-forum meeting hall and marketplace for more than 250 years. Talks are held in the second-floor Great Hall meeting space. Called the "Cradle of Liberty," Faneuil Hall was the site on November 5, 1773, of discussions between John Hancock and other Bostonians about a certain pesky tea tax—and we all know how that turned out.

King's Chapel

Corner of Tremont and School Streets
(617) 227–2155
www.kings-chapel.org

Memorial Day to Labor Day, Monday through Saturday, 10:00 A.M. to 4:00 P.M. (closed on Tuesday and Wednesday, 11:30 A.M. to 1:30 P.M., for noontime services).

Labor Day to Memorial Day, Saturday, 10:00 A.M. to 4:00 P.M.

THE CATCH
} Voluntary donations are accepted. Self-guided tours are $1.00.

America's first architect, Peter Harrison, designed this small church, which was completed in 1754 (the church's predecessor, an Anglican church made of wood, occupied this spot from 1686 until this one was built). The magnificent interior is considered the finest example of Georgian church architecture in North America. A bell cast by Paul Revere still rings before every service. The church is a stop on the Freedom Trail. The "tour" is a talk given frequently to visitors throughout the day.

Massachusetts State House

Corner of Park and Beacon Streets
(617) 727–3676
www.sec.state.ma.us/trs/trsgen/genidx.htm

Weekdays year-round, 10:00 A.M. to 3:30 P.M.; closed on weekends and holidays.

THE CATCH
} Reservations are required for conducted tours.

The Massachusetts State House, a stop on the Freedom Trail, is the oldest building on Beacon Hill and is famous for its enormous golden dome. Built in 1798 and designed by noted local architect Charles Bulfinch, the State House is the seat of government for the Commonwealth as well as the home of the Massachusetts Senate and House of Representatives. During the spring, school class trips are particularly popular; to avoid the hordes of youngsters, pick a tour after 3:00 P.M. Tours last between thirty and forty-five minutes and include an overview of the history and architecture of the building. Tours that highlight the legislative process can be arranged in advance.

Old North Church

193 Salem Street
(617) 523–6676
www.oldnorth.com

Labor Day to Memorial Day, daily, 9:00 A.M. to 5:00 P.M.

Memorial Day to Labor Day, daily, 9:00 A.M. to 6:00 P.M.

THE CATCH: Call ahead for reservations for larger groups. Donations are appreciated.

Built in 1723, Old North is the oldest church building in Boston and continues to serve as an Episcopal church. On April 18, 1775, Robert Newman, sexton of the Old North Church, displayed two lanterns from its steeple to warn Paul Revere and others of the British troop movements. Paul Revere's famous "midnight ride" began with that signal. Tours are geared mostly for school groups, but they'll take big people, too. The location is one of the most popular along the Freedom Trail, so make sure to hit it early in the day.

Old South Meeting House

310 Washington Street (at Milk Street)
(617) 482–6439
www.nps.gov/bost/OSMH.htm
www.oldsouthmeetinghouse.org

July 4 through Labor Day, daily tours at 11:00 A.M. and 2:00 P.M.

THE CATCH: Admission is $5.00 for adults, $4.00 for seniors and students, and $1.00 for children ages six to eighteen. Children under age six are admitted free.

Angry about the tea tax, 5,000 colonials gathered on December 16, 1773, at the Old South Meeting House to devise a way to make sure their displeasure was duly noted by King George. Someone suggested tossing all that tea into the ocean, people seemed to like the idea, and the rest is literally history. Today, as a National Historic Landmark and a stop on the Freedom Trail, it continues to host regular discussions and lectures on the events that shape our world today, just as it did over 200 years ago. In addition to educational tours, the Meeting House hosts regular free and paid events, including readings, concerts, and lectures. From November to March, there are no tours, but the Meeting House is open from 10:00 A.M. to 4:00 P.M. for self-guided tours.

Old State House

206 Washington Street (at State Street)
(617) 720–1713
www.bostonhistory.org

THE CATCH

Admission is $5.00 for adults, $1.00 for children under eighteen. Audio guides are available for an additional $1.00. Senior Bostonians and Boston public school children can visit for free.

The Old State House, which is a stop on the Freedom Trail, was built in 1713, making it the city's oldest public building. It began its life as the seat of the royal government in the New World and became one of the most historically significant places in Boston during the birth of the rebellion. The Boston Massacre happened near here, colonials debated the Stamp Act within its walls, and it was the location of the first public reading in Massachusetts of the Declaration of Independence. Today, the Old State House is a museum of Boston history, with changing exhibits on different aspects of the city's past.

Park Street Church

Park Street at Tremont Street
(617) 523–3383
www.parkstreet.org

Mid-June to mid-August, Tuesday through Saturday, 8:30 A.M. to 3:30 P.M.

This church is where William Lloyd Garrison gave the first abolitionist speech and where the song "America" was first sung. The tour of the 200-year-old church, which is a stop on the Freedom Trail, lasts about fifteen minutes and includes a short video.

Symphony Hall

301 Massachusetts Avenue
(617) 266–1492

October through early May (except during the last three weeks of December), on Wednesday at 4:30 P.M. and on the first Saturday of each month at 1:30 P.M.

This tour takes visitors throughout all nooks and crannies of the stately home of the Boston Symphony Orchestra and tells the symphony's colorful history. The tour takes one hour and begins at the Massachusetts Avenue entrance.

HISTORIC HOMES

Cooper-Frost-Austin House

21 Linnaean Street
Cambridge
(617) 227–3956
www.spnea.org/visit/homes/cooper.htm

Tours by special arrangement May through November.

THE CATCH — Admission is $4.00 but is free to Historic New England members (www.spnea.org; membership: $35 individual, $45 family) and residents of Cambridge.

The oldest house in Cambridge, the Cooper-Frost-Austin House was built in 1690 by Samuel Cooper. Although it was expanded and updated through the years, many pieces of the original frame and original finishes survive today.

Frederick Law Olmsted National Historic Site

99 Warren Street
Brookline
(617) 566–1689
www.nps.gov/frla/index.htm

THE CATCH — This site is scheduled to be closed for renovations until the fall of 2007. Call the National Park Service or visit the Olmsted Web site for more information.

The man responsible for the landscape design of Central Park, the White House Lawn, the Emerald Necklace, and thousands of other world-famous green spaces throughout the country made his home, named Fairsted, and office here in the bucolic fields of Brookline, beginning in 1883. It is free to visit both Fairsted and his office, in which there are over one million design documents relating to some of his most notable projects.

John Fitzgerald Kennedy National Historic Site

83 Beals Street
Brookline
(617) 566–7937
www.nps.gov/jofi

Guided tours Wednesday through Sunday every thirty minutes from 10:00 A.M. to 3:00 P.M. Self-guided tours Wednesday through Sunday from 3:30 to 4:30 P.M. (first and second floor). No self-guided tours mid-May through September.

THE CATCH — Admission is $3.00, but National Park Service Park Pass holders can visit free. Free to kids fifteen and under.

The JFK National Historic Site, the birthplace and first home of President John Fitzgerald Kennedy, was restored by his mother, Rose Kennedy, to the condition it was in when the president was a young child (the family moved when he was four). The site, administered by the Park Service, holds frequent educational workshops for children and older students throughout the summer.

Longfellow National Historic Park

105 Brattle Street
Cambridge
(617) 876–4491
www.nps.gov/long

House tours June through October from Wednesday through Sunday at 10:30 A.M., 11:30 A.M., 1:00 P.M., 2:00 P.M., 3:00 P.M., and 4:00 P.M. The grounds are open daily from dawn to dusk.

THE CATCH
} Admission to the house is $3.00. The NPS Park Pass gets you in free, and children under sixteen may visit for free.

Before Henry Wadsworth Longfellow moved into this stately mansion in 1843 (his descendants occupied it for the next century), it hosted General George Washington between July 1775 and April 1776 while he planned the Siege of Boston to drive the British out of the colonies. The house has an impressive collection of historical artifacts chronicling both the families that have lived here and its many famous visitors, including Julia Ward Howe, Nathaniel Hawthorne, and Ralph Waldo Emerson. The grounds feature expansive gardens, which everyone can visit for free.

Otis House Museum

141 Cambridge Street
(617) 227–3956
www.spnea.org/visit/homes/otis.htm

Tours year-round Wednesday through Sunday every half hour between 11:00 A.M. and 4:30 P.M.

THE CATCH
} Admission is $8.00, with a $24.00 maximum per family. Historic New England members (www.spnea.org; membership: $35 individual, $45 family) and Boston residents are admitted free.

Want to see how the other half lived a couple of centuries ago? A visit to the Otis House is like stepping back in time to witness the elegant lifestyle of Boston's ruling class after the American Revolution. Built in 1796, the house belonged to Harrison Gray Otis, who developed Beacon Hill and was both a U.S. representative and a mayor of Boston. The house was designed by Charles Bulfinch, one of the most noted architects of his time.

The Paul Revere House
Pierce/Hichborn House

19 North Square
(617) 523–2338
www.paulreverehouse.org

Revere House open daily April 15 through October 31 from 9:30 A.M. to 5:15 P.M. and November 1 through April 14 from 9:30 A.M. to 4:15 P.M.; closed on Monday in January, February, and March.

Pierce/Hichborn House by appointment only.

THE CATCH

Admission is $3.00 for adults, $2.50 for seniors and college students, and $1.00 for kids under seventeen.

The home of Paul Revere, built in 1680, is a stop on the Freedom Trail. While there are no formal tours, there are plenty of helpful and knowledgeable staff members throughout the three-story, colonial-style house and courtyard to answer any questions that you might have about our favorite resident patriot, silversmith, and leader. The same admission fee will also get you into the Pierce/Hichborn House, located next door. It is an early Georgian-style home built around 1711 that was owned by Nathaniel Hichborn, Revere's cousin. It is one of the most authentically preserved examples of this type of architecture in the city and is filled with original period furniture and decorations. Because of its small size, it is shown by guided tour only. Hours at the Pierce/Hichborn House change frequently, so call ahead to reserve a tour.

Pierce House

24 Oakton Avenue
Dorchester
(617) 227–3956
www.spnea.org/visit/homes/pierce.htm

THE CATCH

Free tours by prior arrangement May through November.

The Pierce House, built in 1683, is one of the few First Period, or seventeenth-century, houses in Boston. The house was occupied by ten generations of the Pierce family, and it offers a unique glimpse into the evolution of building styles and techniques as well as the lifestyle of one family over more than three centuries.

SEASIDE TOURS

Boston Harbor Islands

(617) 223–8666

www.BostonharborIslands.com

Mid-June to Labor Day.

THE CATCH

} It'll cost you $10 to $12 for the ferry ride to George's Island from Long Wharf off Commercial Street.

The dozens of islands just off the Boston coast offer a wonderful mix of walking trails, historic buildings and forts, camping, and unique features (like a giant lighthouse). It will cost you money to get to George's Island, but once you're there, free shuttles will take you to a variety of other islands. The National Park Service and the Massachusetts Department of Conservation and Recreation offer tours on some of the islands, and they host Family Fun Days every Saturday and Sunday from July 1 to Labor Day. The Fun Day events include Civil War reenactment encampments, underwater animal "show and tell," music, and more. For a current schedule, visit the Boston Harbor Islands Web site.

Boston Natural Areas Network

(617) 542–7696

www.bostonnatural.org/canoe.php

THE CATCH

} Reservations are required.

Canoe with BNAN staff and volunteers along the Neponset River and also Belle Isle Marsh in East Boston and enjoy the beauty and wildlife of Boston. Trips run from April through October. Canoes are provided, or you can bring your own. Trips last two to three hours.

Charlestown Navy Yard

National Park Service Visitor Center

(access via Warren Street off Chelsea Street, near Gate 1)

Charlestown

(617) 242–5601

www.nps.gov/bost/Navy_Yard.htm

Visitor Center: open daily from 9:00 A.M. to 5:00 P.M.

THE CATCH

} Guided tour times vary. Call ahead for an updated schedule.

The ranger-guided, forty-five-minute walking tour explores the Navy Yard's nearly 200-year history by taking visitors past such sites as the Chain Forge, where die-lock anchor chain was first manufactured; the Ropewalk, a quarter-mile-long building designed by famed architect Alexander Parris; and Dry Dock 1, one of the first two dry docks constructed in the nation. There are signs that let you take a self-guided tour as well.

Deer Island Wastewater Treatment Plant

Deer Island
Winthrop
(617) 660–7607
www.mwra.com/03sewer/html/sewditp.htm

Every Tuesday and Thursday from 10:00 A.M. to noon.

THE CATCH
}
There's a thorough previsit security check conducted on all visitors, so book at least a month in advance.

Touring a wastewater treatment facility might not seem like a fun way to spend the day, but if you've ever wondered what happens to all the stuff that you dump down the drain, here's your chance to find out. This secondary treatment facility treats the waste of forty-three Boston area communities. The centerpieces are the 140-foot-high, three-million-gallon egg-shaped digester tanks that are a major focal point of any harbor view. Deer Island also has miles of trails and walkways. When you call to book a tour, the tour director will send you a security form to fill out and return. It takes about two weeks for the security clearance to get processed. This is a surprisingly popular tour, and openings are usually booked several months in advance. Be sure to wear very comfortable shoes and clothing and be ready for bad weather since a portion of this two-hour tour takes place outside.

Fort Independence

Castle Island
South Boston
(617) 727–5290
www.mass.gov/dcr/parks/metroboston/castle.htm

Memorial Day to Labor Day, continuous tours on weekends from noon to 3:30 P.M. and on Thursday from 7:00 P.M. to sunset. Labor Day to Columbus Day, Sunday, noon to 3:30 P.M. Last weekend of October, noon to 4:00 P.M.

THE CATCH
}
Tours run weather permitting.

Fort Independence, atop Castle Island (joined to South Boston by a causeway), began in 1634 as a simple wooden fortification with three cannons built to protect and monitor the mouth of Boston Harbor. Since then, the fort has been built and rebuilt, and today it is a granite and earthwork fort that tells a rich history of revolution and civil war. It is even said that events at the fort inspired Edgar Allan Poe, who served there briefly, to write "The Cask of Amontillado." Fort tours are conducted by the Castle Island Association in the summer months, and there are interpretive signs for self-guided tours. The association also hosts a free kid-friendly "Haunted Fort" event during the last weekend of October.

Harborwalk

(617) 482–1722

www.bostonharborwalk.com

www.tbha.org/events_tbha.htm (current calendar)

The Harborwalk is a walking path that closely follows the shore of Boston Harbor from the North End all the way to the Kennedy Library in Dorchester. The walkway, the result of a massive urban renewal project spanning more than a decade, has reclaimed sections of the waterfront that had long been impassable to pedestrians. Today, the Boston Harbor Association offers walking tours and cruises that highlight the art and history of this unique public resource. There's a current events listing at the BHA Web site, and new events are being planned all the time. You will actually do the city and the waterfront a service by going on one of these tours; the BHA collects comments from tour visitors to incorporate into future proposals for Harborwalk improvements.

USS *Cassin Young*

Pier 1, Charlestown Navy Yard

Charlestown

(617) 242–5601

www.nps.gov/bost/Cassin_Young.htm

December through March, guided tours only, Monday through Wednesday at 11:00 A.M., 2:00 P.M., and 3:00 P.M. April through November, ship's main deck open from 10:00 A.M. to 4:00 P.M.; tours at 11:00 A.M. and 2:00 P.M.

This World War II destroyer was decommissioned in the 1950s and now stands in stark contrast to the USS *Constitution* docked nearby. The forty-five-minute tours take you into parts of the ship not usually open to the public.

USS *Constitution*

Pier 1, Charlestown Navy Yard

Charlestown

(617) 242–5670

www.ussconstitution.navy.mil

November 1 to March 31, Thursday through Sunday, 10:00 A.M. to 3:50 P.M. April 1 to October 31, Tuesday through Sunday, 10:00 A.M. to 5:50 P.M.

THE CATCH You have to go through a security check to get in. } The USS *Constitution* is the oldest commissioned warship in the world. Launched in 1797, she got her nickname "Old Ironsides" during the War of 1812 when cannonballs fired at her bounced off her sides, which are made of three layers of hardwood harvested from all over the United States. The naval officers assigned to the ship give tours every half hour, with the last tour leaving at 3:30 P.M. All visitors are required to go through a screening process. It is a good idea to arrive at least a half hour early to allow time to get through the security tent. Anything that isn't allowed on an airplane is also banned from the *Constitution:* guns, mace, and any sharp objects, such as razors, knives, pocket knives, Swiss army knives, "Leatherman"-type tools, scissors, and letter openers.

ART AND ARCHITECTURE TOURS

Boston Athenæum

10½ Beacon Street
(617) 227–0270
www.bostonathenaeum.org

Tuesday and Thursday at 3:00 P.M.

Taking a guided tour through the Boston Athenæum, a National Historic Landmark, is literally like walking through the heart and soul of Boston's literary and artistic history. Founded in 1807, the Athenæum was the original location of a fledgling Museum of Fine Arts before it moved out to its own facility. Although the MFA took much of its art with it, the Athenæum still contains many sculptures, paintings, and other priceless works that make this lovely old library feel like an art museum in its own right. The Art and Architecture tour will give you an up-close look at these rare treasures.

Boston Public Library

700 Boylston Street (Copley Square)
(617) 536–5400 (ext. 2216 for tour information)
www.bpl.org

Monday at 2:30 P.M., Tuesday at 6:00 P.M., Thursday at 6:00 P.M., Friday at 11:00 A.M., Saturday at 11:00 A.M., and Sunday at 2:00 P.M. (October through May only).

This tour, led by library volunteers, highlights the architecture of Charles Follen McKim and Philip Johnson, the two men from different eras who together conceptualized the two vastly different wings of the first large public library in the United States. The tour also showcases the sculptures, murals, and paintings within the library. The tour takes about an hour and begins in the foyer of the Dartmouth Street entrance of the McKim building (the older building).

John Joseph Moakley U.S. Courthouse

One Courthouse Way (near Fan Pier in South Boston)

John Adams Courthouse

One Pemberton Square (near the State House)
(617) 748–9639
www.discoveringjustice.org

Tuesday through Thursday, 9:00 A.M. to 4:00 P.M. or by appointment.

THE CATCH } You must have two forms of identification, one with a photo, to take part in the tour.

The Moakley Courthouse, one of the most recent additions to the Boston skyline, is noted for its unique curved walls of glass and its clean modern lines. The John Adams Courthouse, built between 1886 and 1894, houses the Commonwealth's Supreme Judicial Court. It was recently renovated to expand its facilities and to restore existing spaces and artwork. Tours of both locations focus on the courthouses' architecture and the art housed within, which at the Moakley includes a series of paintings by Ellsworth. Visitors spend time in a typical courtroom, and some may attend an actual court session in progress. The Moakley has a great public cafeteria with a spectacular view of the city skyline and harbor below.

Trinity Church

Copley Square
(617) 536–0944
www.trinitychurchboston.org

Free tour on Sunday immediately after 11:15 A.M. service (approximately 12:15 to 12:30 P.M.). Tuesday through Saturday, various times between 9:00 A.M. and 4:00 P.M.; Sunday, 1:00 to 4:00 P.M.

THE CATCH
} Every tour except the one after the Sunday service costs $5.00.

The imposing Romanesque spires of Trinity Church dominate the Copley Square landscape and promise untold architectural treasures within. It doesn't disappoint. Completed in 1877, this award-winning architectural marvel recently underwent massive renovations. The tour after the Sunday service meets at the Eagle lectern at the front of the church and encompasses all the art and architecture that has made this place famous, including the Eugene Oudinot stained-glass windows. Visit the Web site for an updated list of free events as well as monthly tour times, which vary.

COOL STUFF

Boston Globe

135 Morrissey Boulevard
(617) 929–2000
www.boston.com

Monday, Thursday, and one Wednesday per month at 10:00 A.M., 11:15 A.M., and 1:15 P.M.

THE CATCH
} Make reservations in advance. Children must be nine or older.

Take a tour of the Fourth Estate! The *Boston Globe* offers tours of its facilities as well as the giant printing presses that pump out over half a million newspapers a day. The tour lasts about one hour.

Harpoon Brewery

Mass Bay Brewing Company
306 Northern Avenue
(888) HARPOON (ext. 522 to schedule private tours)
www.harpoonbrewery.com

Tours on Tuesday through Saturday at 3:00 P.M., plus additional tours on Friday and Saturday at 1:00 P.M.

THE CATCH

Bring an ID if you want to sample the beer. The drinking age in Massachusetts is twenty-one.

Since the 1980s the Harpoon Brewery has been creating award-winning beers. The tours of the brewery last approximately thirty to forty-five minutes. Groups of fifteen or more can make reservations. Harpoon also hosts the 5:30 Club, a group tour of the brewery held Tuesday through Friday from 5:30 to 7:00 P.M. Group size can range from fifteen to eighty people, but it must be scheduled in advance (can you say "office happy hour"?). The brewery charges a nominal $1.00 per person for these events, refundable if the tour is canceled twenty-four hours ahead. Call the private tour phone line to make 5:30 Club reservations.

The Samuel Adams® Brewery

Boston Beer Company
30 Germania Street
Jamaica Plain
(617) 368–5080

Thursday, 2:00 P.M.; Friday, 2:00 and 5:30 P.M.; Saturday, noon, 1:00 P.M., and 2:00 P.M.; additional tours held on Wednesday at 2:00 P.M. from May 1 through August 31.

THE CATCH

Suggested donation is $2.00, but it goes to charity. Bring an ID if you want to taste the beer.

This tour will show you the inner workings of the brewery that put Boston beer makers on the international map. You must be 21 or older to taste their award-winning beer at the end of the tour.

"So, come on and take
a free ride."

—*Edgar Winter Group*

Despite what you may have heard in the old song "Charlie on the MTA," most people do return from their excursions on Boston public transportation. Although Boston's subway system is the oldest in the nation (built in 1898), the Massachusetts Bay Transportation Authority—the T—is undergoing constant expansion and improvement and still has one of the lowest rate structures of any major city. You can get to most cities and towns in eastern Massachusetts using a combination of bus or subway. Throw in the commuter rail, our light rail system, and your options stretch all the way west to Fitchburg and south to Rhode Island. There are also a number of cheap ways to get out of town, or to the airport.

GETTING AROUND BOSTON

City Water Taxi
(617) 422–0392
www.citywatertaxi.com

Hours: Monday through Saturday, 7:00 A.M. to 10:00 P.M.; Sunday, 7:00 A.M. to 8:00 P.M.

THE CATCH } Fares for inner harbor travel start at $10.

These water taxis drop off and pick up at most of the major destinations in the inner harbor, including Logan Airport, the World Trade Center and Boston Convention Center, Rowe's Wharf Hotel, and Charlestown Navy Yard. During rush hour they're a much more pleasant way to get to your destination and often give you better door-to-door access than the bus or subway. There is no fixed schedule. Visit the Web site for a complete list of destinations.

FREE FLEET FEET

In Boston the cheapest and most enjoyable method of transportation is attached to the end of your legs. Walking around Boston is easy and cheap. The city is mostly flat, compact (just don't call it small), and dense. You can walk from one end to the other in a couple of hours. Excellent and highly detailed maps can be downloaded for free from Google Maps, Yahoo Maps, and a variety of other Web-based applications. Maps and other tourist information can also be found at the Boston Common Visitor Center, which is in the Boston Common along Tremont Street across from Temple Place (617–536–4100; open Monday through Saturday from 8:30 A.M. to 5:00 P.M. and Sunday from 10:00 A.M. to 6:00 P.M.). By far the best map of Boston I've ever used is Boston's BikeMap (about $12; available at almost all bicycle and sporting goods stores in the city, or by contacting Rubel BikeMaps, P.O. Box 401035, Cambridge, MA 02140 or www.bikemaps.com). This map is waterproof, extremely durable, and updated frequently, and it has impeccable detail, including attractions. The best part is that the designers have highlighted the least trafficked and most scenic routes throughout the city, which also makes the map ideal for walkers. If you're brave enough to attempt cycling Boston's city streets (where you will be in direct competition with Boston's notoriously bad drivers), the map contains excellent cycling tips, rules about taking your bike on the T, and route directions to get to and from Logan on your bike.

Massachusetts Bay Transportation Authority
(617) 222–5000
www.mbta.com

THE CATCH In a throwback to our Puritanical roots, the Boston public transportation system begins running at 5:30 A.M. and ends at about 12:30 to 1:00 A.M. One day, we'll have twenty-four-hour public transport, but it's not going to be today.

The MBTA, or T as it's called, oversees operation of all the subways, buses, commuter boats, and trains in and around the city of Boston (the boats and commuter rail are operated by contractors). The network is extensive and can be very confusing. Fares vary depending on distance of travel. There are several daily, weekly, and monthly passes available that get you access to as much of the system as you think you're likely to need; prices vary, and details are available on the MBTA Web site. The entire system is in the process of being upgraded to "Charlie Cards"—named after the hapless T traveler who "never returned" from his trip on the subway because he didn't have exit fare (the T still charges exit fares of $1.25 at the Red Line's Braintree and Quincy Adams stops). The Charlie Cards act as fare debit cards and subtract the value of your trips automatically, which is a welcome change—or at least will be once the confusion of the transition is over.

The subway color-coded system is based on the concept of "Inbound" and "Outbound." Inbound means the subway train is heading toward the downtown area (Park Street for Green and Red Lines, Downtown Crossing for the Orange Line, and Government Center for the Blue Line), and Outbound means it's heading away from those stops. The commuter rail departs from North Station, Back Bay Station, and South Station in Boston and will get you to points as far away as Newburyport; Providence, Rhode Island; and Fitchburg. If you get lost or confused when attempting to use the MBTA system, don't despair. I've lived in the city for over twenty years, and I still get screwed up and turned backward regularly.

GETTING OUT OF BOSTON

Logan Airport

Getting to Boston Logan International Airport by public transportation is obscenely cheap—and increasingly convenient with the addition of the Silver Line bus, which goes directly to each airport terminal at Logan from South Station (Red Line) for $1.25. Or you can take the Blue Line (currently $1.25) to the Airport T stop, where the free MBTA shuttle bus will take you directly to your terminal. The water shuttles are a little more pricey (starting at $6.00), but they go from Long Wharf (near the Aquarium) directly to the airport docks, where the shuttle bus will drop you off at your destination. Of course, leave extra time. Additional details can be found at www.mbta.com. A substantial fare increase was proposed at press time, which could double these rates, but even then they'd still be a steal. The only drawback is that most of the bus and subway system doesn't start running until about 5:30 A.M. and stops running around 12:30 A.M., so if your plane is late, or you've got a really early flight, you could be out of luck.

Auto Driveaway Company
480 Neponset Street, 2-B
Canton
(781) 828–4070
www.autodriveaway.com

This service is a great way to drive yourself to your desired destination for just the price of the gas. This national auto delivery service, which has an office in the Boston area, will match you to a car that needs to be driven to a predetermined city, and all you have to do is keep the rubber side down, pay for gas, and arrive in the predetermined number of days. All drivers must be twenty-three years old with a valid driver's license, and all drivers must provide a motor vehicle driver's record, which is generated by your home state's Registry of Motor Vehicles. You'll also need to leave a refundable security deposit of approximately $350. The Web site keeps an updated list of cars needing transport out of Boston. Getting home is up to you—but, because the Auto Driveaway network is nationwide, you can always pick up another car in your destination city to deliver back home to Boston.

ERideShare

P.O. Box 402
Edwardsville, IL 62025
(618) 530–4842
www.erideshare.com/carpool.php?city=Boston

Free membership in this carpooling Web site will give you access to the frequently updated list of carpooling opportunities as well as ride shares to faraway cities. Most ride shares involve paying your share of the gas.

HOUSE-SWAPPING SERVICES

Want a free vacation home in Paris? How about the Swiss Alps? Colorado? Well, they're out there just for the asking. It's called house swapping, and it's becoming all the rage for the savvy traveler. By simply swapping a house with another family, both families get comfortable accommodations in a city they want to visit—for FREE! Obviously there are risks when you open your home to people you've never met, and whom you can't supervise, but travelers who house-swap claim they quickly become addicted. Vacationing this way, they say, gets you entree into the locals' world, allowing you to experience a vacation destination in a much more intimate and complete way, as opposed to being holed up in a sterile hotel. Most house-swapping services charge a small fee to list your home and browse the other house listings. Here are some tried-and-trusted services.

Craig's List

www.boston.craigslist.com/swp/

These are primarily long-term swaps.

Home for Exchange

www.homeforexchange.com

International; $48 for one-year membership.

Home Link International

www.homelink-usa.org

The largest service, serving twenty-two different countries. Annual fee is $80.

Intervac

www.intervacusa.com

The oldest house-swapping service, founded in 1953. Fees are $65 for U.S.-only swaps and $78.88 for U.S. and international swaps. Hard-copy catalogs of listed homes are also available for $50.

RETREATS

East Mountain Retreat Center

Lake Buel Road
Great Barrington
(413) 528–6617
www.eastretreat.org

THE CATCH East Mountain suggests a donation of $30 a day, which includes meals. A suggested donation of $10 a night (not including meals) is requested from bicyclists and hikers who arrive without cars. Reservations are required.

Looking for some serious peace and quiet? This retreat destination, open from April 1 to October 31, except for the last week in July, is a silent retreat tucked away in a forest in the Berkshire Mountains. You'll be expected to cook your own meals, but food is provided. You'll get a private room with bedding and towels. But unless you're either talking to a guide or a teacher at the center or eating, it's expected that you will literally keep your mouth closed for the duration of your stay. The center suggests that you stay at least two days, but no longer than two weeks.

Kripalu Center for Yoga and Health

Kripalu Center
57 Interlaken Road
Stockbridge
(413) 448–3123
www.kripalu.org

THE CATCH If you contribute thirty-five hours of work per week, you gain access to all the center's amenities, plus room and board, for $50 a month.

Kripalu is the yoga lovers' retreat of choice in New England. The lovely, sprawling estate is on the line between Stockbridge and Lenox, Massachusetts, near Tanglewood, the summer home of the Boston Symphony Orchestra. Volunteers help keep the place looking good, feed the paying guests, and clean bathrooms. You may volunteer for one, two, or three months, depending on which type of volunteer program you choose. One is more structured, with a strong personal educational and development component; the other is more laid-back and expects you to lend a hand around the place (as directed by your volunteer coordinator).

Rowe Camp and Conference Center

273 King's Highway Road
Rowe
(413) 339–4954
www.rowecenter.org

Rowe Camp and Conference Center, run by a Unitarian Universalist minister, holds frequent weekend workshops and programs featuring some of the best minds in the country, like Grace Paley and Noam Chomsky, on subjects ranging from meditation to writing to baseball. Set on beautiful grounds in the western part of Massachusetts, the camp is wide open to those willing to put in a little elbow grease in exchange for free room and board. Between Labor Day and late June, the camp offers a work-study sabbatical lasting at least six weeks, and up to a year, depending on your schedule. If you put in thirty-three hours of work, you'll get free room and board and access to many of the conferences and weekend workshops. After late June, there's also a summer volunteer program, requiring at least twenty-eight hours of work a week in exchange for free room and board. If you don't want to do that much work, they'll let you barter some services or skills for reduced rates on workshops and classes, but you'll have to pay for room and board (subject to availability; rates vary).

Starseed Healing Sanctuary and Retreat Center

672 Chapel Road
Savoy
(413) 743–0417

THE CATCH
Stay for free in exchange for doing gardening and landscape work.

This retreat focuses on earth-healing, or connecting with the earth to heal one's past traumas. There are stone sanctuaries in the woods, a sweat lodge by the stream, and a peace labyrinth where you can lose your troubles. Starseed allows visitors to stay in the retreat for free in exchange for working on the land—gardening and other types of property upkeep. Food is not included.

Vipassana Meditation Center

386 Colrain-Shelburne Road
Shelburne Falls
(413) 625–2160
www.dhara.dhamma.org

The ten-day silent meditation course offered at Vipassana can be rigorous in a minimalist way: no exercise, no physical contact with other people, no music, and, above all, no talking. The focus is on silently meditating in complete isolation, using ancient Buddhist techniques. Donations are accepted, but only after you come back for a second ten-day session, when you'll also be expected to prepare meals, keep the center running, and help the new students complete their course. All students must apply and make reservations at least one month in advance for admission.

{ART GALLERIES AND EXHIBITS: }
F R E E   H A N D

"My God! How terrible these
money questions are for an artist!"

– *Paul Gauguin*

There's absolutely no reason why a Cheap Bastard in Boston should spend a penny to see some of the best art in the world—you'll find it for free all over town, displayed in our art galleries, studios, artist cooperatives, and art schools. It doesn't cost a penny to browse through these treasure troves, as long as you can resist the temptation to bring a piece home if you fall in love with it. Many of the galleries listed are tiny spaces able to showcase only a few pieces by one or two artists at a time. Others are veritable museums showcasing the masters. While the bulk of these galleries are located along Newbury Street in the heart of the Back Bay, many galleries are springing up in less obvious locales—the South End, East Boston, Fort Point in South Boston, and Cambridge. Artists' communities have also sprouted up in every Boston neighborhood, and many host annual open-studio events where you can find fresh, new artists doing fabulous work that's selling at "undiscovered artist" prices.

ART GALLERIES

ACME Fine Art
38 Newbury Street, fourth floor (between Arlington and Berkeley Streets)
(617) 585–9551
www.acmefineart.com

Hours: Tuesday through Saturday, 11:00 A.M. to 5:30 P.M., and the first Friday of every month, 11:00 A.M. to 7:30 P.M., or by appointment.

This gallery features modern works, including abstract expressionism, fauvism, cubism, and surrealism, dating from 1900 through 1980.

Allston Skirt Gallery
65 Thayer Street
(617) 482–3652
www.allstonskirt.com

Hours: Wednesday through Saturday, 11:00 A.M. to 5:00 P.M.; closed in August.

This gallery features contemporary art in all media, from both established and emerging artists.

Alpha Gallery

38 Newbury Street
(617) 536–4465
www.Alphagallery.com

Hours: Tuesday through Friday, 10:00 A.M. to 5:30 P.M.; Saturday, 11:00 A.M. to 5:30 P.M.

This spacious gallery exhibits multiple artists and focuses primarily on painting, although other media are represented. It holds frequent New Artist exhibitions but generally features mid-career and established artists. Don't miss their periodic special shows of master artists such as Pablo Picasso, Fairfield Porter, Max Beckmann, and Milton Avery.

Arden Gallery

129 Newbury Street
(617) 247–0610
www.ardengallery.com

Hours: Monday through Saturday, 11:00 A.M. to 5:30 P.M.

Arden represents contemporary living artists. Works vary from realistic portraits to abstract to still life.

Artana

1378 Beacon Street, Suite B (Coolidge Corner)
Brookline
(617) 879–3111
www.Artanagallery.com

Hours: Tuesday through Saturday, 10:00 A.M. to 5:00 P.M.; hours vary during the summer.

Artana's gallery director, Heather Roy, is on a crusade to demystify art collecting and to educate people about art. This gallery reflects her unpretentious spirit. Artana focuses on displaying collectible work created by accomplished New England artists.

Axelle Fine Arts Galerie Newbury

91 Newbury Street
(617) 450–0700
www.axelle.com

Hours: Monday through Saturday, 10:00 A.M. to 6:00 P.M.; Sunday, noon to 6:00 P.M.

One of four Axelle galleries nationwide, this gallery represents contemporary European artists.

BAAK Gallery

35 Brattle Street
Cambridge
(617) 354–0407
www.baakgallery.com

Hours: Monday through Saturday, 10:30 A.M. to 8:00 P.M.; Sunday, 1:00 to 6:00 P.M.

Fine art mixed with fine jewelry (featuring conflict-free diamonds) has earned this gallery in Cambridge accolades from collectors, and awards from local magazines and newspapers.

Barbara Krakow Gallery

10 Newbury Street
(617) 262–4490
www.barbarakrakowgallery.com

Hours: Tuesday through Saturday, 10:00 A.M. to 5:30 P.M.; closed Saturdays in July, the month of August, and the week between Christmas and New Year.

This gallery is known for its minimalist art collection, as well as its conceptual installations, all done by regional and international artists.

Berenberg Gallery

4 Clarendon Street
(617) 536–0800
www.berenberggallery.com

Hours: Tuesday through Saturday, 11:00 A.M. to 6:00 P.M.

This small gallery, which shares space with a framing shop, presents the work of unconventional, sometimes marginalized artists who are institutionalized or have physical and/or emotional disabilities. The work is sometimes disturbing, always compelling, and spans all media except video.

Bernard Toale Gallery

450 Harrison Avenue
(617) 482–2477
www.bernardtoalegallery.com

Hours: Tuesday through Saturday, 10:30 A.M. to 5:30 P.M.; closed Saturdays in July; open by appointment only in August.

This gallery features cutting-edge contemporary art in all media by internationally known as well as emerging artists.

Boston Center for the Arts Mills Gallery

539 Tremont Street
(617) 426–8835
www.bcaonline.org

Hours: Wednesday, Thursday, and Sunday, noon to 5:00 P.M.; Friday and Saturday, noon to 10:00 P.M.

The BCA presents six large-scale exhibitions in its 2,200-square-foot Mills Gallery each year, including contemporary works by established and emerging local, regional, national, and international visual artists. During each show the BCA schedules a variety of opportunities to get to know the artists, including opening receptions, artists' talks, curators' talks, and other events.

Boston Sculptors Gallery

486 Harrison Avenue
(617) 482–7781
www.bostonsculptors.com

Hours: Tuesday through Saturday, 11:00 A.M. to 6:00 P.M.

Boston Sculptors Gallery is a cooperative of twenty-eight participating sculptors, two of whom take over the space for a show each month on a rotating basis. The BSG has gained wide acclaim from art critics for its innovative approach and for the quality of the work presented here since 1992.

Brickbottom Gallery

1 Fitchburg Street
Somerville
(617) 776–3410
www.brickbottomartists.com

Hours: Thursday through Saturday, noon to 5:00 P.M.

Brickbottom Gallery mounts professionally curated exhibitions of contemporary art. Its annual Open Studios, started in 1989, is one of the oldest in Boston.

Bromfield Gallery

450 Harrison Avenue
(617) 451–3605
www.bromfieldartgallery.com

Hours: Tuesday through Saturday, noon to 6:00 P.M.

This is the oldest artist-run cooperative gallery in Boston. Each member presents a solo show every two years. The shows often include pairings of visual arts with music, performance, and poetry.

ART ON THE GO

When James Hull, an artist and gallery owner, moved to the Jamaica Plain neighborhood of Boston in the late 1990s, he got fed up looking at the abandoned storefront of the Green Street MBTA station down the street from his house. Rather than complain, he went to the city to find out if he could open up an art gallery in the space, and to his shock, they said yes. He's been operating the Green Street Gallery ever since, and it has become a beloved community resource that showcases the work of local students as well as some nationally known and emerging artists. The space has become a well-respected presence on the art scene—it's won several awards for spotting emerging talent, including Taylor Davis, who showed her sculpture at the Whitney Biennial. The gallery is funded by donations and the sale of the artwork in a special annual sale, and every year the gallery must rejustify its existence to the MBTA, but so far, so good. You can find the Green Street Gallery at 141 Green Street on the ground floor of the Green Street MBTA stop on the Orange Line in Jamaica Plain. For more information, visit www.green streetgallery.org or call (617) 522-0000.

Brookline Center For The Arts Gallery
86 Monmouth Street
Brookline
(617) 566–5715
www.brooklineartscenter.com

Hours: Monday through Friday, 9:00 A.M. to 4:30 P.M.

This gallery represents artists who work in all media—watercolors, sculptures, oils, photography, and pottery.

Chase Gallery
129 Newbury Street
(617) 859–7222
www.chasegallery.com

Hours: Monday through Saturday, 10:00 A.M. to 5:30 P.M.

Chase represents primarily local contemporary artists through rotating solo exhibits. It also handles resale.

Childs Gallery

169 Newbury Street

(617) 266–1108

www.childsgallery.com

Hours: Tuesday through Friday, 9:00 A.M. to 6:00 P.M.; Monday and Saturday, 10:00 A.M. to 5:00 P.M.

Childs Gallery wants you to buy art, and they'll stop at nothing, including trolling around someone's attic, to find it. Their collection is mostly older works, everything from Renaissance through the 1950s. You'll find the classical and the obscure here.

Claygo Gallery

450 Harrison Avenue (along Thayer Street, a pedestrian way)

(617) 695–0100

www.claygo.com

Hours: Tuesday through Saturday, 11:00 A.M. to 6:00 P.M.

Funky handmade pottery, some of it specially designed for use at local restaurants and pubs, has put this place on the map. They make gorgeous dinnerware and barware that look like art.

Crump McCole Gallery

200 Seaport Boulevard

(617) 330–1133

Hours: Monday, Tuesday, Wednesday, and Friday, 10:00 A.M. to 6:00 P.M.; Thursday, 10:00 A.M. to 8:00 P.M.; Saturday and Sunday, noon to 5:00 P.M.

Two artist friends from South Boston—one a Boston Harbor boat captain, the other a news editor at the *Boston Herald*—rediscovered their shared love of creating and displaying art and started this funky little gallery near the World Trade Center. They show local artists' painting, photography, and sculpture.

DTR Modern Galleries

167 Newbury Street

(617) 424–9700

Hours: Monday through Thursday, 11:00 A.M. to 7:00 P.M.; Friday and Saturday, 11:00 A.M. to 8:00 P.M.; Sunday, 11:00 A.M. to 6:00 P.M.

Showcasing the works of twentieth-century masters, this is one of the best places in town to see the big names in their original format. Recent shows have included "the three Spaniards"—Miró, Picasso, and Dalí. They also show pop and surrealist art.

Fort Point Arts Community Gallery

300 Summer Street
(617) 423–4299
www.fortpointarts.org

Hours: Monday through Friday, 9:00 A.M. to 9:00 P.M.

This gallery, located in the Artist Building in the Fort Point neighborhood, is ground central for the artist community in South Boston. (The Artist Building also has a great cafe.) The large exhibition space showcases Fort Point artists in all media, including large installations.

Galerie d'Orsay

33 Newbury Street
(617) 266–8001
www.galerie-dorsay.com

Hours: Monday through Saturday, 10:00 A.M. to 6:00 P.M.; Sunday, noon to 6:00 P.M.

Want to see some Rembrandt, Renoir, Toulouse-Lautrec, Pissarro, Picasso, Matisse, Chagall, or Miró? Drop by Galerie d'Orsay, which has more masters per square foot than nearly any other gallery in the city. They also feature works by contemporary painters, sculptors, and printmakers.

Gallery AA/B

535 Albany Street, Suite 3B
(617) 574–0022
www.artadvisoryboston.com

Hours: Thursday and Friday, noon to 5:30 P.M.

Gallery AA/B focuses on works by contemporary artists, sculptors, painters, and photographers.

Gallery @ The Piano Factory

791 Tremont Street
(617) 437–9365

Hours: Saturday and Sunday, noon to 5:00 P.M. and by appointment.

This gallery features the work of local artists in all media. Exhibitions rotate monthly.

Gallery Kayafas

450 Harrison Avenue
(617) 482–0411
www.gallerykayafas.com

Hours: Tuesday through Saturday, 11:00 A.M. to 5:30 P.M.; by appointment only during August.

Kayafas specializes in fine art photography.

Gallery NAGA

67 Newbury Street
(617) 267–9060
www.gallerynaga.com

Hours: Tuesday through Saturday, 10:00 A.M. to 5:30 P.M.

Gallery NAGA is one of the most eclectic and diverse of the big-name galleries. Exhibits include painting, photography, prints, sculpture, holography, and furniture.

Genovese/Sullivan Gallery

450 Harrison Avenue
(617) 426–9738
www.genovesesullivan.com

Hours: Tuesday through Saturday, 10:30 A.M. to 5:30 P.M.

Works by contemporary local artists are exhibited in a giant loftlike space.

Hamill Gallery of African Art

2164 Washington Street
(617) 442–8204
www.hamillgallery.com

Hours: Thursday through Saturday, noon to 6:00 P.M.; Sunday, noon to 5:00 P.M.

Boston's only gallery of traditional tribal art is a large, 7,000-square-foot exhibition space showing displays from seventy-five major tribal groups. Works include masks, figures, artifacts, textiles, jewelry, books, and posters.

Howard Yezerski Gallery

14 Newbury Street
(617) 262–0550
www.howardyezerskigallery.com

Hours: Tuesday through Saturday, 10:00 A.M. to 5:30 P.M.; closed between Christmas and New Year's Day.

This gallery features contemporary art, mixed media, prints, and oil paintings.

International Poster Gallery

205 Newbury Street
(617) 375–0076
www.internationalposter.com

Hours: Monday through Saturday, 10:00 A.M. to 6:00 P.M.; Sunday, noon to 6:00 P.M.

More than 10,000 vintage and modern posters, including one of the leading collections of Italian posters, are available in this gallery.

Judi Rotenberg Gallery

130 Newbury Street
(617) 437–1518
www.judirotenberg.com

Hours: Tuesday through Saturday, 10:00 A.M. to 6:00 P.M.

One of the city's premier galleries, Rotenberg Gallery features early and mid-career contemporary artists working in all media, including video and installation projects.

Judy Ann Goldman Fine Art/Beth Urdang Gallery

14 Newbury Street
(617) 424–8468
www.judygoldmanfineart.com

Hours: Tuesday through Saturday, 11:00 A.M. to 5:00 P.M.

This gallery focuses on contemporary artists and features acrylic and oil painters, installation artists, and photographers.

Kidder Smith Gallery

131 Newbury Street
(617) 424–6900
www.kiddersmithgallery.com

Hours: Monday through Saturday, 11:00 A.M. to 5:30 P.M.

The gallery holds solo exhibitions of painting and photography from mid-career contemporary, abstract, and representational artists.

Kingston Gallery

450 Harrison Avenue
(617) 423–4113
www.kingstongallery.com

Hours: Tuesday and Saturday, noon to 5:00 P.M.

Founded in 1982, Kingston Gallery is an artist-run exhibit space that shows emerging artists. Media include wool, paper, steel wool art, and photography.

Lanoue Fine Art

160 Newbury Street
(617) 262–4400
www.lanouefineart.com

Hours: Monday through Saturday, 10:00 A.M. to 6:00 P.M.; Sunday, noon to 5:00 P.M.

Mid-career and established contemporary artists in various media are the focus of Lanoue Fine Art. Works include representational and abstract work by nationally and internationally renowned painters, sculptors, and printmakers.

L'Attitude Gallery

218 Newbury Street
(617) 927–4400
www.lattitudegallery.com

Hours: Monday through Saturday, 10:00 A.M. to 6:00 P.M.; Sunday, noon to 5:00 P.M.

Usable art, sculpture, and crafts— including glass, ceramics, wood, stone, mixed media, and textiles—are the focus at L'Attitude. The gallery presents over seventy-five U.S. and international artists.

Mercury Gallery

8 Newbury Street
(617) 859–0054
www.mercurygallery.com

Hours: Monday through Saturday, 10:00 A.M. to 5:30 P.M.

Expressionism rules at this comfortable gallery space, which resembles a plush living room and features artists in media such as pottery, photography, multi-media, and oil painting.

Mobilia Gallery

358 Huron Avenue
Cambridge
(617) 876–2109
www.mobilia-gallery.com

Hours: Tuesday through Friday, 11:00 A.M. to 6:00 P.M.; Saturday, 10:00 A.M. to 5:00 P.M.

For almost thirty years, this gallery has featured exciting wearable art and furniture, as well as jewelry, glass, ceramics, textile, and beadwork. Their curated exhibits include paintings and mixed-media pieces.

MPG Contemporary

450 Harrison Avenue
(617) 357–8881
www.mpgallery.net

Hours: Tuesday through Saturday, 11:30 A.M. to 5:30 P.M.

MPG is dedicated to contemporary artists working with sculpture, mixed media, and works on paper.

Newbury Fine Arts

29 Newbury Street
(617) 536–0210
www.newburyfinearts.com

Hours: Monday through Saturday, 10:00 A.M. to 6:00 P.M.; Sunday, noon to 5:00 P.M.

This gallery, which focuses on educating consumers, keeps a multi-artist, multi-genre exhibition on display at all times to expose visitors to a variety of styles and media.

Nielsen Gallery

179 Newbury Street
(617) 266–4835
www.nielsengallery.com

Hours: Tuesday through Saturday, 10:00 A.M. to 5:30 P.M.

Nielsen Gallery features contemporary painting and sculpture by nationally recognized artists.

OHT Gallery

450 Harrison Avenue
(617) 423–1677
www.ohtgallery.com

Hours: Tuesday through Saturday, 11:00 A.M. to 5:00 P.M.; by appointment during July and August.

OHT features emerging and mid-career contemporary painters from New York and Boston, with some national artists thrown into the mix.

OSP Gallery

450 Harrison Avenue
(617) 354–5287
www.ospgallery.com

Hours: Monday through Saturday, 11:00 A.M. to 5:00 P.M.

On display at this gallery are emerging contemporary local and national artists working primarily on paper media.

Out of the Blue Art Gallery

106 Prospect Street
Cambridge
(617) 354–5287
www.outoftheblueartgallery.com

Hours: Monday through Sunday, noon to 7:00 P.M.

This noncurated gallery accepts contributions from all local artists, who pay a hanging fee to display their work here. Art ranges from photography to crafts.

Pepper Gallery

38 Newbury Street, fourth floor
(617) 236–4497
www.peppergalleryboston.com

Hours: Tuesday through Friday, 10:00 A.M. to 5:30 P.M.; Saturday, 11:00 A.M. to 5:00 P.M.

Contemporary artwork—mostly painting, sculpture, photography, mixed media, and collage—is presented in an intimate setting. It's worth the four flights of stairs to get to it.

Pucker Gallery

171 Newbury Street
(617) 267–9473
www.puckergallery.com

Hours: Monday through Saturday, 10:00 A.M. to 5:30 P.M.; Sunday, 1:00 to 5:00 P.M.

The Puckers, Bernie and Sue, have been showcasing local and national artists in a variety of media—from watercolor and acrylic to photography and ceramic—since 1967. Their vibrant approach to art has made this gallery a mecca for the local arts scene.

Richardson-Clarke Gallery

38 Newbury Street
(617) 266–3321
www.richardson-clarke.com

Hours: Tuesday through Friday, 10:00 A.M. to 5:00 P.M.; Saturday, 11:00 A.M. to 5:00 P.M.

On display is a continual exhibition of a variety of works by nineteenth- and twentieth-century American and European painters in the genres of the Hudson River, American Impressionism, the Philadelphia Ten, and the Boston School.

ARTS AND APPS

Art isn't all that's free once you get to know the art community in Boston. Exhibition openings mean opening-night parties. With such a thriving art and art patron community, these parties are some of the best events in the city, and they're free to attend. Most have an open wine and beer bar and appetizers. When you visit a gallery that shows art you really like, ask to be added to their mailing list. You'll receive a postcard or e-mail invitation when new exhibitions, and the opening-night party, are scheduled. Then let the arty fun begin.

Robert Klein Gallery
38 Newbury Street
(617) 267–7997
www.robertkleingallery.com

Hours: Tuesday through Friday, 10:00 A.M. to 5:30 P.M.; Saturday, 11:00 A.M. to 5:00 P.M.

If you love photography, you can't miss this gallery. Most work is by renowned nineteenth- and twentieth-century photographers, including Alfred Steiglitz, Annie Leibowitz, and ManRay. Klein also exhibits an impressive array of contemporary photographers.

Victoria Munroe Fine Art
179 Newbury Street
(617) 523–0661
www.victoriamunroefineart.com

Hours: Tuesday through Saturday, 10:00 A.M. to 5:30 P.M.

This gallery offers a fascinating selection of nineteenth- and twentieth-century paintings, as well as a diverse collection of drawings, including eighteenth-, nineteenth-, and twentieth-century European and American architectural, engineering, decorative arts, garden design, and natural science drawings.

Vose Galleries of Boston

238 Newbury Street
(617) 536–6176
www.vosegalleries.com

Hours: Monday through Friday, 9:30 A.M. to 5:30 P.M.; Saturday, 10:00 A.M. to 5:30 P.M.

Established in 1841 as an artist's supply store in Providence, Rhode Island, the Vose Galleries are the grande dame of Boston art galleries. It is the oldest family-owned art gallery in the country and exhibits primarily the work of noncontemporary American artists from the eighteenth, nineteenth, and early twentieth centuries. Several years ago, however, the Vose Galleries broke with an unspoken rule against showing contemporary (living) artists and opened a new gallery showcasing more current work by artists still around to explain what it all means.

OTHER GALLERIES AND EXHIBITS

Adams Gallery

David J. Sargent Hall
Suffolk University Law School
120 Tremont Street
www.suffolk.edu/adams_gallery

Hours: daily, 10:00 A.M. to 6:00 P.M.

This gallery exhibits collections that revolve around a historical theme relevant to life in Boston. Past exhibits have covered subjects like the Red Sox, the Big Dig, photography of the *Boston Herald,* and the Boston Symphony Orchestra's 125th anniversary. The university also presents lectures and discussions related to the topic of the exhibits.

Cambridge Art Association

25 Lowell Street
Cambridge
(617) 876–0246
www.cambridgeart.org

Hours: Tuesday through Saturday, 11:00 A.M. to 5:00 P.M.

Today, the Cambridge Art Association consists of approximately 500 juried artist members—photographers, printmakers, painters, sculptors, textile artists, and glassmakers—and a supporting group of Friend Members. The purpose of the organization, while constantly evolving as artists' needs change, also remains much the same as it was in the 1940s: to enhance the quality of the community by exhibiting art, supporting local artists, and creating diverse opportunities for art education and art appreciation.

Cambridge Multicultural Arts Center

41 Second Street
Cambridge
(617) 577–1400
www.cmacusa.org

Hours: Monday through Friday, 10:00 A.M. to 6:00 P.M., and during special gallery events.

This local arts organization runs frequent exhibitions by local and national artists in various media. The CMAC also offers a variety of visual and performing arts-related programs for Cambridge residents and visitors.

Copley Society of Art

158 Newbury Street
(617) 536–5049
www.copleysociety.org

Hours: Tuesday through Saturday, 11:00 A.M. to 6:00 P.M.; Sunday, noon to 5:00 P.M.

The CoSo is the oldest nonprofit art association in the United States. It has 700 artist members nationwide who must pass peer review to be admitted. CoSo mounts member exhibitions and holds educational outreach programs, workshops, and lectures throughout the year to help build an audience for its young and emerging artists.

Eclipse Gallery

164 Newbury Street
(617) 247–6730
www.eclipsesalonboston.com

Hours: Tuesday through Saturday, 9:00 A.M. to 6:00 P.M.

It's an art gallery. It's a hair salon. Wait! You're both right. It's a hair salon that since 1988 has been mounting well-respected monthly art exhibitions on its walls. Media include oil paintings and photography from emerging and mid-career artists.

New Art Center in Newton

61 Washington Park
Newtonville
(617) 964–3424
www.newartcenter.org

Hours: Monday through Friday, 9:00 A.M. to 5:00 P.M.; Sunday, 1:00 to 5:00 P.M.

Located in a renovated church in the village of Newtonville, this arts education organization offers beginning through advanced classes to children and adults. It hosts frequent exhibitions of student artwork and has several juried shows throughout the year, including works of video, painting, installation, and sculpture.

Samson Projects

450 Harrison Avenue
(617) 357–7177
www.samsonprojects.com

Hours: Wednesday through Saturday, 11:00 A.M. to 6:00 P.M.

Some people aren't sure whether this is an art gallery or a very cool museum, but we don't care as long as it's there. The range of thought-provoking installations and exhibits mounted by the gallery's owners, Camilo Alvarez and Alexandra Cherubini, defy description and aim to be more culturally significant than commercially marketable. Past exhibits have examined themes like "bad behavior" through the use of video, film, performance art, and music.

School of the Museum of Fine Arts

230 The Fenway
(617) 369–3718
www.smfa.edu

Hours: Monday through Saturday, 10:00 A.M. to 5:00 P.M.

You can see the art stars of tomorrow here today in the more than twenty exhibitions mounted at the MFA School annually. Some are solo shows by internationally renowned artists, some are group exhibits, and many are juried. There are alumni, current student, and faculty galleries. The art is contemporary, and all media are explored.

Society of Arts and Crafts

175 Newbury Street
(617) 266–1810
www.societyofcrafts.org

Hours: Monday through Saturday, 10:00 A.M. to 6:00 P.M.; Sunday, noon to 5:00 P.M.

Incorporated in 1897, the Society of Arts and Crafts has been working to elevate the profile of craftsmen and -women for over a century, and its founders helped to fuel the Arts and Craft Movement. The gallery is a two-story space: The first floor is a retail gallery, and there's a more formal exhibition space on the second floor. This organization goes out of its way to find new craft forms and exhibits types of work that may not be considered commercially viable by other galleries.

Zeitgeist Gallery

186 Hampshire Street
Cambridge
(617) 876–6060
www.zeitgeist-gallery.org

Hours vary; call ahead or check the Web site for gallery exhibition hours.

THE CATCH

Most exhibits are free, but some performances request a donation. }

This cutting-edge art/performance/video gallery is an eclectic treasure that refuses to define itself. Zeitgeist has won accolades for its unique approach to the concept of art—one day it features a jazz guitarist, the next day a sale of clothing designed for the coming reign of global warming. Exhibits rotate frequently and are intermixed with performances. Zeitgeist Gallery cohosts events with other local arts organizations at different venues throughout the city.

OPEN STUDIOS

Open studios have become a rite of fall in Boston. That's when the thousands of local artists throw open their studio doors and let us, the clumsy masses, into their inner sanctums to see their work. Open studios are opportunities to see art from accomplished masters as well as experimental work from fledgling artists just testing their wings. Open studios are also wonderful social events, and a great way to meet your neighbors. Here is a list of artist organizations that hold open-studio events. They're usually held over several days, usually a weekend. Some, like the SoWa Group, hold monthly events.

Allston/Brighton Open Studios

Allston Arts District
(617) 254–3333
www.allstonarts.org

It is fitting that the only city in America named for an artist (Allston is named after the painter Washington Allston, who died in 1843 and is buried in Boston) holds an annual open-studio event for two days each winter. Started in 1987, it is one of the longest-running open-studio programs in the city, and the studios of the nearly forty artists who participate annually are within easy walking distance.

Charlestown Third Thursdays

Artist Group of Charlestown
(617) 241–0130
www.artistsgroupofcharlestown.com

Open studios are held at the Stove Factory at 523 Medford Street near Sullivan Square on the third Thursday of April, May, June, September, October, and November.

Dorchester Open Studios

Dorchester Arts Collaborative
www.dorchesterartists.org
www.dorchesteropenstudios.org

For two days in late October, you can tour artists' studios and visit group shows at locations like the Great Hall in Codman Square.

Fort Point Open Studios

Fort Point Arts Community
www.fortpointarts.org

The artists of Fort Point taught the city of Boston about the transformative power of a strong art and culture community. Previously an industrial backwater, Fort Point has seen a cultural and architectural resurgence, thanks largely to the artists' presence. When developers started moving in, buying the buildings where artists had their studios and tossing them out on their ears, the artists banded together and staked their claim. There are now several designated artist live-work buildings in this neighborhood, which makes the Fort Point Open Studios one of the biggest and best. The event takes place during two weekend days in the fall.

Jamaica Plain Open Studios

Jamaica Plain Arts Council
(617) 524–3816
www.jpopenstudios.com

This two-day weekend event in the fall is coordinated by the Jamaica Plain Arts Council. It includes several juried shows, group shows at centrally located landmarks (like the Unitarian Universalist Church), and artists' studios. Comprehensive studio location maps, a participant list, and information are available on the Web site in early fall.

Roslindale Open Studios

(617) 710–3811

www.roslindaleopenstudios.org

The newest addition to the open-studio scene got off to a great start in 2005, with almost thirty artists showing their work. The event spans two days each fall.

Roxbury Open Studios

Act Roxbury Consortium

(617) 541–3900

www.actroxbury.com

The historic neighborhood of Roxbury is teeming with artists, and the Roxbury Open Studios is the most culturally diverse open-studio program in the city. It lasts two days and is usually held in the fall.

South End Open Studios

United South End Artists

www.useaboston.com

This two-day, weekend event in the fall features tours through the wonderful artist studio complexes that line Washington and Harrison Streets.

SoWa Artists Guild First Fridays

450 Harrison Avenue

www.sowaartistsguild.com

On the first Friday of every month, from 5:00 to 8:30 P.M., there's a party going on at 450 Harrison Avenue, as visitors browse the fifteen galleries and fifty artists' studios packed into this artists' colony building. Free drinks and snacks are often provided for the masses. These evening events are very popular, and growing more so by the month.

{ MUSEUMS: }
CUT-RATE CULTURE

"Clear out 800,000 people and pre-
serve it as a museum piece."
—*Frank Lloyd Wright, about the city of Boston*

A city with as much history as Boston is a bit of a museum in and of itself, as Wright so correctly noted. Our Boston forefathers, Cheap Bastards that they were, never threw out anything, and today our museums are packed with their bequests, whether historic artifacts, masterpiece paintings, or obscure curios. Our history of invention, culture, creativity, and exploration is also well documented in a number of local museums, many of which are free to the public all the time or have free hours. If your tastes run more to the eclectic, we can certainly oblige with the world-famous Museum of Bad Art.

ALWAYS FREE

Alexander Graham Bell Museum Tour
Verizon
185 Franklin Street
(617) 743–5440

Hours: open daily at all hours.

"Mr. Watson, come here." That famous moment is portrayed in a re-creation of the garret that Alexander Graham Bell used as his laboratory when he invented the telephone in Boston in 1875. In addition to the depiction of this seminal moment, the exhibit includes original documents and blueprints chronicling Bell's early work as well as examples of early telephones. The museum is in the lobby of Verizon's headquarters building, which is open twenty-four hours a day, seven days a week, just in case you get a hankering for some history at 3:00 A.M. on a Wednesday.

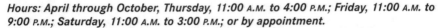

Boston Fire Museum

344 Congress Street (Fort Point)
(617) 482–1344
www.bostonfiremuseum.org

Hours: April through October, Thursday, 11:00 A.M. to 4:00 P.M.; Friday, 11:00 A.M. to 9:00 P.M.; Saturday, 11:00 A.M. to 3:00 P.M.; or by appointment.

This museum memorializes one of the oldest fire departments in the country in a restored firehouse in use since 1891. Exhibits include a hand-operated fire pump that dates to 1793.

Commonwealth Museum

220 Morrissey Boulevard (across from the JFK Museum)
(617) 727–9268
www.sec.state.ma.us/mus/museum/index.htm

Hours: Monday through Friday, 9:00 A.M. to 5:00 P.M.; second and fourth Saturday of the month, 9:00 A.M. to 3:00 P.M.

This museum focuses on the history of the Commonwealth of Massachusetts, from the Puritans to the archaeology of the Central Artery Tunnel Project.

Cyrus Dallin Art Museum

The Jefferson Cutter House
1 Whittemore Park (corner of Massachusetts Avenue, Mystic Street, and Pleasant Street)
Arlington
(781) 641–0747
www.dallin.org

Hours: daily, noon to 4:00 P.M.

Visit a museum dedicated to the work of the man who created the statue of Paul Revere in the North End as well as the beautiful and moving *Appeal to the Great Spirit,* the statue of a Native American atop his horse that stands in front of the Museum of Fine Arts. This museum chronicles the many other works of Cyrus Dallin, including his lifelong efforts to get his Revere statue produced.

Davis Museum and Cultural Center

Wellesley College
106 Central Street
Wellesley
(781) 283–2051
www.davismuseum.wellesley.edu

Hours: Tuesday through Sunday, noon to 4:00 P.M.

THE CATCH

The museum was scheduled to be closed for repairs through the spring of 2007. Call ahead before you visit.

The Davis Museum and Cultural Center was founded in 1889 by the first president of Wellesley College. Today, its collections include examples of the world's fine art, from ancient history through present times. The museum has rotating exhibitions and an active lecture, workshop, and educational program befitting an institution of higher learning.

Longyear Museum

1125 Boylston Street (Route 9)
Chestnut Hill
(617) 278–9000
www.longyear.org

Hours: Monday and Wednesday through Saturday, 10:00 A.M. to 4:00 P.M.; Sunday, 1:00 to 4:00 P.M.

The Longyear Museum is filled with exhibits and resources about the life and achievements of Mary Baker Eddy, founder of the Church of Christ, Scientist, and her early students.

McMullen Museum of Art

Boston College
140 Commonwealth Avenue
Devlin Hall 108
Chestnut Hill
(617) 552–8100
www.bc.edu/bc_org/avp/cas/artmuseum/index.html

Hours: Exhibition dates vary throughout the year. Call for hours. The museum is closed between exhibitions.

This museum features American, Italian, and Flemish paintings by the old masters, as well as three or four exhibits annually that highlight particular artists or themes, often revolving around explorations of religion or religious art.

MIT List Visual Arts Center

20 Ames Street
Cambridge
(617) 253–4680
http://web.mit.edu/lvac

Hours: Tuesday through Thursday, Saturday, and Sunday, noon to 6:00 P.M.; Friday, noon to 8:00 P.M.

The List Visual Arts Center isn't just an art museum with a gallery. It's a collection of dozens of sculptures (by such renowned sculptors as Alexander Calder and Pablo Picasso), paintings, and installations throughout the MIT campus, including students' rooms, classrooms, and professors' and administrators' offices. The museum mounts five to eight exhibits a year in its museum gallery, but the real museum can be found by walking around and looking at all the public art the Institute has amassed since it received its first donation of art from Standard Oil in 1950. That was followed in 1985 by a generous gift from Vera and Albert List that allowed the program to relocate to the first floor of a 1940 I. M. Pei–designed building, where its galleries are today.

MIT Museum's Compton Gallery

MIT Museum
77 Massachusetts Avenue
Building 10, Room 150
Cambridge
(617) 452–2111
http://web.mit.edu/museum/exhibitions/compton.html

Hours: Monday through Friday, 9:30 A.M. to 5:00 P.M.

This is a rotating exhibition space that highlights the work being done by students and professors working at and with MIT's various academic projects. Included is everything from photography, video art, and sketches to the technology itself.

MIT Museum's Hart Nautical Gallery

55 Massachusetts Avenue
Building 5
Cambridge
(617) 253–5942
http://web.mit.edu/museum/exhibitions/hart.html

Hours: daily, 9:00 A.M. to 8:00 P.M.

If you think ship models are cool, this is the place for you. The museum, started in 1922, showcases the work of MIT's Pratt School of Naval Architecture and Marine Engineering, which includes dozens of antique and current model ships.

Museum of Afro-American History

46 Joy Street
(617) 725–0022
www.afroammuseum.org

Hours: Monday through Saturday, 10:00 A.M. to 4:00 P.M.

THE CATCH } Suggested donation is $5.00.

The Museum of Afro-American History is New England's largest museum dedicated to preserving, conserving, and interpreting the contributions of African Americans. The African Meeting House is the oldest African meetinghouse in America, and the adjacent Abiel Smith School is the first building in the nation constructed for the sole purpose of housing a black public school. Today, the Abiel Smith School galleries feature rotating exhibits and a museum store, which is open year-round.

Museum of Bad Art

Basement of Dedham Community Theater
580 High Street
Dedham
(781) 444–6757
www.museumofbadart.org

Hours: Monday through Friday, 2:00 to 10:00 P.M.; Saturday, Sunday, and holidays, 1:00 to 10:00 P.M.

It's so bad, it's good. Since 1995 the Museum of Bad Art has been astounding the art world with its ability to find the absolutely worst art available anywhere. To complete the experience, it is located in the basement of an old building, lit only by the unflattering glow of a large, humming fluorescent light fixture. Their permanent collection includes about 250 pieces, of which two dozen are exhibited at any one time. Which is more than enough.

National Heritage Museum

33 Marrett Road (at the intersection of Route 2A and Massachusetts Avenue)
Lexington
(781) 861–6559
www.nationalheritagemuseum.org

Hours: Monday through Saturday, 10:00 A.M. to 5:00 P.M.; Sunday, noon to 5:00 P.M.

This museum has a selection of exhibits focusing on the history of our nation, with special emphasis on New England. Past exhibits have included a history of the Freemason movement, household items from the past three centuries made in Massachusetts, and, naturally, an exhibit on the Revolutionary War, which had one of its most crucial battles in Lexington/Concord.

GET A FREE PASS

If you have a valid Boston Public Library or Minuteman Library network card (see the Libraries chapter for participating libraries), you can visit the best museums in Boston absolutely free—even when they're charging everyone else.

Both of these library systems make free museum passes available to anyone who asks, but needless to say, they're very hot tickets. You must usually reserve your desired museum pass several weeks before you want to use it. Both library systems will only let you reserve up to four weeks in advance, and you must return the passes either the same day or first thing the next morning. You may book a pass either in person or over the phone. (See Appendix B for a list of branch locations.) The person who reserved the pass must be the person who picks it up. Other rules apply.

Boston Public Library System
The following museum passes are available from all Boston Public Library locations (except the Kirstein Business Branch), with the number of people admitted and the discounted admission fee, if applicable.

> Children's Museum: six people, $2.00
>
> Harvard Museum of Natural History: two people, $1.00
>
> Museum of Fine Arts: two people
>
> Museum of Science: four people
>
> New England Aquarium: four people (September through June)
>
> Wheelock Family Theatre (certain restrictions apply; contact your local branch for information)

The following museum passes are available only at the library location(s) listed.

> DeCordova Museum and Sculpture Park: Copley Square
>
> Harvard Art Museums: Jamaica Plain
>
> Isabella Stewart Gardner Museum: Copley Square, Jamaica Plain, and West Roxbury
>
> Larz Anderson Auto Museum: Jamaica Plain
>
> John F. Kennedy Library and Museum: Jamaica Plain
>
> Zoo New England: Connolly, Dudley, Faneuil, Orient Heights, Roslindale, and West Roxbury

Each of these branch locations has one pass per day, per museum. All passes must be reserved by an adult with a valid library card. Children must be accompanied by an adult.

Cambridge Public Library System

*If you hold a valid Minuteman Library Network card (for a list of partici-
pating libraries, see the Libraries chapter), you can reserve passes for
museums by calling the Cambridge Public Library (617-349-4044) or one
of its branches. A full list of branch locations and phone numbers is available at www.ci.cambridge.ma.us/%7ECPL/hours/libhours.html. You can
reserve passes up to a month in advance. Here's a list of museum passes
available, the number of people the pass will admit, and the discounted
admission price, if applicable.*

> Children's Museum: four people, $2.00
>
> Harvard Art Museum and Harvard Natural History Museum: free
> to all Cambridge Library cardholders; just present card
>
> Isabella Stewart Gardner Museum: four people (Monday through
> Friday) or two people (Saturday and Sunday), $2.00
>
> MIT Museums: four people
>
> Museum of Fine Art: two people, $5.00
>
> Museum of Science: four people
>
> Peabody Essex Museum: two people
>
> Rose Art Museum at Brandeis University: one person (four avail-
> able per cardholder)
>
> Stone and Franklin Park Zoos: two adults, four children
>
> Wheelock Family Theatre: one person (Friday and Saturday per-
> formances)

Perkins School for the Blind History Museum
Main Hall, Howe Building
175 North Beacon Street
Watertown
(617) 924–3434 (school number)
(617) 972–7767 (museum)
www.perkins.org/museum

*Hours: Tuesday and Thursday, 2:00 to 4:00 P.M., September through July; in August call
ahead for appointment.*

For 200 years, the Perkins School for the Blind has been educating blind and
deaf/blind students to the highest levels of academic excellence. The museum
charts the school's history, the history of educating the vision impaired, and the
stories of the people who founded the school, Samuel Gridley Howe and his wife,
Julia Ward Howe, as well as the famous personalities who have been involved with
the school throughout its history. Interactive tactile, visual, and auditory exhibits
are accessible for blind and sighted visitors.

USS *Constitution* Museum
Charlestown Navy Yard
Charlestown
(617) 242–7511
www.ussconstitutionmuseum.org

Hours: daily, May 1 through October 15, 9:00 A.M. to 6:00 P.M.; October 16 through April 30, 10:00 A.M. to 5:00 P.M.

The USS *Constitution,* launched in 1797 and nicknamed "Old Ironsides" after the cannonballs of an attacking warship merely bounced off her triple-thick hardwood sides, is the oldest commissioned warship in the U.S. Navy. This interactive museum tracks the ship's history and the history of its military engagements and offers kid-focused learning exhibits about what life was like for sailors during the ship's heyday.

SOMETIMES FREE

Arthur M. Sackler Museum
485 Broadway
Cambridge
(617) 459–9400
www.artmuseums.harvard.edu

Hours: Monday through Saturday, 10:00 A.M. to 5:00 P.M.; Sunday, 1:00 to 5:00 P.M.

When free: Saturday until noon. Cambridge Public Library cardholders are always admitted free.

The Sackler Museum houses a world-renowned collection of ancient Islamic, Asian, and later Indian art. Its curators boast of having the world's finest collections of archaic Chinese jades, as well as outstanding Chinese bronzes, ceremonial ancient weapons, and Buddhist cave-temple sculpture. The museum also has a collection of ancient Greek, Roman, and other Far East artifacts. The Sackler was named for doctor, businessman, and philanthropist Arthur Sackler, who had a life-long love of the art of Asian cultures. The Sackler's Asian collections were originally housed in the Fogg Museum at Harvard.

MERRY MONTH OF MAY

May is Museum Month in Boston (and in many other cities as well). Sponsored by Bank of America, Museum Month means that most of the major museums in the city are free for you and a guest if you have a Bank of America bankcard or credit card or an MBNA credit card. All you have to do is show your card, and you and a guest are in. For a full listing of participating museums, check out the Web site, www.bankofamericapromotions.com/museums.

DeCordova Museum and Sculpture Park

51 Sandy Pond Road
Lincoln
(781) 259–8355
www.decordova.org

Hours: Tuesday through Sunday, 11:00 A.M. to 5:00 P.M.

When free: The sculpture park is free when the gallery is closed. The gallery is free to Lincoln residents, as well as active-duty military personnel and their dependents.

The DeCordova Museum is in the former home of Julian de Cordova, a self-educated son of a Jamaican merchant, and a prominent local merchant himself. He deeded his home to the town of Lincoln and stipulated that it should be used as a museum after his death. The museum houses contemporary art and sculpture by living artists and focuses much of its efforts on educational workshops and programs.

Fogg Art Museum/Busch-Reisinger Museum

32 Quincy Street
Cambridge
(617) 495–9400
www.artmuseums.harvard.edu

Hours: Monday through Saturday, 10:00 A.M. to 5:00 P.M.; Sunday, 1:00 to 5:00 P.M.

When free: Saturday until noon. Cambridge Public Library cardholders are always admitted free.

The Fogg Art Museum opened to the public in 1895. It's Harvard's oldest art museum, and its collections track the history of Western art from the Middle Ages to the present. It is noted for its Renaissance, British pre-Raphaelite, and nineteenth-century French art. On the second floor, you'll find the Wertheim Collection, noted for its Impressionist and post-Impressionist works. The Busch-Reisinger is accessible from the second floor of the Fogg Museum and is the only museum in North America devoted to the arts of northern and central Europe, especially German-speaking countries.

Harvard Museum of Natural History
26 Oxford Street
Cambridge
(617) 495–3045
www.hmnh.harvard.edu

Peabody Museum of Archaeology and Ethnology
11 Divinity Avenue
Cambridge
(617) 496–1027
www.peabody.harvard.edu

Hours (both): daily, 9:00 A.M. to 5:00 P.M.

When free: For Massachusetts residents, Sunday until noon year-round; Wednesday, 3:00 to 5:00 P.M., September through May.

The Harvard Museum of Natural History (HMNH), the public museum of Harvard University's three natural history academic institutions, explores the theory of evolution through its exhibits and specimens. Founded in 1866, the Peabody Museum is one of the oldest museums in the world devoted to anthropology and houses one of the most comprehensive records of human cultural history in the Western Hemisphere. The two museums are connected, and one admission gets you into both.

Institute of Contemporary Art
100 Northern Avenue
(617) 478–3100
www.icaboston.org

Hours: Tuesday, Wednesday, and Friday, noon to 5:00 P.M.; Thursday, noon to 9:00 P.M.; Saturday and Sunday, 11:00 A.M. to 5:00 P.M.

When free: Thursday after 5:00 P.M.

The ICA is the first art museum to be built in Boston in nearly a hundred years. The 65,000-square-foot building, featuring a cantilever that extends the building out over the waters of Boston Harbor, is already a Boston landmark. The museum explores contemporary art in all media, including performance and video. The new museum's focus is on making contemporary art inclusive through education, workshops, and interactive activities.

Isabella Stewart Gardner Museum
280 The Fenway
(617) 566–1401
www.gardnermuseum.org

Hours: Tuesday through Sunday, 11:00 A.M. to 5:00 P.M.

When free: If your name is Isabella or you're under eighteen.

Since 1903 the grande dame of Boston arts, Isabella Stewart Gardner, has been shocking, delighting, and astounding visitors with her unique and vast collection of art from around the world. The museum is her former home, and though she is no longer there (she died in 1924), the art remains in much the same locations and conditions as it was when she was alive. The courtyard garden in the center of the building is one of the most beautiful and serene places in the entire city of Boston.

MIT Museum

265 Massachusetts Avenue
Cambridge
(617) 253–4444
http://web.mit.edu/museum

Hours: Tuesday through Friday, 10:00 A.M. to 5:00 P.M.; Saturday and Sunday, noon to 5:00 P.M.

When free: third Sunday of each month.

Home to renowned collections in science and technology, holography, architecture, and design, the MIT Museum makes science personal, accessible, and intriguing with constantly rotating exhibits. Go for the futuristic robot exhibit; stay for the cool photography of Harold Edgerton (whose famous high-speed photos of bullets going through various things never ceases to mesmerize).

Museum of Fine Arts

465 Huntington Avenue
(617) 267–9300
www.mfa.org

Hours: Wednesday through Friday, 10:00 A.M. to 9:45 P.M.; Saturday through Tuesday, 10:00 A.M. to 4:45 P.M.

When free: Wednesday after 4:00 P.M.; free for children age seven to seventeen on weekdays after 3:00 P.M., weekends, and public school holidays.

This is the granddaddy of local museums, with a mammoth collection of nearly every form of art from nearly every century and country in which art was ever created. Leave at least four hours to begin to scratch the surface of this local cultural jewel.

EXTREMELY CHEAP

With many of our local museums charging $8.00 to $15.00 to get in during peak hours, these museums offer a welcome price break, especially for families. Some are cheap all the time, and others offer steeply discounted admission hours.

Blue Hills Trailside Museum

1904 Canton Avenue
Milton
(617) 333–0690
www.massaudbon.org/Nature_Connection/Sanctuaries/Blue_Hills/index.php

Hours (museum): Wednesday through Sunday, 10:00 A.M. to 5:00 P.M.

Hours (museum grounds): daily, 9:00 A.M. to 5:00 P.M.

Admission: adults, $3.00; children ages three to fifteen, $1.50.

Blue Hills trails are free and are open daily, dawn to dusk.

THE CATCH · No pets are allowed on the museum grounds. } The Blue Hills Trailside Museum is the interpretive center for the state's 7,000-acre Blue Hills Reservation and is managed by the Massachuetts Audubon Society. Indoor exhibits include displays featuring native wildlife such as wild turkeys, red-tailed hawks, and a snowy owl. Weekend programs on Saturday and Sunday, which are free with museum admission, include naturalist presentations about local wildlife, guided hikes, and other educational lectures.

Boston Children's Museum
300 Congress Street
(617) 426–8855
www.bostonkids.org

Hours: daily, 10:00 A.M. to 5:00 P.M.; Friday, 10:00 A.M. to 9:00 P.M.

Discount hours: $1.00 per person on Friday from 4:00 to 9:00 P.M.

For over ninety years, this museum has featured interactive, educational exhibits that keep kids occupied and enthralled. It includes such exhibits as Black Boston, celebrating Boston's diversity; the science workshop; a turtle-viewing area; and historical toys. There are ongoing special events, and everything at this award-winning museum is hands-on.

Charles River Museum of Industry
154 Moody Street
Waltham
(781) 893–5410
www.crmi.org

Hours: Thursday through Saturday, 10:00 A.M. to 5:00 P.M.

Admission: adults, $5.00; seniors and students, $3.00; children under six, free.

Located in the 1814 Boston Manufacturing Company textile mill, on the National Register of Historic Places as America's first factory, this museum explores the evolution of industrial science. The museum has interactive exhibits and antique examples of industrial inventions, including steam engines, generators, timepieces, machine tools, bicycles, automobiles, and more, as well as detailed histories of the men and women who dreamed it all up.

Larz Anderson Auto Museum
Museum of Transportation
15 Newton Street
Brookline
(617) 522–6547
www.mot.org

Hours: Tuesday through Sunday, 10:00 A.M. to 5:00 P.M.

Admission: adults, $5.00; seniors, students, and children under eighteen and over six, $3.00; children under six, free.

America's oldest collection of automobiles can be found at the Museum of Transportation, which, through its many exhibits, tracks the development of the automobile and related technology, as well as the societal changes that took place during the car's rapid rise.

Museum of the National Center for Afro-American Artists
300 Walnut Avenue
(617) 442–8614
www.ncaaa.org

Hours: Tuesday through Sunday, 1:00 to 5:00 P.M.

Admission: adults, $4.00; seniors and students, $3.00.

The museum is the public face of the National Center for Afro-American Artists, founded by renowned local arts patron Elma Lewis. The museum is dedicated to the exhibition, collection, and criticism of the black visual arts heritage world-wide. From explorations of historical works to contemporary art, the museum's galleries are filled with paintings, sculpture, graphics, photography, and decorative arts that bring the black American experience into vivid perspective.

Rose Art Museum
Brandeis University
415 South Street
Waltham
(781) 736–3434
www.brandeis.edu/rose

Hours: Tuesday through Sunday, noon to 5:00 P.M.

Admission: $3.00.

Founded in 1961, the Rose is an educational and cultural component of Brandeis University. The museum hosts temporary exhibitions and displays throughout the year that present a range of modern art, emerging artists, and displays of the Brandeis University art collections. It is considered to have one of the top academic collections of contemporary art in the country.

{ZOOS:}
FREE RANGE

"My parents used to take me
to the pet department and
tell me it was a zoo."

—*Billy Connolly*

There aren't any completely free zoo options in the greater Boston area, but our two biggest, best (and only) zoos do offer some pretty nice discounts. The New England Aquarium, one of the most popular tourist destinations in the city, doesn't offer any free or reduced-price admission opportunities, so if your kids are really hankering to see some fish, take them to a local lobster pound on Commercial Street along the waterfront or stop by any number of the restaurants in Chinatown where that night's special entree can be seen swimming around in the tanks by the front door.

Franklin Park Zoo

1 Franklin Park Road, Dorchester
(617) 541–5466
www.zoonewengland.com

THE CATCH: Admission is $9.50 for adults and $5.50 for kids ages two to twelve. Tickets are half off on the first Saturday of each month if you enter between 10:00 A.M. and noon.

Gorillas, giraffes, lions, tigers, and butterflies all peacefully coexist at the Franklin Park Zoo. The Tropical Forest is home to baby gorillas, pygmy hippopotamus, and free-flight birds. The Butterfly Landing is like walking into a fluttering dream—in the enclosed tent over 1,000 butterflies live and fly freely. The Serengeti Crossing area is a multi-acre replica of the African plains, complete with ibex, wildebeest, zebra, and ostrich. You can't leave without visiting the Kalahari Kingdom, home to lions, giraffe, and other African wildlife.

Stone Zoo

149 Pond Street, Stoneham
(781) 438–5100
www.zoonewengland.org

THE CATCH: Admission is $7.50 for adults and $4.50 for children ages two to twelve, but you can get half-price admission on the first Saturday of each month if you enter before noon.

The twenty-six-acre Stone Zoo is ten minutes north of Boston, and worth the trip. The zoo hosts colobus monkeys, Canadian lynx, snow leopards, Mexican gray wolves, flamingos, arctic fox, spider monkeys, capybaras, and more. The Treasures of the Sierra Madre exhibit features jaguars, cougars, coyotes, and Gila monsters. At Windows to the Wild, view hyacinth macaws, African crested porcupines, emperor tamarins, Geoldi's monkeys, and silvery-cheeked hornbills. Parking at the zoo is free.

{GARDENS}
AND GARDENING:
BOSTON GARDEN

"The garden is the poor man's apothecary."

—*German proverb*

As the home of world-renowned landscape architect Frederick Law Olmsted, Boston has a rich history of shaping wild nature to suit its whim. From the first public garden in the country to the last remaining World War II Victory Garden, our city is a flower lover's paradise. You can even get in on the horticulture act and grow it yourself in one of the many community gardens that have sprung up in vacant lots throughout every neighborhood of Boston. There are even free gardening classes to get you started. Who knows, with some hard work you may just earn the title "Cheap Botanist."

PUBLIC GARDENS

Adams National Historic Site
135 Adams Street
Quincy
(617) 770–1175
www.nps.gov/adam/index.htm

Hours: mid-April through mid-November, 9:00 A.M. to 5:00 P.M.

Five generations of the Adams family lived in the two historic homes at this location. The "Old House" is surrounded by a formal English garden, which is free to visit. There is a $5.00 admission charge to tour the homes.

The Emerald Necklace

The Emerald Necklace (described in more detail in the Fitness, Fun, and Games chapter under Parks) is a connected series of parks and gardens that were built around the perimeter of the city of Boston, creating a virtual "necklace" of green space. The brainchild of Frederick Law Olmsted, it was completed in 1896 and has grown into one of the most treasured natural resources that the city of Boston possesses. I've highlighted three parks that are particularly noted for their beautiful gardens (and free cost).

Arnold Arboretum

125 Arborway
Jamaica Plain
(617) 524–1718
www.arboretum.harvard.edu
www.emeraldnecklace.org/arboretu.htm

Hours: open year-round from sunrise to sunset.

The Arnold Arboretum has been providing Bostonians an oasis from the city since it was bequeathed to Harvard University in 1872. Today, it is the home to thousands of species of flowering plants, shrubs, and trees and is home to one of the most impressive Bonsai collections in New England. Each Mother's Day, the park hosts its Lilac Festival, which draws thousands (it's also the only day when picnicking is allowed in the park). Trails, both paved and gravel, wind throughout the park, bringing visitors around its many ponds and streams, and into stands of pines, rhododendrons, roses, and other collections for which the Arboretum is renowned. The Hunnewell Building houses the Arboretum's permanent collection, library, and archives. Restrooms are available here as well.

Back Bay Fens

From the Boylston Street overpass at Charlesgate to the Longwood Medical area
www.emeraldnecklace.org/fenway.htm

The Fens was once a foul-smelling tidal creek, until Olmsted's plans reshaped the lands surrounding the Muddy River, which became a freshwater creek after the Charles River was dammed in 1910. The Fens is now home to parks, meandering trails through stands of willows and other deciduous trees, and gorgeous gardens, including the oldest remaining World War II Victory Garden in the United States. (Plots cost $20. Information is available at www.fenwayvictory gardens.com.) The Fens has several war memorials, ball fields, and the Kelleher Rose Garden, which contains over 200 varieties of roses in a magnificently tended and landscaped display. This area is best avoided at night due to crime.

Boston Public Garden
Located between Arlington, Beacon, Charles, and Boylston Streets
www.friendsofthepublicgarden.org

The Public Garden was the first botanical garden in the United States. Here, Swan Boats glide across a twenty-four-acre lagoon, and the meticulously tended rose gardens spring to life each spring. Gardeners plant an ever-changing rotation of seasonal flowering plants. It's a popular spot for wedding photos, reading, picnicking, or just relaxing on a bench under a mammoth weeping willow.

Gore Place
52 Gore Street
Waltham
(781) 894–2798
www.goreplace.org

Hours: year-round, dawn to dusk.

This former summer home of the seventh governor of Massachusetts, Christopher Gore, hosts acres of gardens and lawns fashioned largely on traditional European landscaping ideals (instead of the fastidious and abundant English gardens that were the rage at the time). The elegantly furnished mansion has been called "the Monticello of the North," and architectural historians consider it to be the most significant Federal-period mansion in New England. It costs a lot to tour the mansion, but nothing to wander the glorious open grounds.

Harvard University Botanical Museum Glass Flower Display
26 Oxford Street
Cambridge
(617) 495–3045
www.hmnh.harvard.edu/exhibitions/glassflowers.html

Free on Wednesday from 3:00 to 5:00 P.M. September through May and every Sunday morning (year-round) from 9:00 A.M. to noon.

Starting in 1886 and continuing for more than fifty years, Leopold Blaschka and his son, Rudolph, worked to create this magnificent display of glass flowers. Today, the museum displays their 3,000 works of art representing 830 plant species. When it's cold and snowy outside, this museum is like walking through a permanent spring (without the allergies!).

Lyman Estate Greenhouses

185 Lyman Street
Waltham
(781) 891–1985
www.spnea.org/visit/homes/lyman_estate_greenhouses.htm

Hours: Monday through Saturday, 9:30 A.M. to 4:00 P.M.

THE CATCH } Admission to the greenhouses is by suggested donation of $6.00.

This thirty-seven-acre country estate was designed in the late 1790s following traditional English style, and the three large greenhouses were constructed in 1804 to house exotic and hard-to-find fruits to feed the Lyman family. Today, the greenhouses are filled with a collection of heirloom fruits and plants: The Grape House contains exotic fruit trees, the Camellia House is filled with many types of this flowering shrub, and a world-renowned orchid collection graces another greenhouse. The Lyman Estate also hosts frequent plant sales.

CEMETERIES: GARDENS OF STONE

Until recent decades, cemeteries in Boston served as public gardens and social gathering places—peaceful spots to take a long walk, host a family picnic, or read a book on a blanket. Although that might seem a little creepy today, one trip to these two historic garden cemeteries is guaranteed to change your mind.

Forest Hills Cemetery

95 Forest Hills Avenue
(617) 524–0128
www.foresthillscemetery.com
www.foresthillstrust.org

Hours: open daily, dawn to dusk.

Listed on the National Register of Historic Places, the Forest Hills Cemetery was designed and built in 1848 on 250 acres in the heart of the city, near the Arnold Arboretum and Franklin Park. Forest Hills is particularly renowned not only for its gardens and the famous people buried there (including William Lloyd Garrison and Eugene O'Neill) but also for its sculpture. The Forest Hills Educational Trust hosts juried exhibitions of sculpture here frequently, and guided tours of the art and history of the cemetery take place during the last Sunday of every month at 2:00 P.M.

Mount Auburn Cemetery

580 Mt. Auburn Street
Cambridge
(617) 547–7105
www.mountauburn.org

Based on Père Lachaise Cemetery in Paris, Mount Auburn Cemetery was laid out in 1831 by a group of amateur landscape architects who were part of the Massachusetts Horticultural Society, and today it is a designated National Historic Landmark. Their work includes an impressive collection of over 5,000 trees spread throughout the cemetery's 175 acres of hills, dells, ponds, woodlands, and clearings. The landscape styles include Victorian-era plantings, contemporary gardens, natural woodlands, and formal ornamental gardens. There are hundreds of ornamental sculptures and historic chapels, bridges, and lookouts throughout Mount Auburn, not to mention its famous Boston "residents": members of the Cabot and Lowell families, Julia Ward Howe, Mary Baker Eddy (founder of the Church of Christ, Scientist), Oliver Wendell Holmes, artist Winslow Homer, and many more. Friends of the Mount Auburn Cemetery host frequent tours on various aspects of the cemetery's history, art, architecture, and horticulture. Information on upcoming events is available on the Mount Auburn Web site.

COMMUNITY GARDENS

Boston Natural Areas Network

62 Summer Street
(617) 542–7696
www.bostonnatural.org

There are more than 250 community gardens in neighborhoods throughout Boston. They are collective gardens containing smaller plots that are each "owned" and lovingly tended by those with the gardening bug, but not enough space in their own backyard to plant a proper garden. Each little garden oasis in the city is administered by its own nonprofit organization, but the Boston Natural Areas Network oversees the entire collection of gardening groups and helps organize and advertise plot openings. Many of the garden groups charge a small plot fee (averaging around $20 a year), and some have a sliding scale depending on income. Not only are the community gardens a great way to exercise your green thumb, but they're also a great social connection and a wonderful place to learn tips and tricks from more experienced gardeners. The BNAN presents musical concerts at several of the gardens in the summer months. For a complete calendar of events, visit their Web site.

GARDENING EDUCATION

Boston Natural Areas Network
62 Summer Street
(617) 542–7696
www.bostonnatural.org

The BNAN hosts a number of free gardening education workshops throughout the year, including a master gardeners' class. The class is free, but educational materials cost an additional $35. The BNAN also holds workshops on how to start, fund, and administer your own community garden.

APPENDIX A:

ROMANCE: CHEAP DATES

"I've been asked to say a couple of words about my husband, Fang. How about short and cheap?"

—Phyllis Diller

The eternal debate rages on—who should pay for the first date, the man or the woman? I've got the answer: neither. Here are some ideas for avoiding the whole problem by simply going on dates that don't cost a penny. The best part is that you won't have to worry that your date will think you're Cheap (even though you are). These dates will be so much fun that he or she probably won't even notice that no money changed hands. The dating strategy behind these dates is twofold. First, they're free or cheap—an end unto itself. Second, if the object of your affection seems unimpressed by your frugality at the end of the date, at least you avoided spending gobs of cash trying to impress someone who clearly wasn't right for you. Your true soulmate will simply adore your financial creativity.

The "It Must Be Magic" Date: Nothing sets the mood faster than having someone pull a $20 out from behind your ear. The sense of mystery can't help but infuse the rest of the evening. So head to the Hong Kong on Massachusetts Avenue in Harvard Square on Tuesday night and watch the close-up magic show from 7:00 to 8:00 P.M. in the lounge on the second floor. Who knows what will get pulled out next? For more ideas, check out the Comedy chapter.

The "Hold Me Closer, Tiny Dancer" Date: What is hotter than watching two people dance the dance of love, the tango? Pretty much nothing. Find your way to the Tango by Moonlight event on the Weeks Pedestrian Bridge near Harvard Square at 7:30 P.M. on a full-moon night during the summer, and prepare for one helluva show. If you're brave, go early and take a quick dance lesson. If that doesn't help you two kids to get to know each other fast, I don't know what will. In the winter months, you can keep warm and hang onto your beloved at the same time at the MIT Lindy Hop Society Dance at the MIT Student Center on Wednesday nights. For more information on both, see the Dance chapter.

The "Sunset, Celluloid, and Thou" Date: It's a variation on a tried-and-true winner of a date, but it won't cost you a cent. On any Friday night, pack a picnic and go to Rowes Wharf by the Boston Harbor Hotel, where you can see a classic movie for free, just as the glow from the sunset fades away over the harbor. If the breeze is a little too brisk, check out a film at the Rabb Lecture Hall at the Boston Public Library in Copley Square. One is shown there almost any night of the week, and they're often documentaries or foreign films that don't play in regular cinemas—thus making you appear even more cultured and intelligent than perhaps you really are. For more ideas on ways to get your honey into the dark, see the Film chapter.

The "Phat Cats and Kittens" Date: If your beloved has even hinted that he or she likes music, you simply must go to Wally's, the oldest and best jazz club in the city. The vibe is laid-back, the clientele is diverse, the admission is free, and you will look like a swingin', in-the-know, music aficionado. You'll get major bonus points if a famous music celebrity shows up unannounced and takes the stage with the band—it happens all the time. Your date will talk about this night throughout all the years of your happy, cheap courtship. For more info on ways to impress your little music lover, see the Music chapter.

The "Thinking Man's" Date: If you're afraid you won't have anything to talk about with your date, let someone else do the talking for you. Mix it up with some of the city's famous literati at the Four Stories Reading Series at the Enormous Room on the first Monday of every month in the winter. You and your date will mix and mingle with some of the biggest names in literature, who will read from their work that night. When they're not reading, you can lounge on big comfy couches and listen to the funky song stylings of the guest deejay. Before you know it, you'll have plenty to talk about. When Four Stories is on hiatus in the summer months, check out a rousing political debate at one of the Ford Hall Forum's lecture series, held at venues around the city. Make sure to take a long walk after the lecture so that you can fully explore each other's feelings . . . about the debate, of course. For more ideas on ways to liven up the conversation, see the Readings and Lectures chapter.

The "Night of a Thousand Flavors" Date: Dating a foodie? Head over to Faneuil Hall Marketplace on the first Wednesday evening of every month for A Taste of Quincy Market. Every food store in the cavernous marketplace puts out free samples for you to taste. If you can make it through even half of the samples available, there will be absolutely no reason to think about going out for dinner. You can go straight to the after-dinner festivities . . . whatever those may be. For more free meals, happy hours, and samples, check out the Food chapter.

The "Loaf of Bread, Jug of Wine" Date: Is there anything more romantic than sharing a fine wine with the object of your affection? Yup—sharing fine free wine with the object of your affection. The Wine Gallery in Kenmore Square will let you sample a variety of high-end wines from its "Wine Jukebox," an automatic wine-sample dispenser that's almost as much fun as the wine itself. It's also a great way to find out if your date is drawn more to the very high-end wines on offer (in which case you might want to reconsider the whole date) or the good but inexpensive offerings (grab hold and don't let go!). The Wine and Beer Tastings chapter lists plenty more wine-tasting opportunities throughout the city.

The "Likes Long Walks on the Beach" Date: Castle Island is a perfect place to take that long walk on the beach that people are always talking about in their personal ads. The island, which isn't really an island anymore, is surrounded by a smooth walkway that connects with the walkway along the beaches of South Boston. You could literally walk for hours around Dorchester Bay and finish up on the sloping grassy hills next to Fort Independence. If the wind is right, you can lie on your backs and watch the airplanes land at Logan Airport across Boston Harbor. Imagine where the planes are coming from. Imagine where you two crazy kids are headed. . . . See the Fitness, Fun, and Games chapter for more on Boston's beaches and parks.

APPENDIX B:
PUBLIC LIBRARY AND
BRANCH LOCATIONS

ARLINGTON PUBLIC LIBRARY
www.robbinslibrary.org/index.htm

Robbins Library, 700 Massachusetts Avenue; (781) 316-3200; Children's Library, (781) 316-3234

Fox Branch, 175 Massachusetts Avenue (on the corner of Cleveland Street); (781) 316-3198

BOSTON PUBLIC LIBRARY
ww.bpl.org

ALLSTON/BRIGHTON

Brighton Branch Library, 40 Academy Hill Road; (617) 782-6032

Faneuil Branch Library, 419 Faneuil Street; (617) 782-6705

Honan-Allston Branch Library, 300 North Harvard Street; (617) 787-6313

CHARLESTOWN

Charlestown Branch Library, 179 Main Street; (617) 242-1248

DORCHESTER

Adams Street Branch Library, 690 Adams Street; (617) 436-6900

Codman Square Branch Library, 690 Washington Street; (617) 436-8214

Fields Corner Branch Library, 1520 Dorchester Avenue; (617) 436-2155

Lower Mills Branch Library, 27 Richmond Street; (617) 298-7841

Uphams Corner Branch Library, 500 Columbia Road; (617) 265-0139

EAST BOSTON

East Boston Branch Library, 276 Meridian Street; (617) 569-0271

Orient Heights Branch Library, 18 Barnes Avenue; (617) 567-2516

HYDE PARK

Hyde Park Branch Library, 35 Harvard Avenue; (617) 361-2524

JAMAICA PLAIN

Connolly Branch Library, 433 Centre Street; (617) 522-1960

Jamaica Plain Branch Library, 12 Sedgwick Street; (617) 524-2053

MATTAPAN

Mattapan Branch Library, 10 Hazelton Street; (617) 298-9218

NORTH END

North End Branch Library, 25 Parmenter Street; (617) 227-8135

ROSLINDALE

Roslindale Branch Library, 4238 Washington Street; (617) 323-2343

ROXBURY

Dudley Branch Library, 65 Warren Street; (617) 442-6186

Egleston Square Branch Library, 2044 Columbus Avenue; (617) 445-4340

SOUTH BOSTON

South Boston Branch Library, 646 East Broadway; (617) 268-0180

Washington Village Branch, 1226 Columbia Road; (617) 269-7239

SOUTH END

South End Branch Library, 685 Tremont Street; (617) 536-8241

WEST ROXBURY

West Roxbury Branch, 1961 Centre Street; (617) 325-3147

BROOKLINE PUBLIC LIBRARY
www.town.brookline.ma.us/library

Main Branch, 361 Washington Street; (617) 730-2370

Coolidge Corner Branch, 31 Pleasant Street; (617) 730-2380

Putterham Branch, 959 West Roxbury Parkway; (617) 730-2385

CAMBRIDGE PUBLIC LIBRARY
www.ci.cambridge.ma.us/~cpl

Main Branch, 359 Broadway; (617) 349-4040

Boudreau Branch, 245 Concord Avenue; (617) 349-4017

Central Square Branch, 45 Pearl Street; (617) 349-4020

Collins Branch, 64 Aberdeen Avenue; (617) 349-4021

O'Connell Branch, 48 Sixth Street; (617) 349-4019

O'Neill Branch, 70 Rindge Avenue; (617) 349-4023

Valente Branch, 826 Cambridge Street; (617) 349-4015

EVERETT PUBLIC LIBRARY
www.noblenet.org/everett

Parlin Memorial Library, 410 Broadway; (617) 394-2300

Shute Memorial Library, 781 Broadway; (617) 394-2308

MILTON PUBLIC LIBRARY
www.miltonlibrary.org

Main Branch, 476 Canton Avenue; (617) 698-5757

East Milton Branch, 334 Edgehill Road; (617) 698-1733

NEEDHAM FREE PUBLIC LIBRARY
www.town.needham.ma.us/library

1139 Highland Avenue; (781) 455-7559

NEWTON FREE LIBRARY
www.ci.newton.ma.us/library/default.asp

Main Branch, 330 Homer Street; (617) 796-1360

Auburndale Branch, 375 Auburn Street; (617) 552-7158

Newton Corner Branch, 126 Vernon Street; (617) 552-7157

Nonantum Branch, 144 Bridge Street; (617) 552-7163

Waban Branch, 1608 Beacon Street; (617) 552-7166

SOMERVILLE PUBLIC LIBRARY
www.somervillepubliclibrary.org

Main Library, 79 Highland Avenue; (617) 623-5000

East Branch, 115 Broadway; (617) 623-5000, ext. 2970

West Branch, 40 College Avenue (Davis Square); (617) 623-5000, ext. 2975

THOMAS CRANE PUBLIC LIBRARY (QUINCY)
www.thomascranelibrary.org

Main Library, 40 Washington Street; (617) 376-1300

Adams Shore Branch, 519 Sea Street; (617) 376-1325 (adult), (617) 376-1326 (children)

North Quincy Branch, 381 Hancock Street; (617) 376-1320 (adult), (617) 376-1321 (children)

Wollaston Branch, 41 Beale Street; (617) 376-1330

APPENDIX C:
BOSTON COMMUNITY
CENTER LOCATIONS

Some of these community centers are run by independent community organizations, others by the Boston Centers for Youth & Families. Hours, membership fees, and programming change frequently. Most charge less than $50 for an annual family membership. Call ahead for details.

ALLSTON/BRIGHTON

Jackson/Mann Community Center
500 Cambridge Street
(617) 635–5153

After-school programs, child care, basketball, volleyball, ceramics, gym, karate, volunteer program, recreation activities, special-needs program (Camp Joy), summer program, streetworkers, GED, ABE and ESL, girls' programs, Boston Youth Connection Program.

CHARLESTOWN

Charlestown Community Center
255 Medford Street
(617) 635–5169

Basketball, volleyball, swimming, field trips, volunteer programs, recreation activities, gym, pool, Tiny Tots program, child care, Youth Connection Program, special-needs program (Camp Joy), summer day program, girls' programs, summer pool program.

Clougherty Pool (run by Charlestown Community Centers)
Bunker Hill Street at Doherty Playground
(617) 635–5173

Outdoor pool open during the summer months.

Kent Community Center
50 Bunker Hill Street
(617) 635–5177

Preschool child care, tutoring, recreation activities, child care programs.

CHINATOWN

Boston Chinatown Neighborhood Community Center
885 Washington Street
(617) 635–5129

Child care, tutoring and enrichment programs, after-school programs, summer programs, full recreation program, pool.

DORCHESTER

Cleveland Community Center
11 Charles Street
(617) 635–5141

Tutoring program, basketball, recreation activities, gym, Youth Connection Program, day camp, Youth Challenge Program.

Holland Community Center (closed for repairs at press time)
85 Olney Street
(617) 635–5144

Basketball, volleyball, swimming, karate, softball, weightlifting, exercise class, recreation activities, gym, pool, after-school tutoring, Boston Youth Connection Program, girls' program, summer day program, volunteer and mentoring programs, special events.

Marshall Community Center
35 Westville Street
(617) 635–5148

School-age after-school program, preschool program, recreation activities, Youth Connection Program, swimming lessons and programs, summer day program, summer pool program.

Murphy Community Center
1 Worrell Street
(617) 635–5150

Child care, tennis, volleyball, basketball, swimming, ceramics, quilting, crafts, computers, volunteer program, recreation activities, gym, pool, nursery school program, special-needs program (Camp Joy), tutoring, baseball clinics, summer day program, summer pool program.

Perkins Community Center
155 Talbot Avenue
(617) 635–5146

Basketball, volleyball, swimming, karate, softball, weightlifting, exercise classes, tutoring, arts, theater, plays/shows, volunteer and mentoring programs, recreation activities, gym, pool, girls' programs, after-school child care, school reentry program, after-school tutoring, special-needs program (Camp Joy), adult education, bike program, weekend camping (summer only), summer day program, summer pool program.

EAST BOSTON

Harborside Community Center
312 Border Street
(617) 635–5114

Street hockey, soccer, swimming, swim team, gym, Kid's Club, Saturday Fallout program, baton twirling, Teen Center, special-needs program (Camp Joy), after-school tutoring, Youth Connection Program, volunteer programs, dances, business skills program, ESL, GED and CASA testing, outdoor skate park, summer pool program, summer day program.

Orient Heights Community Center
86 Boardman Street
(617) 635–5120

Senior citizen drop-in, reading program, many recreational leagues and programs including wheelchair basketball, teen trip night, arts and crafts, movie night, special events and more, summer day program.

Paris Street Community Center
112 Paris Street
(617) 635–5125

Weightlifting, karate, basketball, aerobics, track, arts and crafts, volunteer program, girls' program, senior citizen bingo, Boston Youth Connection Program, drama hour, racquetball, cardiovascular room, cake decorating, summer day program.

Paris Street Pool
113 Paris Street
(617) 635–5122

Swimming, swim classes for ages three through adult, aquasize classes, lifeguard certification, swim team, summer pool program.

HYDE PARK

Hyde Park Community Center
1179 River Street
(617) 635–5178

Line dance and evening ceramics for adults, choral group, computer lessons, ESOL, GED, after-school tutoring, Saturday art and tutoring classes, gymnastics, various athletic leagues and activities, volunteer and mentoring programs, Boston Youth Connection Program, chess club, Double Dutch Jump Rope Club, girls' dance step club, teen explorer club, special events, summer day program.

JAMAICA PLAIN

Agassiz Community Center
20 Child Street
(617) 635–5191

Basketball, drug and alcohol counseling, alternative education (reading/math), computer programs, recreation activities, gym, after-school programs, summer day program, volunteer and mentoring programs, Boston Youth Connection Program.

Curtis Hall Community Center
20 South Street
(617) 635–5194

Volleyball, basketball, swimming and swim lessons, lifeguard training, water aerobics, weightlifting, recreation activities, pool, JP for Fours Pre-School, volunteer and mentoring programs, senior fitness, computer classes, summer pool program.

English High Community Center
144 McBride Street
(617) 635–5244

Basketball, soccer, karate, weightlifting, computers, adult education program (ESOL and GED), recreation activities, gym, teen program, summer day program.

Hennigan Community Center
200 Heath Street
(617) 635–5198

Basketball, swimming, tutoring, teen center, high school and college guidance help, recreation activities, gym, pool, after-school programs, Boston Youth Connection Program, teen tutorial computer program, summer pool and day programs.

MATTAPAN

Gallivan Community Center
61 Woodruff Way
(617) 635–5252

Recreational and educational activities, social programs, Osco Study Club, computer program, support groups, Boston Youth Connection Program, summer day program.

Mattahunt Community Center
100 Hebron Street
(617) 635–5159

Basketball, swimming, weightlifting, drop-in center for teens, reading and math classes, volunteer and mentoring programs, recreation activities, gym, pool, after-school child care, after-school tutoring, Boston Youth Connection Program, special-needs program (Camp Joy), aerobics classes, entrepreneurship program, summer pool program, summer day programs.

Mildred Avenue Community Center
5 Mildred Avenue
(617) 635–1328

Gym, exercise studio/weight room, classrooms, dance studio, community rooms, computer room, senior center with kitchenette, swimming pool, recording studio, summer pool program, summer day programs.

NORTH END

Mirabella Pool (run by the Nazzaro Community Center)
475R Commercial Street
(617) 635–5235

Open during the summer months.

Nazzaro Community Center
30 North Bennet Street
(617) 635–5166

Basketball, weightlifting, open gym, tutoring, drop-in center, peer leadership program, volunteer program, recreation activities, gym, pool (Mirabella pool), baseball, swimming lessons, summer day program for ages five to eleven, Boston Youth Connection Program, active senior center.

ROSLINDALE

Archdale Community Center
125 Brookway Road
(617) 635–5256

Recreational and educational activities, social programs, day care, support groups, girls' program, family literacy, after-school tutoring program, school-age child care, Boston Youth Connection Program, G.I.V.E. boys' program, Computer Learning Center, Archdale Steppers, summer day program.

Flaherty Pool (run by Boston Centers for Youth & Families)
160 Florence Street
(617) 635–5181

Swimming activities and programs, swim league, open and lap swim.

Roslindale Community Center
6 Cummins Highway
(617) 635–5185

Gym activities, volunteer program, recreation activities, Tiny Tots program, after-school tutoring, summer day program, GED, teen/youth council, Roslindale Adventures for Youth trips, Marion Shea Computer Center.

ROXBURY

Ellen Jackson Children's Center (run by Mission Hill Community Centers)
1483 Tremont Street
(617) 635–4920, ext. 2123

Child care, sliding scale.

Madison Park Community Center
55 New Dudley Street
(617) 635–5209

Recreational and social programs, gym, pool, sports leagues, girls' tennis, teen room, after-school reading/math tutoring, Rainbow Reading/Math program, Madison Park Red Sox Rookie League program, summer day program.

Mason Pool (run by Boston Centers for Youth & Families)
176 Norfolk Avenue
(617) 635–5241

Adult lap swim, adult lessons, community lessons, swim team, lifeguard training/junior lifeguard training, lifeguard team, synchronized swimming, water aerobics, water polo.

Orchard Gardens Community Center
2 Dearborn Street
(617) 635–5240

Gym, martial arts, youth baseball, reading program, Boston Youth Connection Program, workshops, summer day program.

Shelburne Community Center
2730 Washington Street
(617) 635–5213

Basketball, judo, billiards, recreation activities, gym, after-school tutoring, volunteer and mentoring programs, summer camp, swimming, sports, field trips, tutoring, cultural activities, computer room, aerobics, girls' program, summer day program.

Thomas Johnson Community Center
(Mission Hill Community Centers)
68 Annunciation Road
(617) 635–5212

Basketball, arts and crafts, movie hour, recreation activities, gym, volunteer program.

Tobin Community Center
(Mission Hill Community Centers)
1481 Tremont Street
(617) 635–5216

Basketball/other sport leagues, sports camps, summer day program, teen center, special events, field trips, and more.

Vine Street Community Center
339 Dudley Street
(617) 635–1285

Senior center; teen center; child care center; recreational, educational, and social programs; summer day programs.

SOUTH BOSTON

Condon Community Center
200 D Street
(617) 635–5100

Basketball, swimming, soccer, volunteer program, recreation activities, gym, pool, after-school tutoring, special-needs program (Camp Joy), computer skills training, before-school program, summer day program, summer pool program.

Curley Community Center
1663 Columbia Road
(617) 635–5104

Volleyball, handball, horseshoes, aerobics, racquetball, volunteer program, recreation activities, gym, weight room, Tiny Tots program.

Tynan Community Center
650 East 4th Street
(617) 635–5110

Basketball, volleyball, street hockey, arts and crafts, ceramics, girls' program, volunteer program, recreation activities, gym, after-school tutoring, Boston Youth Connection Program, day camp, summer day programs.

Walsh Community Center
535 East Broadway (behind South Boston Courthouse)
(617) 635–5640

Basketball, boxing, street hockey, roller hockey, tennis, volleyball, summer day programs.

SOUTH END

Blackstone Community Center
50 West Brookline Street
(617) 635–5162

Boston Youth Connection Program, gymnastics, basketball, self-defense, recreation activities, gym, pool, after-school child care, after-school tutoring, volunteer and mentoring programs, streetworkers, GED (also in Spanish) and ESL, girls' soccer, Saturday intensive ESL, babysitting for educational programs, food share, summer pool program, summer day programs.

WEST ROXBURY

Draper Pool (run by Boston Centers for Youth & Families)
5279 Washington Street
(617) 635–5021

Adult lap swim, adult lessons, community swim lessons, swim team, lifeguard training/junior lifeguard training, lifeguard team, water aerobics, water polo.

Ohrenberger Community Center
175 West Boundary Road
(617) 635–5183

Floor hockey, gymnastics, basketball, drama, arts, soccer, roller-skating, volunteer program, recreation activities, gym, after-school child care, nursery school program, Boston Youth Connection Program, computer classes, special-needs program (Camp Joy), tutoring program, summer day program.

Roche Family Community Center
1716 Centre Street
(617) 635–5066

Senior center, senior lunch program, teen center, girls' basketball league, computer room, gym activities, Boston Youth Connection Program, summer day program.

West Roxbury Community Center
at West Roxbury High School
1205 VFW Parkway
(617) 635–5066

Basketball, swimming, quilting, sewing, typing, arts and crafts, volunteer program, recreation activities, gym, pool, special-needs program (Camp Joy), Boston Youth Connection Program, summer day program, summer pool program.

APPENDIX D:
BOSTON COMMUNITY
LEARNING CENTERS

These centers offer after-school programs and educational opportunities for students, as well as adult evening classes. For more information, see the listing in the Children and Teens chapter.

ALLSTON/BRIGHTON

Gardner School CLC, 30 Athol Street, Allston; (617) 635-8365

Garfield School CLC, 95 Beechcroft Street, Brighton; (617) 635-6323

Hamilton School CLC, 198 Strathmore Road, Brighton; (617) 635-5269

Jackson/Mann School CLC, 500 Cambridge Street, Allston; (617) 635-5153

BOSTON

Quincy School CLC, 885 Washington Street; (617) 635-5135

DORCHESTER

Cleveland School CLC, 11 Charles Street; (617) 635-8631

Dever School CLC, 325 Mt. Vernon Street; (617) 695-2300

Holland School CLC, 85 Olney Street; (617) 635-5144

King School CLC, 77 Lawrence Avenue; (617) 635-8217

Lee School CLC, 155 Talbot Avenue; (617) 635-6339

Murphy School CLC, 1 Worrell Street; (617) 635-8781

EAST BOSTON

Guild School CLC, 944 Bennington Street; (617) 567-3249

Otis School CLC, 218 Marion Street; (617) 635-8372

Umana Barnes School CLC, 312 Border Street; (617) 635-6935

JAMAICA PLAIN

Curley School CLC, 40 Pershing Road; (617) 905-7424

Young Achievers CLC, 25 Walk Hill Street; (617) 635-6804

MATTAPAN

Lewenberg School CLC, 20 Outlook Road; (617) 436-2450

Mattahunt School CLC, 100 Hebron Street; (617) 296-6089

Taylor School CLC, 62 Woodruff Way; (617) 635-5252

ROSLINDALE

Bates Elementary School CLC, 426 Beech Street; (617) 469–5151

Irving School CLC, 114 Cummins Highway; (617) 469–0074

Sumner School CLC, 15 Basile Street; (617) 635–8131

ROXBURY

Dearborn School CLC, 35 Greenville Street; (617) 592–6422

Hernandez School CLC, 61 School Street; (617) 635–8187

Lewis School CLC, 131 Walnut Avenue; (617) 427–5300

{ INDEX }

ABOUT THE AUTHOR

Born and bred in rural Massachusetts, **Kris Frieswick** has lived in Boston on and off since she graduated from Emerson College in 1985. She is a freelance journalist and humor columnist and has won numerous awards for her work in various genres. She is a regular contributor to the *Boston Globe Magazine, The Economist, Worth* magazine, *Arrive* magazine, Southwest Airlines's *Spirit* magazine, *Boston* magazine, and many others. For five years, she wrote a regular humor column for *The Phoenix* newspapers, a chain of alt-weeklies based in Boston. Her humor columns have appeared in two humor anthologies, and she's done numerous interviews on television and radio. She has also dabbled in standup monologue at famous comedy clubs the Lizard Lounge and the Hong Kong, both in Cambridge.

Kris and her husband Andrew Robinson live in Boston's South End, the sixth Boston neighborhood that she has called home. She's an avid traveler, skier, cyclist, cook, and bargainist whose proudest Cheap moment was convincing a deli clerk to grind up a leg of lamb and sell it to her for the price of hamburger. The memory still gives her goose bumps.